Praise for

Four Decades of Magic

Four Decades of Magic is a terrific stroll down memory lane for any Disney fan and the perfect tribute for Walt Disney World's 40th anniversary. The book knits together its own "Carousel of Progress" of sorts through a collection of entertaining tales and insightful essays by notable Disney experts about favorite parts of Disney World's magical journey to date. Four Decades is a charming anthology of Disney memories and intriguing behind-the-scenes insights that range from If You Had Wings and *The Hoop Dee Doo Review*, to "resorts that never were" and the Beastly Kingdom section of Disney's Animal Kingdom that never materialized.

Vicki Johnson
Principal/CEO of Vicki Johnson Communications, LLC, former Walt Disney Parks & Resorts executive

Four Decades of Magic brings together fascinating stories about the Walt Disney World Resort. As a former Disney executive who started out as an hourly Cast Member, this collection rekindled fond memories of my favorite parts of the magic that I experienced over the years.

Steven K. Brown
CEO of accesso, former Walt Disney Parks & Resorts executive

FOUR DECADES OF MAGIC

Celebrating the First Forty Years of Disney World

a collection of essays

FOUR DECADES OF MAGIC

Celebrating the First Forty Years of Disney World

a collection of essays

compiled by

Chad Denver Emerson

Cover and book design by 24 Communications, www.2wenty4.com.

Visit us on-line at:
www.ayefourpublishing.com

Printed in the United States of America.

First Printing: 2011

ISBN 978-0-615-43101-7

to Addison Clare Emerson, our special girl

Table of Contents

Foreword

Jim Hill

Given that nearly a billion people have visited Walt Disney World since this destination resort first opened back in October of 1971, it seems kind of hard to believe that there was once a time when Mouse House execs actually felt compelled to try & explain just what Disney World was going to be. How "Project Florida" was going to be different from the original Disneyland Park which Walt had built among the orange groves of Anaheim, CA. back in 1955.

And yet – if you were driving through Central Florida from January 1970 through September 1971 – you could get off I-4 at State Road 535 and then go visit the Walt Disney World Preview Center. Which was the very first building on property that was open to the public.

Inside of this relatively modest structure (which is still there, by the way. It currently houses the offices of the Amateur Athletics Union) were a variety of models and artists renderings. Which then allowed tourists to "ooh" & "aah" at all the WED-designed wonders yet to come. Beautifully themed structures like Thunder Mesa (which was to have housed the Western River Expedition ride) not to mention highly ornate hotels like the Persian Resort with its white columns and huge blue dome.

What's that you say? You've never heard of Western River Expedition? Well, then it's lucky for you that you just now picked up this copy of Four Decades of Magic. For this 379-page paperback happens to feature an excellent essay by Mike Lee which will then tell you all about this never-built attraction.

And if you were previously unaware of the Persian Resort (which was one of the five monorail hotels that were supposed to have been built during "Phase One" of Walt Disney World's construction), then check out the chapter that Lou Mongello contributed to this book. Which will tell you all about many of the other amazing hotels that the Imagineers designed for WDW over the past 40 years that never quite made it off the drawing board.

That – to me, anyway – is the real charm of Four Decades of Magic. This book contains the wisdom of some of Disney World's most dedicated fans, Webmasters, and historians who are now sharing their insights about this Resort. Not to mention all sorts of great behind-the-scenes stories which will then explain why certain rides and shows eventually turned out the way that they did.

The topics covered here run the gamut from unique pieces of entertainment that have been up and running for almost as long as WDW has (see Greg Ehrbar's terrific "Much Ado about Hoop-

Dee-Doo" essay), short-lived attractions (see George Taylor's feature on Discovery Island and then learn of the mystery of Ben Gunn's buried treasure) as well as much-beloved parts of this Resort that have recently disappeared (see Jim Korkis' article about the late, great Pleasure Island). You'll also get the chance to explore whole lands that were never built (see Scott & Carol Holmes' Beastly Kingdom piece) as well as parts of WDW theme parks that didn't quite reach their full potential (check out Tom Corless' Sunset Boulevard story and then find out about all the cool stuff that Disney's Hollywood Studios visitors have missed out on).

In short, Four Decades of Magic is the perfect way to celebrate the rich history and heritage of the Walt Disney World Resort. Which – not that long ago – wasn't really all that much to look at. Just a single modest building built right at the edge of Lake Buena Vista, along what's now known at Hotel Plaza Drive. Some 5 miles southeast of where a huge piece of swampland was being transformed into "The Vacation Kingdom of the World." Which – FYI – is the very clunky catchphrase that Disney executives came up with back in 1969. Back when they were still struggling to come up with a succinct way to describe to would-be WDW visitors what exactly Walt Disney World was going to be like.

What a mouthful, huh? Makes you kind of glad that at least some things have changed over these past 40 years, doesn't it?

Jim Hill
Editor / Publisher
JimHillMedia.com

Introduction

Chad Emerson

As someone who is nearing his 40th birthday, four decades sure seems like a long time. From growing up in the Detroit area to attending school in Nashville, and ultimately settling with my wife and children in Montgomery, Alabama, I've experienced a life full of adventures over the last forty years.

Little did I know upon being born in May 1972 that the life span of Disney World would so closely track mine. I wonder if that's why I enjoy Disney World so much—it's almost as if we've grown up together over these last four decades.

During those years, we've shared many good times and interesting experiences. Everything from elaborate press events to simple family gatherings. All in all, my Disney World past has enjoyed a whole range of experiences. I suspect many of you can say the same thing.

That's what makes Disney World such an interesting place. From around the entire world, people who like to dream (myself included), are quickly comforted by the fact that in the middle of Central Florida there exists a place designed by a dreamer for the purpose of dreaming.

Having passed in 1966, Walter Elias Disney did not live to see the actual opening of Disney World. That's not to say, though, that he never envisioned it in vivid, life-like Technicolor in his mind's eye. While today's version of Disney World is different in many ways from his original plan, it is clear that both share the same goal:

> *Create a place where families can get away from the challenges of everyday life, enjoy time together, and experience those magical stories that had long been merely the province of books and movies.*

Though he was never able to attend the completed Disney World, Walt did live long enough to spend nearly a year visiting the then-open fields and swamps that would amazingly become a worldwide destination. Out of the muck and mire rose a place whose mere mention brings a smile and memories to so many of us.

If there is such a thing as "good ghosts", then the smiling spectre of Walt Disney benevolently haunts these many acres—taking care to notice the joy that something so complex in its creation, yet so simple in its goal, has provided.

We hope that this book triggers more of those smiles and memories for you. We hope that as you read through the stories that these great Disney-focused writers have shared, something will bring back an event or two during these last forty years that brought you happiness.

Maybe it was your first glimpse of the Castle. Or your best seat ever for the 3pm parade down Main Street. It could be a quiet afternoon you spent exploring Fort Wilderness or the mesmerizing music that greets guests entering Epcot.

Whichever memory it is, this is a book about those experiences—a compilation that seeks to share and revive those memorable moments within the reader.

Throughout these pages, we have sought to recreate something special through the voices and muses of a diverse set of Disney-related authors. These varied perspectives are sure to generate a spectrum of emotions. Most of all, we have worked hard to edit lightly in order to allow their own words to fully come through.

As you travel through this book, you may find yourself chuckling, remembering, wondering, tearing up, or just silently nodding as you recall your personal Disney World past. If you do, then we've done our job and, in many ways, honored the man behind the magic and the individual whose namesake theme park resort is now indelibly and fondly marked in our memories.

We hope that you enjoy this reflection on forty years of magic at the Walt Disney World Resort.

Chad Emerson
Ayefour Publishing

The Sunset Boulevard that Was, Is, and Never Will Be

Tom Corless

Sunset Boulevard is a Hollywood icon that immediately brings to mind the glitz and glamour of tinseltown at it's golden age and beyond. For guests at Walt Disney World, it may be the place where they spend the most time when they visit Disney's Hollywood Studios. Thrill rides, groundbreaking entertainment, and inviting shops and restaurants make the Disney version of this west coast landmark a guest favorite. However, the Studios did not open with this intersection on Hollywood Boulevard.

When the park opened as the Disney-MGM Studios on May 1, 1989, guests could only experience one street representing the Hollywood that never was, and only a handful of attractions and shows. The park was purposely designed to be a half-day experience, consisting then of the Studio Backlot Tour, Great Movie Ride, Superstar Television, the Monster Sound Show, and the Indiana Jones Epic Stunt Spectacular (along with some other minor offerings). From the moment the park opened, it regularly closed at maximum capacity. Lines were long, paths were crowded, and seating was hard to come by at any stage show. Disney immediately realized the need for not only more attraction capacity, but for more room for guests to roam, shop, and dine. The creative process immediately begun for Sunset Boulevard, a street that would lead guests off of Hollywood Blvd., but keep the 1930's theme.

While those plans were coming to fruition, the rest of the park tried to cope with crowds by opening up previously closed areas, such as New York Street, to foot traffic and adding major attractions such as Star Tours and Muppetvision 3-D.

Walt Disney Imagineering drew up many different concepts for Sunset Boulevard before finally landing on the plans that would actually be constructed. The earliest concept was ripped from the original post-show plans for EPCOT's movie pavilion, "Mickey's Movieland". "Movieland" would have consisted of a large building modeled after the old Hyperion Studios Disney used in the very early days of the company and would house a number of exhibits that eventually opened as part of "The Magic of Disney Animation".

When the Disney Decade was announced in the early 1990's by then Disney CEO Michael Eisner, revolutionary new attractions and lands for the Disney-MGM Studios were at the forefront. "Dick Tracy's Crime Stoppers" was supposed to be placed on Sunset Boulevard and utilize the brand-new Enhanced Motion Vehicle (EMV). Once the "Dick Tracy" film failed at the box-office, the attraction was cancelled and the Indiana Jones Adventure was designed for Disneyland Park to be the first attraction to use the EMV technology. Dick Tracy did arrive on Sunset Blvd. in a different form, and unfortunately, it was before Sunset was even constructed. The original Theater of the Stars stood where the entrance of Sunset Blvd. is today, and it was at that uncovered, outdoor stage that the "Dick Tracy Diamond Double-Cross" performed from May 21, 1990 until February 16, 1991.

A number of Roger Rabbit themed attractions were also announced as part of the Disney Decade, all of them to be located at the end of Sunset in "Roger Rabbit's Hollywood". Disagreements that led to the cancellation of multiple sequel attempts for "Who Framed Roger Rabbit" also canned plans for "Baby Herman's Runaway Baby Buggy" coaster, the "Toontown Trolley" simulator-based attraction, and "Roger Rabbit's Cartoon Spin". While never realized in Orlando, "Roger Rabbit's Cartoon Spin" did finally open at Disneyland with Mickey's Toontown. Roger Rabbit still has a place at Disney's Hollywood Studios, however, it is not on Sunset Boulevard. Roger, Baby Herman, and Jessica Rabbit can be found on a large billboard for the fictional Maroon Studios just behind Hollywood Boulevard.

While Imagineering was toying with the idea of bringing animated characters and big-budget blockbusters to the park's new street, Disney began talks with Mel Brooks to produce some of his films and lend some of his well-known and already produced films to a major Disney-MGM Studios attraction. It seemed like a natural fit as Mel and his son were huge fans of Disneyland and visited the park regularly. The large plot at the very end of Sunset Blvd. almost became one of two Mel Brook's themed rides that would combine comedy and horror (much like the Haunted Mansion). The first concept was known as "Mel Brooks' Hollywood Horror Hotel", a ride on magical golf carts through the hot set of a new horror film Mr. Brooks is directing; and "Castle Young Frankenstein", based on the classic 1974 comedy "Young Frankenstein" starring Gene Wilder. Mel Brooks walked out on the project after it became too different from what he had originally envisioned (On a side note, Mel never worked with Disney beyond the attraction either). This was around the same time Disney Imagineers began playing with the idea for an elevator-type attraction that would drop guests a number of stories.

While Disneyland Paris was being initially developed, one of the original attractions designed for the park's Frontierland was an "E-Ticket" attraction called Geyser Mountain. Geyser Mountain would have been an entirely new experience for Disney as it would start as a mine train coaster (Similar to Big Thunder Mountain Railroad) and then launch guests directly up through a mine shaft with a ride mechanism hidden by large water jets. When Big Thunder Mountain ended up in the plans for Paris, the concept was redesigned for the park's Discoveryland, slated to go inside a rather large *Space Mountain* structure. The attraction would have been called "Journey to the Center of the Earth" and would have featured an earth-moving elevator dropping "deep" below the earth's surface. Financial problems led that project to be cancelled as well (even though a very different "Journey to the Center of the Earth" attraction would open with Tokyo DisneySea in 2001), but Walt Disney Imagineering refused to let their free-fall elevator concept go away.

Imagineers decided that attraction type would be a perfect draw and addition for the Disney-MGM Studios, which was still struggling to find an opening day attraction for its first major expansion. However, they needed to find a story that would better fit the Studios' theme. Michael Eisner believed the attraction needed to be tied to a strong property, and "The Twilight Zone" seemed like the perfect fit. Once this franchise came into play, ideas to include the 5th dimension and some kind of element where the elevator would move forward, backward, and left to right began. After may attempts to work with long-established elevator design companies such as Otis to develop a working ride system, Disney decided it was best to just invent a custom system to accomplish what they wanted. The AGV, or Autonomous Guided Vehicle was created: a self controlling ride vehicle that could move without track. Although the "5th Dimension" scene where the elevators would mysteriously roll forward was designed with guide-ways for traction, the vehicle itself would run on its own wheels along the floor. Such a vehicle needed to have fast charging onboard power. The inductive power coupling that was designed for Epcot's Universe of Energy traveling theatre cars were a perfect fit because they could recharge the elevator's onboard batteries without a physical connection. This technology was refined for "Tower of Terror", and also used later in Tokyo Disneyland`s "Pooh's Honey Hunt". Onboard computers follow a pre-programmed ride path, and communicate with the Ride Control System through a wireless frequency. A secondary tracking system follows a wire embedded in the floor to keep track of the elevator's location to make sure all is going well. If all this wasn't impressive enough, Disney also wanted the elevators to then fall faster than terminal velocity.

How would the elevator operate like a "Universe of Energy" vehicle and then do that? It wouldn't. This would all be achieved by a second vehicle. As the AGV guides itself into the ride shaft to ascend to the boiler room loading level, it slots into a larger contraption - know as the Vertical Vehicle Conveyance (VVC). This is an elevator car in the true sense, complete with cables and wheels, albeit with wire mesh for walls. It is this that lifts the AGV up through the corridor scene, and to the 5th Dimension level. As the elevator car transfers horizontally, the VVC returns to the basement level to receive the next vehicle that is unloading its guests. For the drop shaft, a beefed up second VVC is brought into play - enough to take the rigors of accelerated free-fall, and with a pulley system not just on its roof to lift it like a conventional elevator, but a complete loop of cable that also pulls the entire carriage downwards as well as up - hence faster than gravity. With this incredible attraction's complex ride system designed, and the proper theme chosen, it was time to open Sunset Boulevard.

On July 22, 1994, "The Twilight Zone Tower of Terror" opened with a very large expansion of the Disney-MGM Studios. As you approach the attraction from Sunset Blvd., you enter through the front gates of the Hollywood Tower Hotel, now with a "Keep Out" sign hanging from them. You continue into the gardens, which are looking a bit overgrown and rundown. You pass a broken fountain and approach the front door of the hotel itself. You then continue into the very creepy lobby, where everything is in its original place from the time the Hollywood Tower Hotel was closed in 1939. Cobwebs cover all of the furniture and beautiful decor. You then approach the bellhop station, where they split you into two pre-show rooms.

At the end of your pre-show a door opens and you enter the boiler room of the hotel and make your way toward one of two loading areas to board your service elevator. Your trip aboard the service elevator begins and quickly stops to reveal the last group of passengers to ride the Hotel's elevator, the movie star and starlet, the bellhop, the child actress and her nanny are all there, waiving to you from down the hall. Suddenly, in what appears to be a surge of electricity, they disappear and the hall begins to glow with electric current. The walls of the halls disappear and turn into a star-field, while at the very end of the hall, the widow begins to float and then shatter ominously. Scenes like this showcase the blending of multiple innovations from Disney's past and present that were necessary to bring every piece of this modern marvel to life.

Guests then move up the elevator shaft and the door that opened for those five passengers in 1939 once again opens for you, bringing you into what is unique and most impressive about Walt Disney World's version of the attraction, the fifth dimension scene. Your elevator car moves out of the shaft and past scenes consisting of strange items such as a giant pocket watch and a large eye offering a look into your own elevator. The eye would actually present a picture of your elevator taken earlier in the ride during the years right after the attraction debuted, the effect now features the same elevator picture over and over again. The elevator then rolls toward a star-field which suddenly converges into a single beam of light opening in half before you. "You are about to discover what lies beyond the fifth dimension. Beyond the deepest darkest corner of the imagination, in the Tower of Terror." This famous phrase begins your single (this will change shortly) rise and fall in the Hollywood Tower Hotel. Your trip to "The Twilight Zone" comes to an end as you are give "A warm welcome back and a friendly word of warning". You then exit through the basement, down a service hallway that leads back into the "guest areas" of the hotel, including a check-in desk where you can pick up your on-ride photo and the hotel gift shop known as "Tower Gifts".

The ride system for the Twilight Zone Tower of Terror was so innovative and different, that it was the first Disney attraction that could be easily updated to feature new ride profiles, even multiple ride profiles at once. In 1995, "The Twilight Zone Tower of Terror II" debuted, dropping guests three times down 13 stories, instead of the original one. On March 1, 1999, "The Twilight Zone Tower of Terror III: Fear Every Drop" added more drops, changed its drop patterns and enhanced the other special effects in the drop shaft. On December 31, 2002, "The Twilight Zone Tower of Terror IV" debuted, placing computers in control of the ride experience for the first time, making each ride sequence unique and random. A temporary change to the attraction was also introduced for Walt Disney World's "Summer Nightastic!" promotion in 2010. The layover lasted from June 6th through August 14th, 2010. During that time, Imagineers brought some audio and lighting changes to the boiler room, new audio to the fifth dimension scene, brought back the photo of your elevator before entering the drop shaft (the effect was now projected directly in front of you rather than in the eyeball), covered the fifth dimension side scenes with a star-field, and added a glow effect to the inside of the drop shaft for nighttime visitors. At this point, it is unknown if the "Summer Nightastic!" version will ever return. It was also at this time that the "4" was dropped from the latest version of the "Twilight Zone Tower of Terror" and the attraction officially went back to the original, simpler name without the version number included.

Since Walt Disney World opened the Tower of Terror in 1994, three more versions have opened around the world. The second version opened at Disney's California Adventure park on May 5, 2004. The third incarnation is located inside Tokyo DisneySea at Tokyo Disneyland Resort and opened on September 4, 2006. The Tokyo attraction is the only version that does not feature "The Twilight Zone" theme, but rather an original story about a rich adventurer and owner of the Hightower Hotel named Harrison Hightower, who vanishes into an elevator going to his penthouse on December 31, 1899 after taking a mysterious idol from Africa. The final version opened at Walt Disney Studios Paris at the Disneyland Resort Paris on December 22, 2007. This version is identical to the attraction that opened at the Disneyland Resort in 2004.

When the Tower of Terror opened to guests in Florida, so did Sunset Boulevard. The expansion brought a wealth of new guest areas into the park, including 3 large buildings containing new shopping experiences and a large outdoor counter service dining location. Sunset also became the new home to the "Theater of the Stars", even thought the theater had already technically existed on that street. In order to allow construction of Sunset Boulevard to begin, the Theater of the Stars had to be moved from its original location right off of Hollywood Boulevard.

The original theater was shuttered in September 1993, moving the popular "*Beauty and the Beast*: Live on Stage" to the Backlot Theater on New York Street temporarily. On June 12, 1994, the show debuted at the new, larger (now seating 1500 guests), covered Theater of the Stars on Sunset Boulevard. From the time it debuted until 2001, the show presented the movie's songs and story out-of-order. A second version of the show debuted in March 2001, correcting the show to match with the actual film. Very similar versions of this show ran at Disneyland Park from 1992-1995, and at Disneyland Paris from 1992-1996. "*Beauty and the Beast*: Live on Stage" has become one of the most legendary stage shows in Disney Theme Park history, lasting an unheard of two decades! That's more years in operation than amazing attractions such as Journey Into Imagination, Horizons, and Body Wars, just to name a select few.

While Tower of Terror, a ton of new shopping & dining venues, and a larger Theater of the Stars helped the Disney-MGM Studios' capacity problems immensely, the park would continue to expand, even breaking away from its working studio component to focus more on Hollywood-type entertainment and attractions. One of the major steps in this change was replacing the Sorcery in the Sky fireworks show for the park with a large scale entertainment spectacular known as *Fantasmic!* Since not many shows were produced in the park anymore, the park needed to have its own productions, and this show was already well-established.

Fantasmic! originated at Disneyland Park where it debuted on a stage at the front of Tom Sawyer Island in 1992, having guests watch the show from across the Rivers of America. The show was a first-time collaboration between the Disneyland entertainment department, Walt Disney Imagineering, and Disney Feature Animation. The Disney-MGM Studios was wildly popular at the time, but was still not a full-day theme park experience. The Sorcery in the Sky show just was not keeping guests in the park as night fell and they needed something that would keep guests in the park for a full day, most likely extending their Walt Disney World vacation. In 1996, it was decided that a version of the *Fantasmic!* show would be added to the Studios rather than placed on the Rivers of America at the Magic

Kingdom, which didn't need such an addition as much as the third WDW park needed it.

Since the Studios did not have a body of water inside the park other than Echo Lake, it was decided that a brand new, state-of-the-art facility be built to house the show. The stadium for *Fantasmic!* would be built right off of Sunset Boulevard and would make use of the imaginary Hollywood Hills Estates name that was created for the backstory of the Hollywood Tower Hotel. The venue would be titled "The Hollywood Hills Amphitheater" and would feature space for 10,000 guests, as well as a custom-built stage and facilities just for this show.

Fantasmic! debuted inside the Hollywood Hills Amphitheater on October 15, 1998. Since the Studios had the special opportunity, unlike Disneyland, to build plenty of seating for the show, which allowed them to make it longer by about 5 minutes. While the basic story-line of the show remains the same for both existing versions, there are a number of scenes exclusive to each resort. The Jungle Book, Pinnochio, Peter Pan, and Ursula (from "The Little Mermaid") scenes from the Disneyland version of the show were cut from Florida to make sure the show included more contemporary Disney animated films. The only piece of the Jungle Book scene that actually made it into the Disney-MGM Studios show was the dancing flower that briefly appears prior to "The Lion King" sequence. As well, rather than having a giant version of Kaa roaming the stage, the snake-form of Jafar battles Mickey in one of the final scenes. In place of these scenes, the Studios version features an animated film bubble montage, as well as Lion King and Pocohontas inspired scenes. Other changes included the removal of Ursula from the Little Mermaid singing "Poor, Unfortunate Souls", the riverboat being custom-built to look like the one from Mickey's debut performance in "Steamboat Willie" (unlike the Mark Twain Riverboat at Disneyland), and the addition of many, many more villains (removing Kaa and the Pink Elephants and adding Hades, Cruella de Vil, Judge Frollo, Scar, and Governor Radcliffe).

The finale scene of *Fantasmic!* at the Studios was also greatly improved with a slightly larger dragon and a giant wall of water that rises to defeat Maleficent. However, Disneyland updated their show even further in the summer of 2009, debuting a new, more realistic Dragon, Crocodile, and Flotsam & Jetsam, along with new lighting effects and high definition water projections as part of a campaign called "Summer Nightastic!" One can only wonder if similar changes will come to the Walt Disney World show anytime soon.

If a wildly popular new nighttime spectacular wasn't enough to make Sunset Boulevard a hot spot at the Disney MGM-Studios, then a second "E-Ticket" thrill ride should do the trick. "Rock 'N' Roller Coaster starring Aerosmith" officially opened adjacent to the Tower of Terror on July 29, 1999, with an invitation-only party featuring Aerosmith as the guests of honor. A local radio station held a contest in which listeners could win tickets for themselves and three friends to attend the special event. Winners rode to the park in stretch limousines and were treated to an all-you-can-eat buffet and bar. After a special performance by painter Denny Dent, winners were given the opportunity to ride the attraction with one of the Aerosmith band members. At the exit of the ride, just outside of the "Rock Around the Shop", hangs a picture from the special event. The paintings Denny Dent made of the five band members hang in various employee office locations on Walt Disney World property.

Keeping the theme of Sunset Boulevard despite having a more contemporary story, guests enter through the arches of the fictional G-Force Records, with the physical studio building resembling the real-life RKO/Desilu studio in Hollywood. The main plaza features the longest background music loop at the Disney Parks, clocking in at 60 hours of rock and roll music. Guests wind through the studio, eventually leading them back "outside" into the parking garage loading area titled "Lock 'N' Roll Parking Systems". This structure is patterned after the Walt Disney Studios Animation parking lot, with the interior pattern following that of the Walt Disney Imagineering parking structure in California.

There are 5 speakers in the headrests of every seat in the "super-stretch limo" vehicle, making a total of 120 speakers per roller-coaster train. Aerosmith worked with Walt Disney Imagineering to create a customized soundtrack for the attraction. The Aerosmith songs featured in the attraction have all been altered in some way, such as "Love in an Elevator" becoming "Love in a Roller Coaster". The Limo vehicles can be identified by their license plates and the music they play. 1QKLIMO plays the song "Nine Lives", UGOGIRL plays "Love in an Elevator" and "Walk This Way", BUHBYE plays "Young Lust", "F.I.N.E.", and "Love in a Roller Coaster", H8TRFFC plays "Back in the Saddle" and "Dude Looks Like a Lady", and 2FAST4U plays "Sweet Emotion".

While many guests think that the track layout for Rock'N' Roller Coaster is designed specifically for this attraction like most other Disney rides, they would be wrong. While the Orlando coaster was first to open, the same track layout and ride system was used by Vekoma for "Superman: The Ride" (now Xpress) at Walibi World in the Netherlands. The success of the Disney project also made way for a slightly altered version of "Rock 'N' Roller Coaster starring Aerosmith" that opened with the Walt Disney Studios park at the Disneyland Resort Paris in 2002.

While Sunset Boulevard has not experienced many major changes for the better part of a decade, it's not hard to understand why. This expansion street has continued to draw a majority of the park's crowd to its headlining attractions and entertainment, while the rest of the park has had a much harder time transitioning from working Studios to theme park attractions. It was really until Toy Story Midway Mania opened in 2008 that Rock 'N' Roller Coaster and Tower of Terror even had competition as the most popular attractions at the newly christened Disney's Hollywood Studios. Can "Star Tours: The Adventures Continue" bring balance to the guest flow (and the force) at the park, or will Sunset Blvd. always be the most popular guest area? Regardless, it's safe to say that even though many projects were cancelled, what guests have enjoyed and enjoy today on Sunset Boulevard is incredible. For a few hours, guests can hang out in a haunted hotel, become VIPs at an Aerosmith concert, and simply get lost in the Hollywood that never actually was, but always is in our minds.

About Tom Corless

With almost 100 trips to the Walt Disney World Resort over the last 22 years, Tom Corless feels like he has grown up in the Magic Kingdom. Using his experience, Tom founded WDW News Today and the WDWNT Network of Disney-inspired websites and podcasts in 2007. Walt Disney World isn't a vacation for Tom, it's his life.

When is the 3 O'Clock Parade? Then, Now, and Forever

Tom Corless

Since Disneyland opened in 1955, parades have marched down Main Street U.S.A. There were several daytime and nighttime parades held at Disneyland before Walt Disney World existed that celebrated Disney films, attraction openings, and seasonal holidays with characters, music, and large floats. When Walt Disney World opened in 1971, it did not feature a daily afternoon parade. This tradition was not adopted until the June 1975 debut of America on Parade.

With America's huge Bicentennial celebration coming in 1976, the Disney Parks were looking for a big way to celebrate. A parade seemed the best way to celebrate, so they began to develop a parade celebrating the america of the past, present, and future in 1973. Two years later, America on Parade debuted at both Disneyland and The Magic Kingdom with over 50 floats and 150 performers. It was the first parade designed for both daytime and nighttime performances, it even was the first parade to replace the Main Street Electrical Parade at Disneyland. The parade featured some rather odd floats such as a giant sandwich, a giant box of popcorn, an 18-foot tall American Eagle, a 20-foot high rocking chair, an 18-foot tall turkey, and a 240-inch television set. These floats represented American history, treasures and pastimes. Alongside the floats were also 300 8-foot tall costumes with oversized heads called the "People of America". The soundtrack included songs such as Yankee Doodle Dandy, Turkey in the Straw, Take Me Out to the Ball-game, In My Merry Oldsmobile, Zip-a-Dee-Doo-Dah and God Bless America. The parade was popular, but could not trump a parade made of electric lights. In response, the parade ended a year earlier than expected in September 1976 with a special appearance by a 1000 piece band. This change was made so that the Main Street Electrical Parade could return to Disneyland and debut at Walt Disney World in 1977.

The Main Street Electrical Parade was an instant hit at Walt Disney World, but it was forced to take another break for a historic company milestone. In 1978, Mickey Mouse celebrated his 50th anniversary. Once again, a parade was created for both the Magic Kingdom and Disneyland to mark the occasion. The Mickey Mouse 50th Birthday parade ran only in 1978 and featured a plethora of Disney characters along with giant cupcakes, birthday gifts, and a cake with 50 candles.

For 1979, the Magic Kingdom created a parade devoted to a classic animated film, but for the first time not to promote any special anniversary, re-release, or home video release. It was "Dumbo's Circus Parade". The parade was littered with clown characters and featured Dumbo and Mickey Mouse as the only recognizable members of the cast. While this parade may have been strange, it was only a place holder while Disney developed a parade to celebrate Walt Disney World's 10th anniversary.

The Walt Disney World Tencennial Parade was a celebration of the Magic Kingdom and its theme lands. The parade used recycled music from Disneyland's 25th anniversary to create the "Disney World is Your World" theme song. The parade opened with the logo float carrying Mickey and Minnie Mouse, followed by sections dedicated to the lands of the Magic Kingdom at the time, minus Liberty Square. Main Street U.S.A. was represented by the horse drawn trolly and a large bandstand. The Adventureland portion had a tribal hut featuring Jungle Book characters. Frontierland featured the Country Bears and performers from the Diamond Horseshoe Saloon Revue danced on a moving stage. Tomorrowland presented the strangest unit, featuring a futuristic punk rock band. Fantasyland was represented by Cinderella in her royal carriage pulled by 6 miniature white horses. The Tencennial parade concluded with the anniversary festivities in September 1982.

A placeholder afternoon parade called the Mickey Mouse Character Parade ran for a short period from October 1983 through May 1984. A much larger scale parade debuted directly afterwards celebrating Donald Duck's 50th Birthday. This parade began May 19, 1984 with the voice of Donald (Clarence Nash) and 50 real ducks leading their way down Main Street. The live ducks would actually be a regular part of the parade, requiring a "duck handler" to follow floats and make sure they did not get hurt or escape. Donald's parade lasted through the end of 1984.

Another forgettable placeholder parade debuted in January 1985 called "Mickey's Street Party". The parade used neon colors for everything, a disco soundtrack, and glittery decorations on the mostly recycled parade floats. "Mickey's Street Party" performed for the last time in September of 1986.

The 15 Years of Magic Parade debuted on October 1, 1986. The parade kicked off by telling guests that they had "only just begun", a nod to the EPCOT Center theme of "We've Just Begun to Dream". The opening float had Mickey and Minnie with the 15th anniversary logo that combined Cinderella Castle and Spaceship Earth into a single icon. The second float featured a rag-tag rock 'n' roll band of Chip, Dale, Pluto, Tigger, Brer Bear, and the Big Bad Wolf. The third unit carried Perla, Cinderella, Clara Cluck, Donald Duck, and the Three Little Pigs. The fourth float featured a kitchen where Liverlips, Wendell, and Shaker from the Country Bear Jamboree had accidentally built an upside-down birthday cake. The fifth float featured some very 80's dressed dancers on a smaller version of the float that would follow. This final float marked the arrival of a parade unit that is actually still in use today, the large blue and silver castle float. In the 15th anniversay parade, the float carried more dancers, a live band, and Goofy. Giant presents, rollerblading dancers, and tons of characters rounded out this extremely popular parade. The parade concluded with the anniversary festivities in September 1987.

The short-lived "All-America Parade" performed sporadically from late-1987 until September 1989. The history of this parade is not well documented, searches for photographs, video, or any information on this offering are incredibly hard to come by. The only known Disney description listed the parade as "a 17 float long extravaganza celebrating 200 years of America". This was really just a filler for after the 15th anniversary festivities had concluded.

Disney's Character Hit Parade, which debuted in October 1989, was the first to truly begin the afternoon parade tradition. The 3PM start time was locked as the permanent start time during this period and the Magic Kingdom has not gone a full day of operation without an afternoon parade since. It was also one afternoon parade where Disney truly got everything right. Instead of developing a single, forced, theme for the parade, Disney decided to put 100 characters and 14 moments from classic films in one performance to really give the guests what they wanted. The pre-parade featured the grand marshall car and the Main Street Philharmonic performing an instrumental version of the parade theme song. If this sounds familiar, it should. This idea was once again adopted 20 years later. The first float of the parade featured the "S.S. Mickey Mouse" steamboat carrying Roger Rabbit, Chip, Dale, and a number of the core Disney characters. The second unit celebrated The Jungle Book and featured Baloo, King Louie, and Mowgli wrestling with each-other. The third float was Winnie the

Pooh's house featuring all of the characters from the Hundred Acre Woods. This float is still in use today in the Magic Kingdom's holiday parades. The fourth float had the Alice in Wonderland characters under a moving gazebo or in roaming teacups. The Country Bear and Davy Crockett rode down Main Street on a Frontierland theme float. The sixth unit had Captain Hook and Mr. Smee trying to escape from the crocodile on a small boat. They were followed by Snow White and her prince on a water-wheel, followed by the marching Seven Dwarfs. Following Snow White, Cinderella's horse-drawn coach from the Tencennial parade returned. The next unit had Mary Poppins on the rooftops of London. Guests would then see Stromboli looking over Pinocchio dancing with the can-can marionettes. The finale float featured Mickey, Minnie, the Gummi Bears, the Three Little Pigs, the Big Bad Wolf, Bongo, The Rescuers, Robin Hood, and more. This parade was loaded with characters from top to bottom, so it was hard for guests not to walk away with a smile after having seen at least a few of their personal favorites. The Character Hit Parade came to an end in September 1991 so that the Magic Kingdom could once again celebrate an anniversary with a new parade. However, many of the concepts introduced for this parade still live on today.

To celebrate Walt Disney World's 20th anniversary, the Magic Kingdom received the popular "Party Gras Parade" from Disneyland's 35th anniversary and re-named it "The 20th Anniversary Surprise Celebration Parade". The parade didn't quite fit any theme for the anniversary festivities, so this was one case where even the least experienced guests might be confused. It was a combination of themes such as Mardi Gras, Carnival del Rio, and Venetian carnivals. 35-40 foot tall balloons of Roger Rabbit, Minnie Mouse, Donald Duck, and Pluto were featured on the main floats. After the 20th Anniversary festivities concluded, the parade was simply renamed "The Surprise Celebration Parade" and continued to perform through May 1994.

Beginning June 1st, 1994 was the Mickey Mania parade. Focusing on trying to make Mickey Mouse hip and edgy for the 1990's, the parade was the first (and still only) parade to use rap/hip hop music. Over 100 performers were featured, some dressed as a part of Mickey or his legacy (ex. giant white gloves). The overload of Mickey memorabilia and characters doing non-sensical things like riding bicycles and going down slides may have been too much for any Disney fan to handle. The attempt to rebrand Mickey wasn't very successful, but the parade certainly had mixed reviews. Mickey Mania came to an end the day before Walt Disney World's 25th anniversary celebration began.

For Walt Disney World's 25th Anniversary, the slogan was "Remember the Magic". It was only fitting that the Magic Kingdom's new parade be called the "Remember the Magic Parade". The parade introduced Walt Disney World guests to "show-stops", where the parade would come to a stop and do a short performance of some kind at that point. For this parade, "parade coaches" would come out prior to 3PM and pick select gusts in the crowd to come out when the parade stopped in front of them. They were given different instructions depending on which float they performed with (each float had a different activity for guests to take part in). The show-stops were cut long before the parades final performances. The legendary castle float returned (slightly remodeled), carrying Cinderella and her prince, Pluto, Minnie, Goofy Donald, Chip, Dale, and the Fairy Godmother. Sorcerer Mickey was at the top of the float since the anniversary logo featured Mickey from his role in Fantasia. The Little Mermaid float was next, featuring Ariel, Sebastian, and an audio-animatronic band with Sebastian. Since this was the first parade to ever feature audio-animatronic characters, rumors have circulated that they were recycled from the cancelled Little Mermaid dark ride for Disneyland Paris. The Sebastian animatronic would be added to Spectromagic after the conclusion of this parade. The third unit celebrated "Beauty and the Beast". Belle and Beast were located on the float, accompanied by spinning plates and an audio-animatonic version of Lumiere. Again, rumors indicate this was from the cancelled Beauty and the Beast dark ride planned for Disneyland Paris. The next float featured Aladdin, recycling a number of props from Aladdin's Royal Caravan parade at the Disney-MGM Studios. The Lion King unit featured 4 audio-animatronic characters: Simba, Zazu, Timon, and Pumbaa. These figures were not as advanced as the others seen in the parade. The Lion King float made a surprise appearance in 2003 at Animal Kingdom to promote the DVD release of the film. The finale float was the Fantasy Forest unit, featuring Snow White and the Seven Dwarfs, Pooh, Eeyore, Tigger, Alice, the

White Rabbit, King Louie, Baloo, Mary Poppins, Pocohontas, Peter Pan, Captain Hook, Pinocchio, and Gepetto. On January 1, 1998, the parade became "Disney's Magical Moments Parade" to mark the end of the 25th anniversary marketing campaign. The parade continued to perform under the new name until September 2001.

The "Share a Dream Come True Parade" debuted as part of the 100 years of magic celebration that was to kick-off October 1, 2001. Each WDW theme park was to receive a new or updated parade for the celebration, but this one was the centerpiece. The parade focused on Walt Disney's legacy, the characters he created and that carry on the Disney story, and the sharing in Walt's vision when you step into a Walt Disney World theme park. The original introduction featured Julie Andrews (most famous for portraying Mary Poppins in the classic Disney film) stating "Hello everyone and welcome. This is Julie Andrews and I'd like to tell you a story. In 1901 a little boy named Walt Disney was born and a dream began. The dream of imagination that today, 100 years later, has touched every one of our lives. I once had the privilege to know the dreamer, Walt Disney. His imagination inspired and built his dreams into reality for all of us to share and he made them practically perfect in every way. Today we celebrate and share the legacy of Walt Disney filled with pixie dust, princesses, fairy tales, and fantasies and above all the magic of dreams." The chorus of children would then sing the main theme and the actual parade announcement would come on.

The introductory float featured an actor dressed as Walt Disney drawing the first Mickey Mouse. The float was pushed down the street by two parade performers dressed as studio artists from the early days of the Disney company. Each of the large floats featured a character in a giant snow-globe and was named after a famous quote from somewhere in Disney history. The first snow-globe float featured Mickey Mouse and was titled "It Was All Started By a Mouse". The base of the float featured film reels with Mickey running, while the upper portion had large moving figures of Mickey through the years including Steamboat Willie, The Band Concert, The Brave Little Tailor, Plane Crazy, The Clock Cleaners, Nifty Nineties, A Christmas Carol, and, Fantasia. The top of Mickey's globe features a small film projector. Foul fellow and Gideon marked the arrival of the Pinnochio

"Wish Upon a Star" unit, and were joined by some of the donkey boys from Pleasure Island. On the front of this float, The Blue Fairy carried her wand and Gepetto played the accordion. A moving figure of Figaro also tried to catch Cleo the fish in her bowl. Pinnochio was inside the globe. The back of the float celebrated "Snow White and the Seven Dwarves", with all 8 characters featured, as well as a mine car full of jewels. "Alice in Wonderland" characters would walk behind the dwarves, followed by Piglet, Tigger, and Eeyore with kites. The "A Thousand Dreams to See" unit captured Disney characters in flight, featuring Winnie the Pooh in a pile of leaves carrying his balloon, Mr. Stork from Dumbo, and Aladdin on his Magic Carpet inside the the globe. A large version of the Genie is holding the globe. The back of the float featured some rooftops of London along with Mary Poppins flying on her Umbrella. The float was followed by some chimney sweeps. The villains float is preceded by Wendy, The Lost Boys, Captain Hook, Mr. Smee, and some pirates. "Face the Darkest Fears", as the float is titled, features the Evil Queen from Snow White in the globe portion, held by Chernabog from Fantasia. The driver on this float was actually visible as a pirate in a ditch on the right side. The front of the float has Jafar and Maleficent standing. The back of the float featured the Magic Mirror and Ursula. "A Dream is a Wish Your Heart Makes" was lead in by dancing brides along with Flora, Fauna, and Merryweather. This was a triple snow-globe unit, with the Fairy Godmother leading on a small, elevated pedestal. The first globe featured Cinderella and her prince surrounded by glistening pumpkins. The second was a stairway with an oblong dome around Belle and the Beast. The third and final had Ariel and Eric along with a wave of water and swans, followed by Flounder. They are followed by more brides, as well as Suzy and Perla. The "As Long as There's Imagination Left in the World" float carried Donald, Goofy, and Minnie on the front, with Peter Pan on a pedestal carrying a lantern holding Tinker Bell. The globe portion featured a double bubble with a carousel topped with a Castle turret. A large swirl and a gold ring surround the globe. The carousel had crystal horses being rode by Mushu, Lucky the Dalmatian, the Cheshire Cat, and Timon. The float also has some smaller globes scattered with crystal statues of Simba, Thumper, Timothy, and Abu. The float also had crystal turrets and the back had an opening with the famous picture of Walt walking through Sleeping Beauty Castle at Disneyland etched in glass.

Each float had a show stop sequence when the parade debuted. This was Disney's second attempt to have show-stops in a Magic Kingdom parade. Most floats would simply feature a spinning centerpiece inside the globe, turning the character inside in a full circle. There was also a pixie dust effect inside the float. The villains float featured a uniqie effect; the Evil Queen would transform into the Old Hag. These stops first had their effects removed, then the show-stops were shortened, and finally cut altogether at the end of the 100 years of magic celebration in March 2003.

On February 11, 2004, a parade performer playing Pluto was struck and killed by the Princess Unit in the parade as the parade was making its entrance through Frontierland. While the accident did not happen on-stage, it made national news. It was the first cast member death to occur on the job since an incident with the Magic Kingdom Skyway in 1999. The accident forced the removal of the float from the parade and forced them to bring back the large castle unit last used in the "Remember the Magic Parade" to carry the princesses. The parade would run in this style for the next 2 years.

In 2006, Disney announced the Year of a Million Dreams, a first of it's kind event celebrating the power of dreams and the dream making magic of Disney cast members. A number of entertainment changes would be made for the celebration. One that was not announced publicly was the changes to the daily Magic Kingdom parade. On August 9, 2006, the parade made it's final performance as the Share a Dream Come True Parade. On August 10, two months before the Year of a Million Dreams even began, the parade became the Disney Dreams Come True Parade. The first notable change was the soundtrack, which was now music recycled from the Tokyo Disneyland 20th Anniversary Parade given completely new lyrics. The opening float with Walt Disney was simply given a name change. In addition, the small globe was removed (since the globes in the parade were now history). The "It was all started by a mouse" float features Mickey in a blue "Dream" suit added for the Year of a Million Dreams. All snow-globes in the parade were removed and replaced with new set-pieces. More film reel was added forming a larger Mickey Icon behind Mickey. The window cleaner Mickey was moved behind it, and the Christmas carol Mickey was placed on the left side. New choreography for characters and performers was also added. The "Wish Upon a Star" Unit added a large wooden archway above. Gepetto lost his accordion and Jimminy Cricket has replaced the Blue Fairy on the float. The "A Thousand Dreams to See" Unit added towers belonging to the palace of Agrabah, which the genie now held onto instead of the snow-globe. "Face the Darkest Fears" no longer featured Wendy and the Lost Boys, but more chimney sweeps follow the "A Thousand Dreams to See" Float. However, more pirates now followed Captian Hook and Mr. Smee carrying pirate flags. The villains float added Cruella De Vil and had a gothic archway added for Chernabog to hold onto. This float was now followed by the "As Long as There's Imagination Left in the World" float. The cast preceding the float included a strange bunch: Meeko, Stitch, Brer Bear, Brer Fox, Baloo, Rafiki, Robin Hood, and Friar Tuck. The float removed Minnie, Donald, and Goofy and added Wendy to stand across from Peter Pan. The triple princess float returned for this version of the parade after 2 years away, adding more brides and moving Suzy and Pearla in front of the float. The globe around Cinderella and her Prince was replaced with gold rods to look like her coach, topped with a pumpkin. Belle and the Beast were now covered by a floral archway, and Ariel and Eric have a coral archway decorated with sea horses and starfish. The float is now followed by Flora, Fauna, and Merryweather from "Sleeping Beauty". The castle float is the final float now and is titled "A Kingdom of Dreams". The float carries Chip, Dale, Pluto, Donald, Goofy, and Minnie and is followed by the parade rope. The rope was at first just a line of small banners with the Disney D on them. It was replaced in 2008 with an illustrated farewell banner. The Disney Dreams Come True Parade would run a few weeks past The Year of a Million Dreams, ending on January 2, 2009.

In the weeks prior to the end of The Disney Dreams Come True Parade, some odd changes were seen by guests. In December 2008, Mickey's float was removed and he was placed onto the castle finale float. This change was made so the float could be converted to match a new name and theme for the parade in 2009, centered around Disney's "What Will You Celebrate?" campaign. On January 23, 2009 (23 days into the celebration), the "Celebrate a Dream Come True Parade" debuted.

The parade added a new soundtrack that did not only consist of the already created "Celebrate You" theme song for the current campaign, but it was a completely original arrangement containing parts of famous Disney themes with an original song mixed in.

The opening unit with Walt Disney was removed and replaced by a banner with the parade name and the grand marshall car carrying some guests celebrating a special occasion. Some generic dancers in some pastel outfits were now placed between each float, each group performing a very different set of choreography. The Mickey Mouse float returned with a radical new look, now featuring streamers, invitations, and what appeared to be spools of ribbon with "Celebrate Today!" written on them. The float now carried Mickey, and his love interest Minnie, dressed in colorful outfits that match the groups of dancers now in the parade. For the most part, characters were removed and replaced by the dancers. This would be a major guest complaint over the next few weeks. The only other major changes were found on the finale castle float, which was now decorated with clouds and Mickey balloons, carrying Chip, Dale, Pluto, Donald, and Goofy in party outfits. The parade also had a show-stop where the performers danced to a different version of the "Celebrate You!" theme song. This was cut and added back a number of times before being officially retired in 2010.

Thanks to negative response to the parade changes from guests and the online Disney community, the parade debuted a second version on May 3, 2009. As part of the changes, Chip, Dale, and Pluto were moved into the first group of dancers from the finale float. As well, Fowlfellow, Gideon, Jafar, The Genie, Abu, Captain Hook, Mr. Smee, Tweedle Dee, Tweedle Dum, Suzy, Perla, Lady Tremaine, Anastasia, Drizella, Lilo, Stitch, Woody, Jessie, King Louie, and Baloo were all added in to counter guest complaints about the lack of Disney characters in the parade. However, Winnie the Pooh and Dopey were removed, and the parade was shortened with the removal of the Villains float. The show-stops now had Disney characters leaving floats to join in the dancing as well.

The parade altered it's layout, units, and float order multiple times over its year-and-a-half. The most recent changes came in August

2010 the Princess float being shortened to one unit, removing the Little Mermaid and Beauty and the Beast sections. As of the time of this article, rumors indicate this is in preparation for a 4th overlay of this parade to tie-in to the 2011 marketing campaign, “Let The Memories Begin”. For the record, the Magic Kingdom has not debuted an entirely new parade since 2001, a record to say the least.

Parades play an important role in Walt Disney World’s 40 year history and have been a tradition carried out through all four decades. For many, they embody what the Disney experience is all about. Every afternoon, Disney characters and whimsical floats fill the streets of the Magic Kingdom, entertaining thousands of children and children at heart. Even the most jaded guests can’t help but smile every time the infectious (yet always repetitive) parade music plays throughout the park. The love of the Disney characters, the admiration for the incredible spectacle of the floats, and the electrifying atmosphere of the parades ensure guests will be lining the streets for hours to see the three o’clock parade.

Tomorrow's Windows: Looking Back at Horizons

Michael Crawford

For that those who love the EPCOT Center that once was, no single attraction better conveyed the themes of that park than *Horizons*. While other Future World pavilions examine individual topics, *Horizons* tied those concepts together to show how advances in various fields would lead to better lifestyles in the future. *Horizons* represented a thesis statement for the park, and perhaps of all the pavilions it best evoked the ethos of Walt Disney's own EPCOT. For this reason and many others, not the least of which were the ride's technological wizardry, style, and humor, *Horizons* remains beloved to fans long after its closure.

Horizons' roots go back to as far as 1958 when Walt and his Imagineers proposed an expansion to Disneyland called Edison Square. Although never built, the concept evolved into the *Carousel of Progress*, which debuted as part of General Electric's Progressland pavilion at the New York World's Fair in 1964.

General Electric continued to sponsor the *Carousel of Progress* after it moved to the Magic Kingdom in 1975, and by the time of EPCOT's 1979 groundbreaking it was in negotiations to underwrite an attraction for the new park. In late 1979, it was announced that G.E. would sponsor an EPCOT pavilion called "Science and Invention."

G.E. hoped the new pavilion would show how their products could improve guests' lives and, by doing so, usher in the future. Their slogan at the time was "we bring good things to life," and that's what they wanted for the new show – something forward looking and progressive. G.E. advisors thought it critical to emphasize that the future will provide individuals many options for how to lead their lives.

The first designers assigned to the pavilion in 1979 were George McGinnis and Collin Campbell, who proposed something called the "Edison Lab." Much like the old Edison Square plans, this would have looked back at Thomas Edison and the origins of G.E. before surveying the company's history of technological feats.

This concept was rejected by Reginald Jones, then the chairman of G.E. Or, as Marty Sklar would later say, "They told us our idea stunk." The sponsor wanted something forward looking and spectacular; in their words, the new show "must not dwell on the past, it must be dedicated to the future." With a mandate that "the future should be exciting and thus the G.E. presentation should be a ride – a thrilling ride – to and through an exciting tomorrow," the Imagineers returned to the drawing board.

Several G.E. team members had worked with Disney since the World's Fair, and after some feedback the idea emerged to make the pavilion a follow-up to the *Carousel of Progress*. Whereas that show follows a family from the 1890s to the present, the new attraction would begin with a humorous look at the futurism of yesteryear before meeting up with the *Carousel* family in the next century – following them into a world of space colonies, undersea cities, and desert farms.

Family was important to the *Horizons* story. McGinnis said at the time, "We kept 'people' details in mind, too. We're convinced that even though environments will change, people won't. Teenagers in our show still monopolize the phone; kids and dogs still exasperate mom and dad. We believe one of the main differences high technology will make is that it will give us more choices."

Early designs were hashed out by a large team from both Imagineering and G.E., including McGinnis, Campbell, and Claude Coates. Coates, who took an early pass on many EPCOT attractions, served as Show Designer until McGinnis took over the role later on. Coates, along with Architect Bill Norton and Industrial Designer Bob Kurzweil, hammered out the preliminary layout for the attraction. After the designers determined a final storyline and layout, Tom Fitzgerald's story team honed the narrative to add humanizing detail to the overarching themes established by McGinnis, Sklar, and John Hench.

Ned Landon, a 30-year G.E. veteran, joined the team as the company's representative in 1979. The sponsor did more than just cut a check; several of its divisions contributed technical expertise in relevant areas. Advice ran the gamut from pavilion lighting and what a kitchen of the future might look like, to input from the Medical Systems division on how diagnostic equipment might be used in space.

The contributions didn't end there. Ride vehicles, made from Lexan polycarbonate, were operated with G.E. motors and drive systems. The company provided everything from wiring to transformers, infrared control systems to mobile radio applications. A G.E.-made robot, combined with their "Gemlink" video transmitter system, provided a live aerial view of the park to the pavilion's corporate lounge.

The pavilion was originally called *Century 3*; with America fresh off the excitement of the 1976 bicentennial, the pavilion intended to show what America could achieve in its third century. From a 1980 press release:

> *The Century 3 Pavilion, presented by General Electric, will celebrate the envisioned technological achievements of America's third century... the years of the 21st Century leading to the U.S. Tricentennial in 2076... and what these advances will mean to each of our lives.*
>
> *Visitors to the pavilion will see the ever-expanding opportunities and choices for tomorrow's world... and the important role their decisions will play in making those visions come true in Century 3.*

Imagineers eventually realized that *Century 3* might prove cryptic to foreign visitors; according to Landon, "the allusion to our own nation's history seemed too parochial." When G.E. officially signed on in October 1980, the name of the pavilion had been changed to *Future Probe*.

Renderings of the pavilion's exterior from 1980 appear indistinguishable from the building's final gemlike, space-age design by architect George Rester. The pavilion was called *Futureprobe* as late as April 1981, when it was decided that another renaming was in order. As Ned Landon famously said about the *Futureprobe* name, "We always thought it had a rather uncomfortable medical connotation." Several new titles were proposed, including *Great Expectations*, but in late 1981 the team settled on *Horizons*. As Landon would go on to say, "We thought *Horizons* was just right. There always is a horizon out there. If you try hard enough, you can get to where it is - and when you do, you find there's still another horizon to challenge you, and another beyond that."

Site work on *Horizons* began August 5th, 1981; construction commenced in January 1982 with opening day scheduled for October 1st, 1983. The show's specifications were daunting; with a ride time of 14 minutes 35 seconds, *Horizons* featured 35 scenes in its three-acre show building. Its 1,346-foot track could carry 2,660 guests per hour past the show's 49 audio-animatronic figures, 17 sets, 583 props,

456 plants – and 110 lighting effects which required 177 miles of fiber optics. The 78-foot high pavilion needed 3,700 tons of structural steel to enclose its 137,000 square feet of show space.

A trip aboard *Horizons* began in the FuturePort - a transportation hub of tomorrow. Kaleidoscopic travel posters, using artwork by Robert McCall, depicted potential destinations. There was the magnificent floating resort of Sea Castle in the Pacific Ocean; Mesa Verde, a flourishing city reclaimed from the desert; and Brava Centauri, the latest of the Centauri class of space stations.

The FuturePort, designed by Gil Keppler, also featured the pavilion's theme song - *New Horizons*, by George Wilkins. Legendary songwriters Richard and Robert Sherman were originally assigned to write the ride's theme, but their compositions were never used. One attempt, for *Century 3* in June 1980, was entitled *Tomorrow's Windows*. In October of that year, they wrote *Tomorrow is the Rainbow*; it seems to have also been called *New Horizons*. Another, *Reach for New Horizons*, circulates amongst fans; several versions are known to exist. Ultimately, the Shermans' material was rejected by G.E. who desired something that felt more fresh. They thought the songs seemed like traditional Disney fare, which was incongruous with their mandate for the show.

Aboard the attraction, on "Horizons Flight 83," riders sat four abreast in a unique variant of the time-tested Omnimover. Unlike other rides, *Horizons* vehicles faced only the left side of the track as, hanging from an overhead rail, they moved horizontally through the attraction. The ride's soundtrack, recorded digitally, was transmitted to receivers in each vehicle via infrared light.

After Mission Control signaled that "Horizons One" was ready to depart for the twenty-first century, a pair of narrators chimed in over the in-car loudspeakers to promise a look at the future, complete with desert farms, floating cities and colonies in space. Passengers then entered a "time travel" tunnel designed by WED Special Effects Manager Dean Sharits. Layers of hand-sculpted, sandblasted acrylic clouds concealed and diffused 22,000 points of shifting colored light – an effect requiring 40 miles of fiber optic cable.

Horizons' first act, "Looking Back at Tomorrow", examined the future through the eyes of past visionaries. Said Tom Fitzgerald, "The technologies that men like Verne and Wells envisioned were 100 years ahead of their time, but the designs remained rooted in their own time." These scenes were developed by Campbell and McGinnis before McGinnis became the attraction's Show Designer. A series of projections resembling woodcut illustrations introduced the concept; here was the Icarus of ancient legend, a man flying with the assistance of caged birds, Verne's own ship to the moon, and other improbable aviation schemes from antiquity.

Verne appeared next, aboard his ballistic craft from 1865's *From the Earth to the Moon.* Seemingly ill-prepared for zero gravity, the author's pet dog and an uncaged chicken floated freely in his lavishly-appointed Victorian spacecraft. Verne succeeds in reaching the moon, in a gag referencing the story's 1902 film adaptation by Georges Méliès.

The whimsical Paris of 1950 as envisioned by French author and illustrator Albert Robida (1848–1926) came next. Robida's future was a busy place; the sky filled with soaring craft shaped like fish or birds, while streams of nattily-attired tourists boarded "les Tubes" – air-propelled cylinders providing mass transit service to Madrid.

Around the corner appeared a vision more distinctly American – the Art Deco future of the 1930s and 40s, where easy living was guaranteed via automatic labor and push-button convenience. A leisurely gent stood, long-stemmed cigarette at his side, gazing out the window at an atomic-powered metropolis while a robotic butler vacuumed behind him. Above, a fashionable blonde soaked contentedly in a bubble bath as she watched television – a mammoth, black-and-white model which bore more of a resemblance to the radios of the era. Onscreen, a dapper fellow in a tuxedo crooned an adaptation of the classic Disney anthem *There's a Great, Big Beautiful Tomorrow.*

Originally penned by Richard and Robert Sherman for the *Carousel of Progress* in 1964, the song had long since been replaced in that attraction by another tune. Even after the song returned to the *Carousel of Progress* in 1994, its inclusion in *Horizons* remained a sly nod to Disney history. As performed by character actor Larry Cedar, the *Horizons* adaptation was a pastiche of big band-era crooners.

The Art Deco scene featured two of *Horizons*' best-remembered visions of retro-futurism. An older gentleman relaxing in a recliner received a haircut and shoeshine from robotic arms, while he enjoyed a tropical breeze from a device that could recreate everything from balmy trade winds to arctic gusts. A sunlamp overhead was adjustable to provide tans from Hawaii, the Bahamas, or Florida. Unnoticed, in the kitchen, was a glimpse at how the conveniences of the future might not prove foolproof; a robotic chef had gone haywire and was wreaking havoc. As the smiling automaton's head spun wildly around, its many arms flailed at stacks of dirty dishes and ruined food. The only beneficiary of this chaos was the cat of the house who lapped happily at the constantly-replenishing pool of spilt milk on the floor.

The next "look back at tomorrow" came through the films of the past. Black-lit theatre marquees, giving the appearance of multicolored neon, advertised science fiction films from the early years of cinema – *Metropolis* (1927), *Things to Come* (1936), and *Modern Times* (1939) were among those featured. As stylized theater marquees gave way to mid-century ranch houses and television aerials, 1930s sci-fi was replaced by televised futurism of the 1960s as seen in Disney's Ward Kimball-produced *Mars and Beyond* and *Magic Highway USA*.

The Neon City's visual style – fluorescent paint lit by ultraviolet lamps – continued in a scene depicting the "future from the 50s". The far-out panorama represented the jet-age futurism familiar from *The Jetsons*, complete with personal hovercraft and rocket packs.

The scene's minimalist look owed to budget cuts late in *Horizons*' development; early plans called for fully dimensional sets and animatronics but it was decided to use black-lit wire frames to save money. The savings were somewhat offset, though, when John Hench decreed that the scene wasn't using its allocated space well. Hench thought the cavernous area needed a large spire to draw the eye, and so the towering "Sky High School" was constructed to use the full height of the building.

Leaving the distant past, *Horizons* passengers entered the Omnisphere for a look at cutting-edge technologies of the current day – circa 1983. To create this most memorable element of the attraction, Imagineers placed two Omnimax screens together for the first time anywhere to create a massive projection surface 240 feet wide and 80 feet high.

The idea of using an IMAX screen in *Horizons* was first raised by Imagineer Dave Burke. Marty Sklar, then Executive Vice President for Creative Development at WED, brought the concept to McGinnis and asked him to incorporate it into the attraction. McGinnis, who had tinkered with curved Omnimax screens for a previous unproduced project, selected that process instead. McGinnis's original plans called for the Omnisphere – formed by three adjacent screens – to serve as the ride's grand finale; it was later moved to the attraction's midpoint by the story team.

Filmmaker Eddie Garrick was in charge of shooting the Omnimax scenes. Using 70mm film, he captured subjects ranging from undersea divers to a space shuttle launch. When the equipment required to film other desired subjects did not exist, Garrick and his team helped designed the necessary technology themselves. The result was innovative in several ways; shots of a spiraling DNA chain and the wire-frame of a space station represented the first use of computer animation in an Omnimax film. The micro-photography of growing crystals was another Omnimax first, as was the computer-enhanced Landsat satellite photography.

A booming score by George Wilkins rounded out the experience, with synthesizer work by Michael Boddicker and a grandiose solo on the pipe organ by Richard Bolks. For added kick, low-frequency sonic transducers were placed in ride vehicles near the base of each passenger's spine to add a rumbling effect during the film's space shuttle launch.

The ride reached its maximum height of 65 feet in the Omnisphere, placing guests at the "sweet spot" for viewing in the center of the screen. With walls three feet thick, the enormous theater was the largest single element of the pavilion and its placement greatly determined architect George Rester's final design for the building.

In Claude Coates's original layout for the attraction, vehicles approached the Omnisphere by rising along a spiraling track past a montage of artwork from pulp science-fiction magazines. McGinnis and Campbell researched these publications at the University of Redlands Science Fiction Library, and had a wealth of material from which to draw. The plan was for riders to enter the Omnisphere on the second floor where, surrounded by *three* screens, they would make two complete downward circuits around a central column before exiting. On the ground floor once more, vehicles would rise back to the second floor and enter the third act of the show.

During development, the *Horizons* team was asked to cut $10 million from the project's budget. One of the three Omnimax screens was eliminated, as was 600 feet of ride track comprising the upward and downward track spirals. In the final ride, vehicles rose to the second floor via one single, 90-second pass of two Omnimax screens. The pulp magazine montage was removed, and that space was instead used for the "future from the fifties" scene.

The third act of *Horizons*, "Tomorrow's Windows," jumped ahead to showcase life in the 21st century. While the future suggested by the Omnisphere might seem fantastic, the narrators assured that it wasn't science fiction; after all, they said, they lived there.

The tour of the future began in the "Urban Habitat" – home to the attraction's unnamed narrators. The ride's story shifted here to the family; Tom Fitzgerald said at the time, "We wanted to emphasize the family unit. Some people think that it may not exist in the future, but our feeling was that advances in transportation and communication will bring families closer together." Of course it's no coincidence that the narrator and his family strongly resembled the cast of the *Carousel of Progress* – right down to the familiar family dog.

The Nova Cite apartment overlooked soaring skyscrapers and swooping maglev trains. Our host, playing a tune on his "symphosizer," welcomed guests while his wife conversed with their daughter on the holographic telephone. After passing through the couple's hydroponic garden (designed, by the way, to actually work), the next stop was the desert farm of Mesa Verde where the narrators' daughter and her family lived.

As riders entered the citrus grove, a puff of scented air was blown towards the track by the Imagineering "smellitzer" scent cannon. The rich perfume of oranges brought the desert orchard to life and quickly became a hallmark of the attraction. To this day, fans continue to track down the elusive chemical formula from its original manufacturer in an attempt to evoke – if ever so slightly – the *Horizons* experience.

Mesa Verde, once desert, had been converted into a lush oasis thanks to advanced technology. Fields of generically engineered citrus stretched into the distance, monitored by the woman previously seen via hologram. Robotic harvesters farmed the fields in the background, while helium lifters loaded the crops for transport to market. The scene, originally developed by Claude Coates, used forced perspective to great effect in making the small show space appear to be a vast desert.

The technologies depicted, fantastic though they seemed, were developed with the help of expert consultants. Said McGinnis, "Both Disney and GE were anxious to show that desert, sea, and space could be interesting and practical places to live and work. We got some concepts and models together and tried them out on the experts." Assisting with the desert farm was Dr. Carl Hodges, founder of the Environmental Research Laboratory at the University of Arizona, and a key advisor on EPCOT's The Land pavilion.

Alex Taylor created the genetically engineered plants and trees that occupied the future farm, although at first he encountered some difficulties. "Every time I designed something I thought was totally new, I would take it over to our horticulturists and they would tell me it already existed," said Taylor. "I began to despair of coming up with something nature hadn't already done." Eventually he got the hang of it. Perhaps his most famous creation was the "Lorange," an elongated hybrid citrus fruit engineered to grow on the outside of the tree for easier harvesting. There were also "Pepcumbers" (a red pepper/cucumber hybrid), "Flavor Grapes" (clusters of multicolored grapes with different flavors), Siamese Apples (a "triple apple"), and Pinanas (a pineapple/banana hybrid). Said Taylor, "I designed a whole bunch of different kinds of these vegetables and then invited people in to look at them and decide which ones looked good enough to eat." Inspiration came from many directions – from the electric eel came the idea for the "Golden Glow"; from an ancient musical instrument came the "Aeolian Harp", which produced music from passing breezes; the kinked patterns of the circuit board inspired "Circuit Egg Ivy." Explained Taylor, "Carl Hodges told me that using the principles of genetic engineering, I could let my imagination run wild, and I did."

Back at Mesa Verde, the farmer has received a video call from her husband to warn that a storm is approaching. Passing her personal hovercraft, guests found the couple's desert home tucked into a natural landscape amongst desert rocks and a garden of tropical flowers. By a waterfall's pool, a housecat pawed unsuccessfully, at a jumping fish.

The habitat, with its glass floors and large windows, was designed and detailed by Gil Keppler, who had also helped McGinnis design the desert farm's control room. In the kitchen, the man of the house was trying to decorate an elaborate birthday cake, but his son seemed more interested in misdirecting the voice-activated cabinets. Meanwhile, a teenaged girl in the next room was supposed to be doing her chemistry homework (on her "Athene 2500" microcomputer) but, to her grandfather's chagrin, she's actually talking to her boyfriend on an enormous wall-sized videophone. The boyfriend, whom the narrator pejoratively refers to as a "beach boy," is studying marine biology on a floating city; his girlfriend's main concern seemed to be his potential tardiness for the upcoming family festivities. Tom Fitzgerald portrayed the boyfriend on film; the ride's designers dubbed his animatronic counterpart in the next scene "Tom II."

Slowly descending, riders entered the undersea world of Sea Castle. In the "solosub" bay, Tom II worked to repair a single-passenger submarine while chatting with his girlfriend. On the deck below, a class of young children – and their pet seal Rover – impatiently prepared for a diving expedition as their teacher reviewed the safety rules one last time. Two of the students were modeled on show designer McGinnis's own children; Scott (then 5) appeared as the boy getting licked by the seal and Shana (7) became the young blonde girl who sat tapping her toes impatiently.

Outside the floating city, in a scene detailed by Tom Scherman, diners could be seen enjoying dinner through a row of bubble-shaped windows. The young divers then re-appeared, swimming underneath the vast city in a projected effect. As the narrators touted the wealth of riches available in our oceans, riders passed robots harvesting manganese nodules and kelp from the seafloor.

Horizons' final destination was space station Brava Centauri. Originally, a special effect designed by Don Iwerks was to bridge sea and space; the submarines of Sea Castle and shuttles of Brava Centauri were designed with similar profiles, allowing for a projected submarine to morph into a space pod as viewers transitioned between the two scenes. Ultimately, the projector built for the effect proved susceptible to the vibrations of passing ride vehicles, rendering the concept impractical.

Once in orbit, construction workers were seen building a series of stations that rotated in the distance. Consulting on their design was Princeton physicist Gerard K. O'Neill, a staunch advocate for space colonization and designer of the "O'Neill Cylinder," on which the designs for Brava Centauri were heavily based. Inside the colony, past the airlock and shuttle bay, was a zero-g gymnasium where station inhabitants could exercise in rowing or bicycling simulators, or perhaps enjoy a game of low-gravity basketball. Outside a long, windowed tunnel rotated the interior of the cylindrical colony. An eight-foot spherical model was built for this effect, which was filmed from inside with a 19mm Kowa lens. It required 8,000 miniature lights to bring life to Shim Yokoyama's painting of the homes, green space, and recreational facilities of the station interior. Sharp-eyed guests might have even noticed a hidden Disneyland among the station's features.

The shuttle *Santa Maria* had arrived in the docking port and its passengers were adjusting to their new habitat. As little Tommy floated around the room with his dog Napoleon, his father tried to retrieve the child's stray magnetic boots. Meanwhile, the family's baggage slowly started to drift away. Tom Fitzgerald's story team had proposed adding the family to introduce warmth to the scene; young Tommy was modeled after McGinnis's son Reed, then 5.

Input from NASA and the Jet Propulsion Laboratory inspired a facility where giant crystals grew in microgravity, but riders could not linger - it was time for a party. Everyone had gathered to wish a happy birthday to the narrators' grandson, living with his parents on the space colony. Appearing via holophone were the narrators, their granddaughter from Mesa Verde, and her "beach boy" boyfriend. Always a stickler for authenticity, Disney actually had to pay the copyright holder for the rights to the song *Happy Birthday to You.*

In the pavilion's early design process, a show writer at WED named Marc Nowadnick had developed a post-show area called "FutureFair" to highlight G.E. products and services. Jack Welch, who had become chair of G.E., actually vetoed the idea of a post-show because, remarkably, he thought it seemed too commercial. The post-show's $28 million budget was instead funneled into the ride itself.

One proposal for the post-show was for a tunnel through which guests would pass on a moving belt. Inside, they would be followed by images highlighting the businesses that comprised the G.E. empire. The concept was inspired by journal articles McGinnis had read describing the projection of advertisements in subway tunnels alongside moving trains. Having studied the mechanics of synchronizing projections to ride vehicles, McGinnis salvaged his idea when the story team moved his Omnisphere finale to the ride's midpoint. Sklar asked McGinnis for a new ending, so the idea from the rejected post-show was adapted into *Horizons*' famous "Choose Your Tomorrow" sequence.

It was originally proposed to use the ride's finale to poll guests on various issues about their future, but G.E. rejected that idea. Claiming they could just as easily get meaningful polling data from surveying a small sample of guests as they exited, they decided instead to use the interactive technology to allow guests to select the ride's finale. After leaving Brava Centauri, "Horizons One" passengers were to return home via transportation of their own choosing.

Marty Kindel took McGinnis's idea for moving projections and developed it into a 50-foot-long traveling picture that, combined with tilting vehicles and low-frequency vibrations, provided a primitive simulator experience. Riders chose one of three destinations via a console in their vehicle; the result with the most votes would be the return route to the FuturePort. Options included a hovercraft flight over the desert, a solosub from Sea Castle, and an intercolony shuttle to Omega Centauri. Plans originally included a fourth film, a maglev train ride through Nova Cite, but that was scrapped.

Special effects veteran Dave Jones, who had worked on *Star Wars*, spent two years designing, constructing and filming the miniature sets. According to Jones, the desert film was the longest continuous sequence ever done with miniatures, and required an 86-foot model – all for 31 seconds of video. Disney's ACES computer-guided motion control camera provided the precise camera movements needed, and a special gantry was built so that the camera wouldn't cast a shadow on the model. It was filmed in an enormous hangar at the Burbank airport, while the space sequence was shot on Soundstage 3 at the Disney lot. The undersea scene was shot dry; smoke was blown onto the set to create the illusion of oceanic haze.

The 35mm films were transferred to videodisc and rear projected onto screens in-ride with G.E. Talaria PJ-5055 light-valve video projectors. These projectors were capable of the resolution needed to project large video images on screens close to the viewer. Concerned about visual intrusion from neighboring vehicles' films, G.E. team members requested that flaps be added between ride vehicles.

After riders unloaded, they originally passed by an enormous 19-by-60 foot mural by renowned artist Robert McCall. McCall, who had done conceptual artwork for *2001: A Space Odyssey* and *The Black Hole*, spent three months at his Arizona studio developing the concept, which he called "The Prologue and the Promise." This was followed by six months at the Disney studio in Burbank painting the actual mural with the help of his wife Louise, finishing in March of 1983. McCall originally created a sketch of his idea, and then a 10-foot master image. This was sectioned off into one-inch grid squares, which were projected onto a large canvas to allow McCall to sketch a perfectly scaled final image.

According to McCall, the mural represented the "flow of civilized man from the past into the present and toward the future." The result was spectacular – a vast panorama of human achievement beginning with prehistory and culminating in a towering space-age metropolis. Unfortunately, exit polls showed that guests weren't associating sponsor G.E. with the attraction, and McCall's masterpiece was replaced just a few short years after its debut. In its place was a rainbow-lit, mirrored hallway leading to a G.E. logo, casting off sparks as it rotated behind a giant lens.

G.E. eventually abandoned the pavilion it helped create when its sponsorship ended on September 30th, 1993. *Horizons* continued to operate without a sponsor, but with no one coming forward to fund a much-needed refurbishment (and Disney leadership unwilling to pay for an update), the pavilion closed in late 1994. Thought was given to converting the building into a new space-based attraction, but again Disney balked at the cost. *Horizons* re-opened in December 1995, after delays pushed back Test Track's opening, and it continued to operate until it entertained its last guest on the 9th of January, 1999. The pavilion remained intact until March of 2000; it was then slowly emptied and demolished over the span of several months.

While *Horizons* is now long gone, its memory lives on in generations of fans – some of whom were never even able to experience it in person. It lives on in countless online tributes, fan-produced videos, and homemade t-shirts. Most importantly, it lives on in a vision of the future that, regardless of outdated color schemes or polyester outfits, remains just as distant, elusive and inspiring as it was in 1983.

Michael Crawford *is a writer living in Chapel Hill, N.C. A lifelong fan of Walt Disney and his works, and obsessed since an early age with the inner workings, history and secrets of Walt Disney World, he is the publisher of Progress City, U.S.A.(progresscityusa.com).*

A Brief History of the Future: From EPCOT to EPCOT Center

Michael Crawford

When Walt Disney announced EPCOT in 1966, the Experimental Prototype Community of Tomorrow was billed as a living, working, model city of the future intended for Disney's expansive property in central Florida. A constantly changing showplace for American innovation and industry, it would serve as a "living laboratory" for new concepts in urban planning. Today's Epcot, which debuted as EPCOT Center in 1982, differs greatly from those original plans. Similar to the great World's Fairs of the 20th century, Epcot is far from Walt's city of the future. Yet it has remained popular since its debut and its unique spin on the theme park genre has earned it generations of devoted fans.

These are the two faces of EPCOT that most Disney fans know – Walt's futuristic city, and the theme park designed by his successors. Yet between Disney's death in 1966 and EPCOT Center's 1982 opening, the Imagineers at WED Enterprises struggled for more than a decade to create a workable approach to the concept.

Most retrospectives make it seem as if EPCOT changed from community of tomorrow to theme park overnight, or even gloss over the issue to make it seem as if EPCOT Center was designed according to Walt's plans. To do so does a great disservice to the literally thousands of talented conceptualists, artists, craftspeople, designers, engineers, writers, and many others who spent so much time bringing EPCOT to life. Its creation was an achievement, and a look at how the project actually developed makes its evolution seem much more organic and understandable.

It's impossible to contextualize EPCOT Center or Walt Disney World without revisiting Walt's original plans for his Florida property. After all, his main interest in the Florida project was EPCOT; while the Magic Kingdom would contain new and exciting attractions, theme parks were a realm that Walt had already conquered. For him there was always a new and exciting challenge to face, and as planning ramped up on his 27,000 acres in Florida that new challenge was EPCOT.

While Disney had considered the idea of a "city of tomorrow" for some time, he revealed little at the press conference announcing the Florida project in 1965. Acknowledging the difficulties of keeping such a project up-to-date, he admitted that one idea under consideration was for the two cities proposed for his property to have different themes – "Yesterday" and "Tomorrow." While two municipalities, the cities of Bay Lake and Lake Buena Vista, were eventually established to govern Disney's holdings, Walt's idea for "Tomorrow" would evolve into EPCOT.

In August of 1966, a memo from Economic Research Associates (ERA) outlined the objectives of EPCOT: to create a city representing optimal patterns of urban living 25 years in the future, to fashion "an environment without equal or precedent" that would act as a model for other cities, and "to effectuate an experimental prototype city that will never cease to introduce, test and demonstrate new ideas and technologies which will contribute to the civilized growth and well-being of man."

EPCOT would draw as little as possible from strategies of the past. It would strive to be dynamic and also relatable on a human scale. Each element of the city would integrate into the whole, but also retain a distinct identity to provide a sense of orientation and familiarity. Interaction between neighborhoods would encourage a feeling of community, as would the economic diversity built into neighborhoods themselves. It was crucial, according to the ERA report, that EPCOT not become a "country-club" district, with housing "available only to whites in the upper-third income group at best."

At the start, EPCOT seems to have been as much of a social experiment as it was a technological one. Walt's quote that his city would have no slums because "we won't let them develop" is often cited to imply some sinister draconian intent, but in actuality it indicated the hope that these problems could be prevented by altering the social systems that create them.

The city would introduce innovative systems, such as advanced telecommunications networks, and techniques like new building methods and materials. To allow the maximum amount of flexibility in their experimentation, Disney required special legislation from the state of Florida before construction proceeded. These demands were eventually met with the creation of the Reedy Creek Improvement District in 1967.

Planning continued throughout 1966 and Walt's vision quickly became more concrete. Notes from planning meetings that October indicate that EPCOT would be a company town; everyone living there would be employed either in Disney's own operations or in nearby industrial centers. The population would not actually own their residences (and, therefore, would not have local voting rights). Retirees were not allowed; everyone living in EPCOT would be a working part of the experiment.

On October 27th, 1966, a mere month before his death, Walt outlined his utopian plans in the famous "EPCOT film." Intended to solicit corporate participation in the endeavor and to encourage support for needed legislation, the 24-minute film showed what the impresario had in mind for his "Disney World" project.

Drawing from the work of Victor Gruen and Ebenezer Howard, the city's radial design evoked Howard's "garden city" concept and featured a high-density, enclosed downtown area at its center. A 30-story hotel and convention center towered overhead; below, the public had access to fifty acres of businesses, shopping areas and entertainment and recreation districts. Encircling the high-density core, a greenbelt provided recreation as well as civic services; beyond that sat low-density suburban housing. Public transportation connected all areas by either WEDWAY *PeopleMover* or monorail; links to the north led to the Magic Kingdom and its resort hotels, while to the south a 1,000 acre industrial park would provide jobs to city residents. The far southern terminus of the monorail line connected to the entrance plaza for the entire resort, as well as an "airport of the future."

EPCOT was dealt a critical blow with Walt's death in December, 1966, but his city of tomorrow remained the centerpiece of the company's plans when they were announced in Orlando on February 2, 1967. After showing the "EPCOT film", Roy O. Disney was careful to point out that while Walt's focus in that presentation was the city, a theme park would also be a key part of the resort and would be the first element built.

Disney suspended long-term master planning in Florida in 1967, in order to focus all of the company's attention and resources on the development and construction of the theme park and resort areas. The company tended to kick the ball down the field whenever EPCOT came up; while still planned, its scope and cost led Disney to predict a target date roughly a decade after phase one's completion. As a Disney spokesman said in December 1968, "We could build it faster if we would use other people's money. We won't because we want to control it."

Nevertheless, development of Disney World was billed as "leading up" to the eventual realization of EPCOT – predicted, in 1971, as still being about a decade away. In mid-1971, Roy O. Disney commissioned a report by the firm of Hart, Krivatsy, and Stubee to assess the company's long-term planning options. Three potential plans were presented in January of 1972; one, billed as the most difficult to enact, was a modified version of Walt's prototype city. Sadly, Roy Disney had passed away in December 1971; it's therefore impossible to know how he would have chosen to proceed.

By 1972, construction was underway at Lake Buena Vista on what would much later be known as the Disney Village Resort. A smaller city that had its origin in plans for a retirement community for EPCOT residents, it was designed as a second-home community; again, Disney would retain ownership of the land but residents would buy their homes or townhouses under a "condominium-form" model.

Lake Buena Vista was promoted as a testing ground; it was a place where technologies and ideas proposed for EPCOT could be tried and refined in advance. While it marked the beginning of Disney World's second phase, the company underscored that Lake Buena Vista was not EPCOT. Gen. William E. Potter, vice president of the Walt Disney World Co., told interviewers that "it's not to be confused with EPCOT. Lake Buena Vista is a precursor of EPCOT." Disney chairman Donn Tatum underlined this point, saying that the community "will provide an introduction for concepts we think will be appropriate for inclusion in EPCOT, but, I repeat, this is not EPCOT." The big project was still "far down the road," according to Disney, and if Lake Buena Vista proved unsuccessful EPCOT's timetable would be moved "a little further down the road."

Despite this ambivalence, Disney president Card Walker announced in October 1972 that groundbreaking for EPCOT was scheduled for 1974. Six months later, spokesman Charlie Ridgeway said that construction was at least five years away. Eventually it became clear that momentum was cooling on the project. This was decried by some in the Florida legislature, which had granted Disney special jurisdictional powers for building EPCOT. It was even noted by the *New York Times* in October of 1972, in an article that referred to the city as the Disney organization's "impossible dream." Even Bill Stubee, whose firm was helping Disney draft their master plan for the site, told the *Times*, "The Disney organization is fascinated by technical experimentation, but scared to death of social concerns." The company still used Walt's quotes about EPCOT to describe the upcoming project, but it's uncertain how close any plan could come to his vision when a partner in the planning firm helping design its layout was quoted as saying, "The monorail is a futuristic idea whose time has passed."

In December of 1973, word came that Disney had decided to proceed with EPCOT; it was announced once more by Card Walker in May 1974. In a speech to the American Marketing Association, Walker gave lip service to EPCOT's original concept while indicating the new direction in which development would proceed.

Quoting liberally from Walt's film, Walker then pointed out that Disney "[did] not seek the commitment of individuals and families to permanent residence." Housing, intended primarily for "transients," would be the last element of EPCOT constructed. First would come an "international showcase" displaying the cultures and wares of various nations. An "American industry showcase" would follow, then low and high-density housing and, finally, the city core. Walker indicated that during the next year the company would organize a number of research teams composed of leading "businessmen, industrialists, scientists and artists" to determine how to best deal with the problems EPCOT sought to address.

Whether due to the energy crisis of 1973-74, which ended a number of other planned projects, or as a result of natural creative processes, Walt's EPCOT had clearly been abandoned by end of 1974. Walt Disney Productions soon gave up any pretense that it was going to build a city of the future in Florida; in July 1975, a Disney spokesman publicly stated that "the concept that was originally envisioned is no longer relevant." Disney had to do something, though; after all, concessions that the company had obtained from the state of Florida were predicated on the assumption that they were necessary for building EPCOT. Outside of the legislature, the public clamored for information. Walt's futuristic city had been well publicized in the run-up to Walt Disney World's opening, and people would not forget it easily. It was clear that despite Walker's back-pedaling, EPCOT was not going to go away. In fact, it was just beginning.

A turning point came in 1975 when Disney announced that it would begin "concentrated planning and design for the 'centers of activity' within EPCOT." Walker reiterated his commitment that February, telling the Christian Science Monitor that "this is not double-talk ... It's serious. We are really getting it off the ground." EPCOT, said Walker, would address "what is the best method of solar energy ... new types of crop rotation ... the whole field of solid waste disposal."
Why 1975? According to Walker, it marked the end of Phase I of Walt Disney World's development. The metric for this was the theoretical rides-per-hour capacity of the Magic Kingdom; the addition of several new attractions had pushed the park's capacity to 70,000, matching that of Disneyland. The endpoint of Phase I had been something of a moving target; prior to the park's opening the company gave themselves five years to achieve an annual attendance of 10 million guests, after which they would proceed with EPCOT. When the resort surpassed that benchmark in its first year, the timetable was recalibrated. According to Walker, this meant that studies for EPCOT were announced two years ahead of schedule. By early 1975, Disney was working with General Electric, RCA, the National Science Foundation and the Jet Propulsion Lab to develop concepts for EPCOT. Said Walker, "We think we can do it, and if we can, it'll be one of the most exciting things the company has ever done. It's bigger than us, but because we're us we might be able to get it done. We're communicators; why not be able to communicate technology as well as entertainment?"

On July 14th, 1975, Walker and Tatum announced the company's plans for EPCOT – again - for media, guests, and visiting dignitaries. Clearly recognizing a different concept from what Walt had originally announced, the headline in the Miami News read, "Disney's 'City of Tomorrow' will be built – without residents." Walker, later reporting on the new "dynamic and achievable" approach to EPCOT, said that Disney "must avoid building a huge, traditional 'brick and mortar' community which might possibly become obsolete, in EPCOT terms, as soon as it is completed."

"We believe," Walker continued, "we must develop a community system oriented to the communication of new ideas, rather than to serving the day-to-day needs of a limited number of permanent residents."

Disney slowly began to promote the narrative that Walt Disney World itself, with its innovative use of technology and prototype systems, was EPCOT made real. EPCOT was never meant to be an actual city, the story would go, but instead it laid out the values upon which the Florida property was modeled. Up to and beyond EPCOT Center's 1982 opening, Disney pushed the idea that EPCOT and Walt Disney World were one and the same, and that the resort's innovations were exactly what Walt was talking about back in 1966. The company became increasingly defensive about the issue over time, later pointing at the thousands of people sleeping every night on Disney property as examples of EPCOT's "residents." In 1975, the memory of Walt's soaring skyscrapers and swooping *PeopleMover*s was still too fresh in the public consciousness for this story to have completely worked, so the company would occasionally admit that they had changed EPCOT into a form with which they were more comfortable. Many of EPCOT's ideas would be incorporated into the resort to service its population of tourists and corporate personnel; these elements would be accessible to the public through a series of attractions that would inform guests about various EPCOT initiatives and allow them to experience the innovations firsthand.

In 1974, it had been revealed that EPCOT would take the form of a series of "satellites." The EPCOT satellite sites were a loosely-defined variety of projects meant to publicly demonstrate innovations in relevant fields of study. These could include any of the innovations already used for the working infrastructure of Walt Disney World, or they could be off-site sponsored research projects. EPCOT thus became more of a philosophical construct than a physical one; the satellites could be anything from new attractions to the systems supporting Disney operations – systems like the AVAC trash disposal system, or the innovative water treatment and power generation facilities. An EPCOT "satellite" need not even be a physical facility; Disney defined it as a "function or activity that affects the quality of life, defines and develops new concepts to meet the needs of mankind, or helps to stimulate understanding between the peoples of the world." Examples cited were "centers for corporate training and industrial research, energy and the environment, design and the arts, communications and the media, educational research, the sciences, experimental and prototype living environments, a health and medical data bank, [and] a major computer center." The satellites would be open to guests, allowing them to see cutting-edge research and development in progress.

The first satellite, announced in 1974, would be the World Showcase. This new attraction was to be "the first major step in the evolution of EPCOT."

The concept of a Disney-built international exposition went back to at least 1955, when International Street was designed for Disneyland. The idea was never realized, but emerged later as an international shopping complex in EPCOT's enclosed downtown area. When EPCOT ceased to be an actual city, its international area was revived as the first of the EPCOT satellites.

World Showcase would provide a few dozen nations the chance to introduce guests to their history, culture and industries. International pavilions would occupy two large semi-circular buildings, resembling the style of the Magic Kingdom's Tomorrowland. Encircling the "Courtyard of Nations," the modernist structures overlooked a large plaza featuring extensive theater and performance facilities. Overhead, a towering spire and observation deck provided a view of the area surrounding the Showcase's 100-acre site adjacent to the Transportation and Ticket Center.

Around the perimeter of the courtyard, WEDWAY *PeopleMover*s provided internal transportation as well as a link to the Ticket and Transportation Center. Weaving in and out of the pavilions, they also allowed a sneak peek at the park's attractions. Monorails provided access to the Magic Kingdom and its resorts, as well as Lake Buena Vista. Disney planned to charge a single admission for the World Showcase, which was a new concept for the company at that time.

To promote a sense of goodwill, each pavilion had equal facing on the plaza. Buildings were modular, so that nations wishing to sponsor more extensive shows could push back the rear wall for increased space; pavilions would thus have equal widths but varying depths. The pavilions were enclosed, but inside they were not unlike World Showcase today. Plans called for themed restaurants, shops, and cultural presentations; there were also to be facilities for business conferences, and commercial elements like product exhibits and industrial displays. Despite their modernist facades, their interiors would feature famous landmarks and scenes from participating nations. Each pavilion was to feature a Disney-designed ride or attraction; renderings show a Mexico pavilion similar to today's, complete with boat ride, while others depict a simulated bullet train ride through the Japanese countryside.

Presentations were made throughout 1975 to at least 31 different nations; ambassadorial-level discussions were held in Orlando, New York, and Washington, D.C.. Nations were asked to sign a minimum ten-year lease for their spot in World Showcase; they would also be responsible for the costs of designing, developing and constructing the pavilion and all of its attractions. Nations would also cover the cost of housing international cast members.

Disney announced that construction on World Showcase would begin in 1978 and open in 1980; later in 1975, it was announced that there had been so much interest in the project that the timetable had been moved up. Construction was now to commence in 1976 with a targeted opening day of October 1st, 1979.

Aside from the satellite sites, a crucial part of the EPCOT plan announced in 1975 was The EPCOT Institute. This independent organization would provide the administrative structure necessary to facilitate participation in EPCOT and its satellite research activities by all interested parties. It would also act as a conduit to sponsors and the public to disseminate the benefits of EPCOT-related research. A series of "expert advisory boards" would be established to guarantee the credibility of these projects.

The company seems to have taken the scientific mission of EPCOT seriously; at the announcement of the project, Card Walker said that "EPCOT will be a 'forum,' where creative men and women of science, industry, government and the arts, from around the world, can present and demonstrate new concepts and systems … no one company, no one nation alone could accomplish the goal of EPCOT."

To help coordinate the recruitment of sponsors and participants, Disney brought aboard two prominent executives to act as the public faces of new EPCOT initiatives. L. Gordon Cooper, scientist and celebrity astronaut due to his membership in the fabled Mercury 7, led the technological aspects of the project as Vice President of Research and Development for EPCOT. C. Langhorne Washburn, the Assistant Secretary of Commerce for Tourism, resigned his political appointment to become the World Showcase Vice President. Washburn would coordinate the diplomatic efforts required to ensure international participation in the EPCOT project.

The real innovation of the 1975 plan was the Future World Theme Center. A single site in which the research underway in the EPCOT satellites would be accessible to guests, it would provide a nexus for the various EPCOT initiatives. Intended for the site later occupied by EPCOT Center, the Theme Center marked the emergence of what would evolve into the Future World we know today.

There would be no fee for guests to visit the Future World Theme Center; it was to be a "long-range, non-profit project." Admission would be charged to the World Showcase and other satellite sites. The Theme Center and World Showcase would be connected by monorail, and other future satellite sites would be tied into the resort transportation system as well.

Entrance to the Theme Center would be through the Communications Corridor or "Communicore." Guests would first experience the "EPCOT Overview Circle-Vision Theaters," inside which, according to the Spring 1976 *Disney News*, "360-degree movie screens and various displays will offer guests an overview of current EPCOT projects. Guests can then visit the area, called satellites, of particular interest to them." The show would also inform EPCOT guests of scheduled activities at the satellite sites on the day of their visit.

The "Information Gallery" led guests to the center of the park, where the World City Model would depict the evolution of major cities by the use of miniatures and a variety of special effects. It would culminate in a model community of the future, similar to Disney's "Progress City" model of years past.

Branching out from the center of the park were three major "theme center pavilions." These pavilions, Science and Technology, Community, and Communications and the Arts, were to feature themed attractions sponsored by corporations, private groups, or governments.

Announced in July of 1975, the Future World Theme Center was to begin construction in 1978. As to cost, officials stated that World Showcase by itself could "reach dimensions and expenditures similar to that of the current Magic Kingdom theme park." Another spokesman said that the Florida property currently represented "an investment of $650 million now. We don't have a figure on how much money is to be involved in the new attractions, but it's possible that it could involve the same amount." Over time, that would of course prove an understatement.

The EPCOT of 1975 is very different from the EPCOT Center that opened in 1982, but we can see the germination of many ideas that would develop into that later park. For the very first time, we had early versions of both Future World and World Showcase, and over the next year those concepts would be combined into a single park. What's interesting is how this version of EPCOT was a very functional environment for active research and development. Instead of just addressing themes relating to the future, the EPCOT satellite centers would feature working installations of cutting-edge systems and the latest developments of public and private institutions and corporations.

The new momentum behind EPCOT can be seen in the increasingly aggressive marketing of the concept throughout 1975. In September of that year, Disney took advantage of the annual conference of the Southern Governors' Association to help promote EPCOT. The conference, which not coincidentally was held at the Contemporary Resort on Disney property, brought a number of notable politicians to Orlando where they were a captive audience for Disney's presentations.

Aiding efforts was Florida Governor Reuben Askew, who assisted Disney in making their EPCOT presentation to Secretary of State Henry Kissinger, Senate Majority Leader Mike Mansfield (D-MT), and EPA Administrator Russell Train. The dignitaries were said to have "expressed their enthusiasm" for the concept. According to Governor Mills E. Godwin, Jr., of Virginia, upon witnessing the presentation, "The depth of planning and the vision that went into the concept, I am certain, will assure its success." Georgia Governor George D. Busbee said, "It is a concept that I feel certain will do a great deal for our own country and for the cause of world peace." Secretary Kissinger assigned two of his top aides to view the presentation, and the State Department arranged meetings for the Disney marketing department in Amsterdam, Athens, Copenhagen, Brussels and Paris. Disney eventually opened an office in Washington, D.C. where Washburn could more easily present the EPCOT concept to diplomats and politicians. One of these meetings took place in December 1975, when Disney executives made a presentation to members of Congress in the theater of the Rayburn House Office Building.

Throughout 1976, Disney worked to sign sponsors for the project. When corporations and governments failed to sign on the dotted line, however, Disney knew it couldn't fund both the World Showcase and the Future World Theme Center. There just wasn't enough backing out there to fully realize both projects, so in late 1976 there came the fateful day when a decision had to be made. Not wanting to completely eliminate one of the two concepts, Imagineers pushed the two models together and EPCOT Center was born.

Early EPCOT Center might still seem alien to the modern viewer. Entrance to the park was through World Showcase, which would act as a "Main Street" area. This World Showcase was still the sleek, modern, semicircular breezeway from earlier plans; the idea of open-air pavilions with iconic national architecture had yet to emerge. Spaceship Earth had yet to sprout, too; renderings show large spires reaching into the sky where the two sections of the park met.

The park's themes were stated as "Man and His World Today" and "Man and His World Tomorrow." In World Showcase, pavilions were designed for major nations, each featuring a show or attraction, a restaurant, a shopping "street," and an area focusing on trade and travel. Examples of attractions included an omnimover ride through Japan, Venezuelan cable cars through the rainforest, and a cruise down the rivers of Germany. Work began on ideas for an American pavilion which Disney claimed would be "worth the price of admission" to the park by itself.

Plans for Future World were vague, but there were ideas for a major introductory show "about man and his spaceship earth." This "one-of-a-kind" theater would combine film and "automated techniques" to tell a story about man's future potential. Guests would then disperse into Future World to learn about a number of topics including energy, health and medicine, communications, and several more.

Things began to snap into place in 1977 when, with great fanfare, the company rather breathlessly heralded the "conceptual breakthrough" of Master Plan 5 – their newest vision for EPCOT. For the first time, models of the park are recognizably "EPCOT Center." Future World and World Showcase were in the proper arrangement, World Showcase consisted of individual, themed show buildings (an idea envisioned and promoted by designer Harper Goff), and there's even a Spaceship Earth – even if it was gold, and not completely off the ground yet.

Surprisingly, though, the vision for Future World matched fairly closely on a pavilion-by-pavilion basis the park that opened in 1982. World Showcase took the form of a double promenade, providing far more space for potential pavilions than the final layout. The American Adventure, labeled on the model as "U.S.A.", sits not at the far end of the World Showcase lagoon, but instead straddles the path from Future World to World Showcase. It would remain in this spot until

1979. Although things were still in flux, it seemed, at last, that the Imagineers had found a concept that they liked.

If, that was, they could secure the funding. Things remained dicey until General Motors signed on as EPCOT's first major sponsor in January of 1978. Exxon followed later that month. The slow accumulation of sponsors gave Disney leadership the confidence to proceed with another – and this time final – announcement on October 2nd, 1978. Speaking before the 26th World Congress of the International Chamber of Commerce at Walt Disney World, Walker announced that EPCOT Center would open on October 1st, 1982.

There were still innumerable additions and changes to make to the EPCOT design both before and after its 1979 groundbreaking, but the general layout of the park remained fairly faithful to that outlined in the 1978 announcement. Pavilions would come and go on that giant site model in the WED Enterprises warehouse; some, like the "Life and Health" pavilion would be delayed until later years, while others like the massive Space pavilion, Tony Baxter's intriguing alternate version of The Land, and the impressive dark ride planned for The Living Seas would never be realized. In World Showcase, many national pavilions were designed and even announced before fading into the mists of history.

It would take three more years for EPCOT Center to open, and in that time it would become the largest private construction project in the world. Astounding as that is, it should not overshadow the many years preceding groundbreaking during which Walt Disney created a visionary city of the future and his creative heirs worked to turn those ideals into a theme park unlike any the world had ever seen.

The Walt Disney World Monorail System

Jason Diffendal

¡Por favor manténgase alejado de las puertas!

If this line is the first thing that comes to mind when someone mentions the Walt Disney World Monorail System, then you've probably ridden the monorail more times than you care to admit. The admonition to "Please stand clear of the doors!" was recorded by Jack Wagner, "the Voice of Disneyland," in both English and Spanish for the Walt Disney World Monorail System. This part of the spiel can still be heard today aboard the "Highway in the Sky."

The monorail is often a favorite "attraction" of children visiting the Walt Disney World Resort, notwithstanding the fact that it's located outside of the theme parks. I can remember as a child staying at the Contemporary Resort, and how excited my sister and I were at the sight of the monorail silently gliding through our hotel. We couldn't wait to board this futuristic transportation system, as it was such a unique and exciting way to get to the Magic Kingdom or EPCOT Center. Walt Disney World provided many guests with their first monorail experience, and the Walt Disney World Monorail is the subject of many fond memories.

Origins: The Disneyland-ALWEG Monorail System

Though the Walt Disney World Resort opened in 1971, the origins of the Walt Disney World Monorail System go back much further. Walt Disney World's monorails are actually the fourth iteration of the Disney monorail design. The original design debuted in Disneyland on June 14, 1959 as the Disneyland-ALWEG Monorail System. The first incarnation of Walt Disney's original vision for the future of urban transportation was designed jointly by WED Enterprises and the Alweg Company in 1958, and constructed by Disney in California. (WED is derived from the initials of Walter Elias Disney. WED Enterprises – known today as WDI, Walt Disney Imagineering – was founded on December 16, 1952 as the design and development arm of the company. ALWEG is an acronym derived from the name of the company's founder, Dr. Axel Lennart Wenner-Gren, a Swedish industrial magnate.)

Since the conception of Disneyland, Walt Disney had envisioned installing a monorail at the park. During a visit to Europe in 1957, Admiral Joe Fowler and other Disney engineers visited the Alweg test site near Cologne, Germany. The Alweg Company had been operating their experimental prototype monorail on a one-mile curving beamway since 1952. The engineers reported that the Alweg design would be suitable not only for Disneyland, but for urban installations as well. This was important since Walt wanted Disneyland's monorail to serve as a practical example for municipalities to use as the basis of their own mass transit solutions.

In 1958, WED joined with the Alweg Company to develop a practical monorail system for Disneyland based on the Alweg design. The Disneyland track layout had been purposely designed to include features which would commonly be required in metropolitan areas: curvatures with a 120-foot radius, overpasses, and grades of up to seven percent. These features would reinforce the practicality of the system. The entire cost of the system was about one million dollars.

Disneyland's original Mark I fleet consisted of two 3-car trains, Red and Blue. The Bob Gurr-designed Buck Rogers-inspired trains ran along a track eight-tenths of a mile long. In 1961, a third train, Gold, with four cars, was added to the fleet, and the original two trains were lengthened to four cars; these three trains then received the Mark II designation. This expansion was necessitated by the extension of the system to the Disneyland Hotel. The track length nearly tripled, measuring 12,300 feet upon completion of the work.

In 1964, Bob Gurr's years of experience with the monorails led him to begin work on a new Learjet-inspired monorail design. This new five-car design became the Mark III trains which replaced the Mark II fleet in 1969. WED Transportation Systems Inc, a division of WED Enterprises, manufactured a set of four trains at a cost of over two million dollars. This same design was used for the fleet of monorails that would debut at the opening of Walt Disney World in 1971.

The Walt Disney World Monorail System Debuts with Mark IV Trains

The plans for Walt Disney World called for monorail transportation as a major part of the resort's utopian urban planning design. In fact, in a 1980s-vintage publication on the monorail system, Disney claimed that the "economic viability of the entire Walt Disney World Resort Area is hinged on the performance and reliability of the Mark IV Monorail System." Two concentric loops surround the Seven Seas Lagoon; the outer express loop shuttles passengers between the Transportation and Ticket Center (TTC) and the Magic Kingdom, while the inner loop acts as the local line, connecting the Magic Kingdom and the TTC with the Contemporary Resort, the Polynesian Resort (originally the Polynesian Village Resort), and, when it opened in 1988, the Grand Floridian Resort & Spa (originally the Grand Floridian Beach Resort).

A fleet of ten Mark IV trains were built by Martin Marietta in 1971-1972 at a cost of about six million dollars. The cars were shipped individually and during installation were permanently coupled with articulated joints. Each of the five-car, 171-foot-long, 92,000-pound white monorail trains had a unique colored stripe used as identification. Monorails Orange (delivered April 5), Green (delivered May 20), and Gold (delivered June 15) were the first trains to enter service, on September 1, 1971. Monorail Blue was the fourth train, and entered service on September 20. These four trains were the only ones that had been delivered prior to the opening of the Walt Disney World Resort on October 1, so the resort operated with four trains from opening day until Monorail Red began service on November 7. Monorail Yellow was placed into service on December 3, and was the last of the monorails to arrive in 1971. Another seven months passed until Monorail Pink arrived on July 3, 1972, with Monorail Silver (August 16), Monorail Purple (November 14), and Monorail Black (December 22) rounding out the fleet.

Two additional Mark IV monorails, the six-car, 201-foot-long Coral and Lime trains, were added to the fleet in 1977. To help distinguish them from Pink and Green, their colored stripes had deltas. Monorail Coral's stripe had white deltas, while Monorail Lime's deltas were blue, paying homage to the monorail cast member uniform colors of lime and blue. Eventually, all of the Mark IV trains except Gold were converted to six cars. Each car had four air-actuated doors per side, giving the trains a "through-loading" capability where disembarking guests exited on one side while embarking guests entered simultaneously from the opposite side. This increased efficiency by decreasing station dwell times at the theme park and TTC stations. The central car had double doors to accommodate wheelchairs. The doors were opened from a control panel outside the cab door, and had to be closed manually. The interior configuration consisted of four seating compartments per car, each having a set of two facing five-person benches across the width of the monorail, allowing each car to seat 40 passengers and bringing the total capacity of the six-car trains to 244 passengers (including four in the nosecone) and one or two pilots.

After their retirement from service at WDW, two monorails, Coral and Lime, were sold for a reported $3.5 million each to MGM Grand-Bally's Monorail, LLC in Las Vegas for use on the monorail system linking the two casinos, which opened June 14, 1995. These two monorails were retired for the second time on Sunday, January 26, 2003 after more than seven years of operation in Las Vegas.

Monorail Red was decommissioned on January 23, 1993, and over its 20 years of service had logged 943,976 miles. Nine years later, on May 27, 2002, Disney put the nosecone of Monorail Red up for auction at Disney Auctions on eBay. The auction closed on June 6, and the winning bidder was Chip Young of Georgia with a bid of $20,000 plus shipping expenses.

Infrastructure and Specifications

Each train has twelve axles fitted with 18-ply, 46.6-inch diameter, 17.8-inch wide pneumatic load tires. In addition, each train has forty-eight 21.5-inch diameter guide tires which provide horizontal stabilization, two steering tires under each cab to assist with steering, and sixty nylon safety wheels which can guide the train in case of a flat tire. The tires are filled with nitrogen to help prevent fires. The passenger compartments are suspended over each load tire by air bag cushions, which are automatically inflated or deflated depending on the passenger load to ensure a smooth ride.

Propulsion is accomplished by eight 100-horsepower electric traction motors on each train, located on axles three through ten. Power is provided to the monorail through eight carbon collector shoes from the 600 volts DC carried by the aluminum and stainless steel buss bars attached to the side of the beam below the train (positive is on the right side of the train's forward motion, and negative is on the left). The buss bars are fed with 2000 amps of current from several power rectifier stations along the track, the most noticeable of which, Rectifier 3, is located along World Drive midway between Epcot Center Drive and Vista Boulevard. The rectifiers convert 13,200 volts AC to the 600 volts DC supplied to the buss bar. In the monorail, the unstable 600 volts DC is converted to a stable 370 volts DC, then further converted to 230 volts AC for the air compressor. A low voltage power supply converts the 600 volts DC from the buss bar to 37.5 volts to power the doors, horns, floor lights, outside lights, computers, radios, onboard communication systems, and the cab console.

The maximum speed permitted for monorails in typical operation is 40 miles per hour. The Train Control System (TCS), often called the Vehicle On Board Controller (VOBC), is responsible for speed control. The Propulsion Electronic Control Unit (PECU) and the Brake Electronic Control Unit (BECU) are components of the TCS. Monorails incorporate two separate braking systems. Dynamic braking, which slow the train, uses the motors as generators to generate electricity, which slows the motors, thus slowing the train. The generated electricity is dissipated in resistor banks between the cars, which can reach 800 degrees Fahrenheit. Air-actuated 18-inch mechanical disk brakes, located on axles three through ten, are used to bring the monorail to a full stop. A monorail with no passengers can make an emergency stop from a speed of 40 miles per hour in approximately 300 feet.

Monorail storage and maintenance takes place at a building located behind the Magic Kingdom, known as the monorail shop, often called the "roundhouse" or "monorail barn." It is located on the second floor of the same building that houses the Walt Disney World Railroad's Steam Trains. The shop has eleven slots. One is used for the three work tractors, which are diesel-powered vehicles used to tow broken-down trains and inspect and repair track. The other ten slots are available for monorails to be parked after closing. One of the slots has an enclosure which is used when the trains are painted, and one has a removable section of track that can be wheeled out of the way when maintenance is performed on a load tire. Since only ten trains can be accommodated here, the other two must be parked in stations along the route. In the event of a hurricane, four trains can be parked on the track inside the Contemporary Resort, and the hurricane doors closed. Once, on May 9, 2001, Monorail Yellow and Monorail Red were parked nose to nose about eight inches apart on the Epcot beam at the TTC due to construction on the switch beam.

The 14.7 miles of track at Walt Disney World includes the 7.6-mile Epcot line, the concentric beams around Seven Seas Lagoon which measure 2.8 miles each, and additional spur lines to connect to the monorail shop. The Mark IV monorails averaged 67,500 miles each year in 18-hour-a-day operation, with a system-wide capacity of 10,000 seated passengers per hour. In their first ten years of operation, the Mark IV trains logged over five million miles and carried 250 million passengers with a 99.9% operational readiness record, at a total operating cost of less than eight cents per passenger mile.

The monorail beamway is constructed of 26-inch wide sections of prestressed concrete and steel around a polystyrene core. The sections of track, four feet tall at midspan, and most between 90 and 110 feet long, were cast in Oregon and transported by truck to Florida, where they were installed onto the tapered precast concrete columns. Once in place, post-tensioning provided the final alignment of the beamway to reduce any remaining discontinuities. The monorail track at its highest point is 60 feet above the ground, where it enters the Contemporary Resort.

The monorail system incorporates several switches throughout the system. Switchbeams 1 and 2 are located between the Magic Kingdom and the Contemporary Resort. These "pivoting beam" switches allow monorails to travel between the spur to the monorail barn and the express loop, and between the express loop and resort loop. Five pivoting beam switches (Switchbeams 3-7) are located adjacent to the monorail shop, and connect the eleven slots to the single beam of the spur leading to the rest of the system. Switchbeam 8 is located just north of the TTC and allows monorails to transfer between the express line and the spur. Switchbeam 9 is located just northeast of the intersection of World Drive and Timberline Drive, and allows monorails to transfer between the Epcot line and the spur. Switchbeams 8 and 9 are new "beam replacement" switches in which a straight section of beam pivots to the side while a curved section moves into place. These switches allow for higher speed operation through the switch, and can cycle in twelve seconds.

The monorails maintain a safe spacing during normal operation via a moving blocklight system (MBS). This system is often called the "MAPO system," a term which comes from the movie *Mary Poppins*. It provides the pilot with information on how far ahead the leading train is located. Spacing is measured in "blocks," which are segments of roughly 500-1000 feet. In general operation, pilots must maintain spacing of at least two blocks, and the system gives the pilot a green MAPO signal. If only one block separates the trains, the system gives the pilot an amber signal. If the leading train is in the very next block (or the same block), the system gives the pilot a red MAPO signal, locks out the pilot's controls, and applies emergency brakes. This emergency stop is called a "MAPO" or "MAPO stop," and the pilot can be disciplined if these happen too frequently. Additionally, after the 1985 fire (detailed below), the trains were also equipped with an Alison heat detection system. This will alert the pilot if any of the heat sensors, located in axle compartments and PECUs, registers an over-temperature situation. Each monorail carries 14 fire extinguishers distributed throughout the passenger compartments and cabs.

The Walt Disney World Monorail System Welcomes the Arrival of the Mark VI Trains

Twelve 203.5-foot-long, six-car Mark VI trains were manufactured by TGI (Transportation Group Inc.), a subsidiary of Montreal-based transportation giant Bombardier, in La Pocatiere, Canada. These trains were manufactured of fiberglass over a steel framework, in contrast to the aluminum bodies of the Mark IV trains. The door and seating configuration of these cars is different than the Mark IV cars. Each car has two bus-style double doors per side that open and close automatically. The interior configuration comprises two compartments per car, each with two facing five-person benches. This allowed much more space between the sets of benches, thus each car is able to accommodate 40 standees in addition to the seated guests. This gave the Mark VI monorails a capacity of 364 passengers plus one pilot, a 50% increase in capacity over the Mark IV trains. To allow for standing inside, these trains are slightly taller than the Mark IV trains. Two vertical handrails were installed in the center of the standing area, with fold-down seats between them to allow for more seating during less crowded times of the day. In practice, these were rarely used, and eventually removed to provide more room for the standees. When the seats were removed, four new vertical handrails replaced the original two, and the floors were also redone; a new, more durable flooring replaced the carpeting.

The Mark VI trains came online from 1989 through 1991, about one every other month, and slowly replaced the aging Mark IV fleet as they were retired. The same twelve color designations used for the Mark IV trains were used for the Mark VI trains. Monorail Lime's blue deltas were changed to white when the monorail was repainted in 2003.

The Mark VI trains were designed and built to mass transit standards, and incorporating slightly more powerful 113-horsepower DC motors. Many of the same systems originally used in the Mark IV monorails (or later retrofitted to the Mark IV monorails) were incorporated into the Mark VI monorails. These systems had served the monorails well for years, so the same basic systems, with some upgrades, were expected to continue to work well in the future. In the case of the safety and communications systems specifically, this was by necessity; for several years, both Mark IV and Mark VI monorails were in use simultaneously at Walt Disney World, so the safety and communication systems had to be interoperable. The Mark VI design (with some modifications) was used for the new Las Vegas Monorails when the original two Mark IV trains purchased from Disney were replaced in 2003.

Monorail Teal was built using parts of the two trains, Pink and Purple, involved in a fatal crash on July 5, 2009 (more information below). Monorail Teal entered service in November 2009, and Monorail Maroon is expected to be added to the fleet to bring the total back to 12 trains. The monorail colors Pink and Purple have been retired.

Epilogue

The Walt Disney World Monorail system is a marvel of engineering. The fact that the same basic design has operated for almost forty years is a testament to the Imagineers who designed and built this amazing transportation system. Although the monorail is technically not an attraction, children of all ages are attracted to the monorails gliding nearly silently along the "Highway in the Sky." A ride on the Walt Disney World Monorail System always brings a smile to my face. I quite enjoy the first "ride" of the day, well before I even walk through the Magic Kingdom's turnstiles.

Appendix: Incidents

Very few major incidents have been reported in the decades of operation of the Walt Disney World Monorail System. The most significant ones are detailed below.

On February 12, 1974, Monorail Blue, as it was entering the Magic Kingdom station, lost air pressure in its brakes, and rear-ended Monorail Red as it was leaving the station filled with passengers. The pilot of Monorail Blue and two guests were slightly injured.

On June 26, 1985, a flat guide tire caught fire in the rear car of the Mark IV Monorail Silver on the Epcot beam en route to the TTC. Passengers broke out the window in a door, then used the exterior emergency release handle to open the door, then used it as a step to climb onto the roof and away from the fire. The Reedy Creek Fire Department rescued the passengers and evacuated the rest of the train. Seven passengers were hospitalized for smoke inhalation or other minor injuries.

A monorail train collided with a diesel maintenance work tractor near the Contemporary Resort on August 30, 1991. Monorail Red was closely following Work Tractor 1 as it was being filmed for a commercial just north of the Contemporary Resort. The cause of the accident was attributed to the work tractor's engine failing while in motion. Two cast members were injured.

An electrical fire occurred on August 12, 1996 as a monorail entered the Magic Kingdom station. Only five passengers were on the train, all of which exited safely. Two cast members were treated for smoke inhalation.

On November 19, 2005, a work tractor was preparing to tow Monorail Yellow which had broken down on the express beam near the Contemporary Resort. The work tractor accelerated suddenly and crashed into the nosecone of Monorail Yellow, crushing the hook operator as he was attempting to connect the work tractor to the disabled monorail.

The first fatal accident in the monorail's history occurred on July 5, 2009. Monorail Pink was attempting a switchover from the Epcot line to the Magic Kingdom express line. The switch was not in the correct position and Monorail Pink traveled in reverse on the Epcot beam into the TTC station, where Monorail Purple was parked. The trains collided, killing Monorail Purple's pilot, 21-year-old Austin Wuennenberg.

Jason Diffendal *is co-founder of the Disney fan organization WDWCelebrations, dedicated to "Celebrating the magic of the past, present, and future, together," by hosting fan gatherings commemorating the anniversaries of Disney theme parks. Jason was instrumental in the planning of Celebration 25, the unofficial fan gathering for Epcot's 25th Anniversary on October 1, 2007, which inspired the creation of WDWCelebrations. More information about upcoming fan events, including a celebration of Walt Disney World's 40th Anniversary on October 1, 2011, is available at WDWCelebrations.com.*

Spaceship Earth

Jason Diffendal

My first visit to EPCOT Center was in 1983, when I was eight years old. With annual or biennial visits, I feel like I grew up with EPCOT Center. From my first visit, I fell in love with the park, and it has remained my favorite park at Walt Disney World. I vividly remember all of the original Future World attractions, but my favorite one is the central icon of the park, Spaceship Earth. A compelling show inside an incredible structure, with a very memorable and meaningful theme song (from 1986 to 1994) made Spaceship Earth, to me, the most perfect pavilion in Future World. The combination of the impressive structure and spectacular attraction is something no other park icon can match. I'm sure many agree, as more guests have ridden Spaceship Earth than any other attraction at Walt Disney World.

Spaceship Earth, the visual and thematic centerpiece of Epcot, gives visitors a sense of awe and inspiration, a perfect foreshadowing of what is to come as the guests enter Future World. Its placement at the front of the park allows guests to easily see this magnificent structure as they approach the turnstiles from the parking lot. And as you enter the park, the sheer magnitude of the 180-foot-tall sphere is magnified as you approach and walk directly under it.

Structure Design and Construction

The structure of Spaceship Earth is typically referred to as a "geosphere," a shortening of "geodesic sphere," namely, a complete sphere derived from a geodesic dome, an architectural structure developed by American architect, inventor, mathematician, and author Buckminster Fuller. The name of the attraction, "Spaceship Earth," was also coined by Fuller in his 1968 essay "Operating Manual for Spaceship Earth."

Prior to the construction of Epcot, a geodesic sphere had never been built before. Perhaps the closest structure was the United States pavilion at Expo 67 in Montreal, which is 4/5 of a full sphere in height. Initially the concept for Spaceship Earth started out as a dome. But planners desired to make the icon a dramatic entranceway to the park, and it would enhance the storyline of the attraction to have guests actually go up into the sphere instead of simply entering a door in its side. Gordon Hoopes, WED's project designer for Spaceship Earth, stated that "we knew that having the entire sphere raised above the ground would cause substantial engineering problems, but the psychological uplift for our guests would be worth it." (WED is derived from the initials of Walter Elias Disney. WED Enterprises – known today as WDI, Walt Disney Imagineering – was founded on December 16, 1952 as the design and development arm of the company.)

In early 1979, WED Enterprises retained the structural engineering firm of Simpson, Gumpertz & Heger Inc., and the architectural firm of Wallace, Floyd, Associates Inc., to develop the design of the Spaceship Earth pavilion from WED's concept sketches. Supporting a full sphere was one of the biggest design challenges. Legendary Imagineer John Hench devised a solution: build two partial spheres, one supported by and one suspended from a center table. Six legs support a 12-foot-thick steel ring and truss assembly 52 feet off the ground, on which rests the upper portion of the sphere. In a sense, this is exactly like building the geodesic dome of Expo 67 on a 52-foot-high table supported by legs. This platform also supports the entire ride and show system structure, independent of and not connected at any point to the sphere itself. The lower dome is hung from this steel ring, and though it does not contain any ride or show elements, it does house mechanical equipment, and the service elevator (housed in the mirrored column under the sphere) is used to access this area. The design required both extensive computer analysis and thorough testing of a 1/16 in. = 1 ft. scale model in a wind tunnel at the Wright Brothers Memorial Institute at the Massachusetts Institute of Technology. Because of the complexity of the structure, WED built a 4-ft-high scale model to the engineering firm's drawings to assist bidding contractors in evaluating the fabrication and erection of the sphere.

The external appearance of Spaceship Earth is also quite interesting. The mathematical model that forms the basis of the design is a pentakis dodecahedron (which has 60 flat faces). The faces of the dodecahedron are broken down into smaller triangles, most of which form hexagons (each set of three individual panels (isosceles triangles) forms an equilateral triangle. Six of these equilateral triangles form a hexagon. However, in order to make the structure more spherical, a bit of modification was required, and thus there are actually a number of pentagons interspersed between the hexagons. A fun but sometimes dizzying task is to see how many you can find!

Construction of Spaceship Earth required 26 months and 40,800 labor hours. The unique design enabled the structure to be built without the use of any interior supports. Except for the external covering, the structure is all steel – 1700 tons to be precise. The external skeleton of the sphere is made of Alucobond, which is an aluminum composite material consisting of two sheets of thin, smooth aluminum thermobonded to a polyethylene core in a continuous process. This lightweight skin is supported 24 inches away from the inner waterproof neoprene surface of the structure itself by 467 four-inch diameter aluminum pipes. The open gaps between the 11,324

Alucobond panels allow rainwater to penetrate this outer skin and be collected into a specially-designed system of hidden gutters at the sphere's equator. Thus, no water drips off the bottom of Spaceship Earth during the thunderstorms so common during Florida summers. This is much appreciated by guests who often will take shelter under the mammoth sphere during inclement weather! The collected rainwater is channeled through the supporting legs to a treatment area where any pollutants are removed. The placement of the legs of the structure and the shops between the legs actually creates a wind tunnel below spaceship earth.

The Attraction, Version 1: 1982-1986

Spaceship Earth opened with EPCOT Center on October 1, 1982. The attraction housed in the iconic sphere tells the story of the evolution of human communication through the ages. The opening-day sponsor of the attraction was the Bell System, quite appropriate for a ride dealing with communication. However, when the Bell System was broken up effective January 1, 1984, AT&T, the parent company, took over the sponsorship. All signage was changed at that time to reflect the new sponsor.

As guests approach the entrance to the attraction, a huge mural by Claudio Mazzoli, depicting man's conquest of space for communication purposes, offers a prelude of what is to come inside. Guests then board one of the 152 four-passenger "time machines" for the 13-minute 26-second ride. The Omnimover-based ride system can accommodate 2400 guests per hour as it moves along at an average of 1½ feet per second.

The original narrator of the attraction is the subject of debate. It was generally agreed that the narrator was Vic Perrin, best remembered as the "Control Voice" in the original version of the TV series *The Outer Limits*. However, in 2008, Imagineer Marty Sklar recalled that the narration was done by Larry Dobson. Much of the original script was written by Ray Bradbury, based on research assembled by Peggie Fariss. This original script was by most accounts too fact-filled and educational, even for EPCOT Center. However, this historically-accurate narration did give rise to a number of favorite memorable lines.

The following paragraphs describe what a guest in 1982 would have experienced during a typical ride through the attraction. This narrative is presented in the present tense to help you, the reader, envision yourself experiencing the attraction.

After boarding, our vehicle ascends into the sphere through a tunnel of fog. Upon entering the geosphere, through swirls of light and fog, we see projections of two Cro-Magnon men as they try to escape an approaching wild animal. As we come to the "dawn of recorded time," we see the first of numerous Audio-Animatronics in this attraction: a caveman tells stories to youngsters around a campfire, while another attempts to record the information by painting the story on the cave walls. The next scene depicts ancient Egypt, and a man carving hieroglyphics on the wall of a temple. We then see a pharaoh dictating to his scribe, who is now writing on papyrus scrolls. The Phoenicians in the next scene are the logical transporters of this new portable form of recorded communications. The captains of two ships are trading scrolls, thus sharing the knowledge across the known world using their new alphabet.

As the alphabet spreads to Greece, playwrights devise a new form of expression. "The theater is born." Several actors are performing a play by Sophocles. The Roman network of roads allowed knowledge to spread to the far reaches of the empire. In a scene of Rome after dark, we see a projection of a chariot rushing down the street. Soon a Smellitzer (a "scent cannon" of sorts, which ejects fragrances toward passing vehicles) provides us one of the most well-known scents in all of Walt Disney World: the burning of Rome. The fall of Rome didn't take all knowledge with it: the vast Islamic empire preserved information in its libraries. We see Islamic scholars discussing a manuscript, followed by a scene of a medieval monastery with monks toiling to preserve knowledge by duplicating books by hand. And here is one of the more light-hearted scenes in the attraction: a monk has fallen asleep at his desk.

In stark contrast to handwritten books, Johann Gutenberg's printing press in the next scene provides a much easier method for ideas to be preserved, duplicated, and shared. The exponential spread of knowledge leads us to the Renaissance, where we pass musicians, an artist, and a sculptor as they practice their craft. Our vehicles then travel under scaffolding supporting Michelangelo as he toils by candlelight: "Behold the majesty of the Sistine ceiling."

The Renaissance sparks a communications explosion, and the scenes now begin to meld together as an illustration of the incredible pace of communications evolution in the last century. A newsboy screams "Extra! Extra! *New York Daily*," as he sells newspapers mass-produced in a large steam-powered printing press nearby. Soon after, Guglielmo Marconi's revolutionary wireless telegraph is presented as an early form of wireless communication. By this time, Alexander Graham Bell's telephone has developed into a widespread network, and we see switchboard operators busily plugging wires, attempting to connect a call, only to report that "the line is busy." This leads to scenes depicting the advances in wireless broadcasting and entertainment: a radio station studio, a cinema, and a family in their 1960s living room watching television. Two sets involving personal computers come next, and then we visit a computer-controlled Network Operations Center, with maps showing the communication network spanning the earth, the continental United States, and Florida. (This scene contained the logo of the sponsor; a small Bell System symbol appeared above the map, but was removed in 1984.)

The culmination of our ascent approaches as we travel through a tunnel which opens into "180top," the highest point in the attraction, where the concave interior ceiling of the sphere is used as a planetarium with projections of stars and our very own tiny planet, Spaceship Earth. Now in outer space, our time machines rotate backward for the steep descent as we travel past several astronauts working on a space station into which the track enters. After we pass under an outline of the space station illuminated in red, a girl can be seen looking out of a space station window, monitoring the repair progress. (Incidentally, during the first weeks of operation, the mechanism that actually rotated the vehicles was not operating correctly, requiring cast members to be stationed here to manually rotate the vehicles for the descent!)

As we descend back to earth, literally and figuratively, projection screens depict the applications of our communications technology.

Satellite images, computer graphics, and electronic circuits all serve to heighten our awareness of just how far we have come since the first forms of communication. "Ours is the age of knowledge." As we disembark our time machines, we are inspired at what the future holds for us and our children.

Exiting into Earth Station, also known as EPCOT Center Information, seven large projection screens above us display a slide show of the wonders that await us in Future World and World Showcase. This area serves as the park's Guest Relations area, and two staffed booths are available. But the biggest draw is the WorldKey Information Service, developed for EPCOT Center by the Bell System, comprised of a wall of touch-screens that connect us to remote Cast Members ready to assist us with answers to our questions or dining reservations. I can distinctly remember during visits in the early 80s, we would skip the attraction and head immediately to Earth Station to ensure that we could secure our reservation for dinner at Alfredo's. During the system's heyday, twenty-three of these interactive terminals were scattered throughout the park, ten here in Earth Station, five in a kiosk near the Odyssey Restaurant, six in a kiosk at the Germany pavilion, and two in the VIP lounge above Earth Station.

The Attraction, Version 2: 1986-1994

Based on feedback regarding the lackluster script, serious discussions to refurbish the attraction began in late 1984. After a year and a half of planning, the attraction closed for its first refurbishment on May 25, 1986. Upon reopening on May 29, 1986, two significant changes were apparent. Veteran broadcast journalist Walter Cronkite was the narrator, reading from a similarly-themed but updated script by Tom Fitzgerald. The classic song "Tomorrow's Child" by Ron Ovadia and Peter Stougaard now inspired riders as they descended to the unload area through an updated descent sequence. Spaceship Earth finally had a fitting theme song, something it had been lacking since opening (but which almost all other Future World pavilions and many World Showcase pavilions did have).

The Cronkite narration is my favorite, mostly because this is the version of the attraction I literally grew up with. Cronkite's epic tone and perfect delivery were an excellent fit for such a classic attraction.

The new script kept many of the quotable lines from the first version, and added several more, while Cronkite's voice made the lines even more memorable. And I must admit that "Tomorrow's Child" is my absolute favorite song from EPCOT Center. The narration and song made a significant impression on me as I rode the attraction many times during my teen years; the finale song was a very inspiring end to a very inspiring ride, and served as a great segue to the rest of Future World.

Several major show scenes were redone as well during the 1986 refurbishment. The Network Operations Center remained but was renamed the AT&T Worldwide Intelligent Network. The descent tunnel lost the scientific and computer images; they were replaced with rotating light projections and silhouetted projections of children which, coupled with the new song, conveyed the idea that today's children are our future.

Several minor changes were also made. The fog machine was removed from the ascent tunnel, and twinkling lights representative of stars were added. An added warning message at 180top notified riders of the impending rotation: "Attention Time Travelers: Your time machine is about to rotate for your return to earth. Please remain seated at all times."

The Attraction, Version 3: 1994-2007

On August 15, 1994, Spaceship Earth closed for its second major refurbishment, reopening on November 23. As in 1986, the major changes again were related to the narration, the final present-day scenes just before 180top, and the descent. A new script was written by Tom Fitzgerald, with Jeremy Irons narrating. A new score composed by Edo Guidotti accompanied the new narration. Much of the ascent remained the same, with very minor changes. Monitors were installed in the ascent tube, warning guests that their vehicle would rotate during the ride. The two now-outdated computer scenes and the AT&T Worldwide Intelligent Network scene were replaced by a single large scene depicting transatlantic video conferencing between a boy and a girl. The system automatically translated languages, so the boy heard the girl in his native language, while the girl heard the boy in her native language. This scene contains one of the more-quotable lines from this version of the attraction: “But will these seemingly infinite communications become a flood of electronic babble?”

A globe-shaped scaffold was added which enveloped the track between the transatlantic communication scene and the tunnel to 180top. This tunnel had many lighting effects added, and a new laser highlighted the entrance. The projection system for the stars and planet earth in 180top was upgraded. The satellite sets of 180top were no longer part of the storyline – two smaller props were completely removed, and the large space station the track enters for the descent was painted black to be hidden from view. The animatronic girl was removed and the window covered. The warning spiel as the vehicles rotate was also updated and broadcast from a new set of louder speakers.

At the beginning of the descent, a new laser was installed to shine through a cloud of mist (though this effect caused several problems related to the mist and was soon deactivated). A new virtual classroom scene was suspended above the track, as well as new projection screens. Moving star effects replaced other projection screens. New scenes depicting worldwide communications were added to the right side of the track. The new finale scene depicted communications beaming from scientists underground via fiber optics across an ocean to a large city. These fiber optic communication transmissions continued above our heads and around a small model of Spaceship Earth, and again above the track as we approach the unload area. The classic “Tomorrow’s Child” song was removed, once again leaving the attraction without a theme song.

This version of the attraction is the favorite of many fans. Certainly many more guests experienced this version than the Cronkite version, as it was simply around longer, and at least some of these guests never experienced the Cronkite version at all. Personally, I like this version as well. Jeremy Irons is a fitting replacement for Walter Cronkite. The new score is excellent and fits the attraction well. The new descent scenes with the fiber optics were significant improvements. But I was most upset by the loss of the fantastic “Tomorrow’s Child” song. No longer was there an inspirational and meaningful song that I found myself humming as I left the attraction. And this loss of the theme song was compounded by the many changes taking place to other Future World pavilions around this same time, in which many of them also lost or had changed their original, memorable tunes. Between 1993 and 1996, Universe of Energy, The Land, and World of Motion all lost their original songs. Imagination and Horizons followed in 1998 and 1999, respectively. (Some of these original songs were not heard again in their entirety in the park until October 1, 2007, during the 25th Anniversary celebration, when they played (with lyrics) as guests left the park at the end of the evening.)

It was during this refurbishment that the postshow area was completely overhauled as well. Earth Station was replaced by the Global Neighborhood, a communications-focused interactive area each hands-on exhibit having an AT&T theme. Guest Relations and the WorldKey Information Service terminals were moved a short distance to Communicore East. A number of exhibits were created by WDI (Walt Disney Imagineering, the successor to WED Enterprises) using technology developed by AT&T Bell Laboratories: Interactive Wonderland, You Don't Say, Communication Breakthrough, Neighborhood Games, What's In a Word, and Ride the AT&T Network. Story Teller Phones allowed guests to call friends and use sound effects of a jungle, haunted house, or cartoon world. An AT&T press release stated, "When visitors leave our pavilion, we want them to understand that our communications technology is easy-to-use. They'll see that AT&T makes it easy for them to communicate with the important people in their lives -- anytime, anywhere."

Global Neighborhood was updated in November 1999 for the Millennium Celebration to the New Global Neighborhood. The communications theme remained, but several new exhibits replaced old, dated ones. The centerpiece of the area was a huge, wiry, leafless "communications tree" with lighted wires tracing its limbs, which supported monitors at the ends, and roots which were visible under a glass floor. AT&T announced that it was ending its sponsorship of all Disney attractions effective January 2003. The New Global Neighborhood stayed open without a sponsor for more than a year before closing in 2004. Between 2004 and 2007, guests exited the attraction into a narrow corridor of blue walls with nothing to see.

The Attraction, Version 4: 2007-present

On November 8, 2005, Siemens and Disney announced a 12-year strategic alliance. In addition to sponsoring IllumiNations: Reflections of Earth (along with the Osborne Family Spectacle of Dancing Lights at Disney's Hollywood Studios and Disney's Electrical Parade at Disney's California Adventure) via the Sylvania lighting division, Siemens itself sponsored Spaceship Earth. Spaceship Earth's third major refurbishment began on July 9, 2007. The ride soft-opened for previews on December 7, 2007, with tweaking occurring during January, and finally the official rededication took place on February 15, 2008. A new icon, strongly influenced by the original 1982 icon, was developed for the attraction and appeared on a new marquee installed at the entrance. The supports at the entrance area were also painted in two complementary shades of blue.

As with past refurbishments, this one also brought a new narrator, new score, and new descent. Dame Judi Dench replaced Jeremy Irons as narrator with an updated script, and a new soundtrack was composed by Bruce Broughton. But even more significant changes took place. Touch-screen monitors were added to all ride vehicles. A camera was installed in the ascent tube to take an on-ride photo of each rider, for use during a new interactive descent.

With Siemens being a technology company, not a communications company, the storyline had to be modified to reflect an evolution of technology in general, not just communication. This necessitated several show scenes being slightly modified to better fit the new story. The lighting, projections, sets, and animatronics of the ascent were overhauled and received major upgrades. Previously-static slide projections in the Cro-Magnon man and caveman scenes were replaced with full-motion video projections. Animatronics were shifted between scenes to enhance the new storyline.

The final scene prior to entering the tunnel to 180top was again completely replaced. Now, early room-size computers occupy the scenes on the left and right of the track. A new outdoor scene of a man building the first home computer in his garage was also added. We then enter the tunnel to 180top, which has completely new projection effects replacing the light tubes. The projectors in 180top itself have again been upgraded.

The most significant changes were made to the descent. Most of the existing show scenes were completely removed or covered, and replaced with nothing. (Some dimly-lit triangles were added later.) This is where the touch-screens in your vehicle are activated and ask a series of questions. Based on your answers, an animated Jetsons-style rendition of your future is played. The on-ride photo taken at the beginning of the ascent is processed through facial-recognition software, and your head is displayed on an animated body. Your picture is also displayed on a large globe as you enter the postshow area.

The Siemens-sponsored Spaceship Earth post show, Project Tomorrow was officially rededicated on March 4, 2008. Originally called Project Tomorrow: Inventing the World of Tomorrow, it opened in phases beginning in March 2007. The name was soon changed to Project Tomorrow: Inventing the Wonders of the Future. It features a series of interactive exhibits related to an array of Siemens technologies. Super Driver is an interactive racing game that provides information about Siemens mobility solutions. Similar to Siemens Imaging technology, the InnerVision experience gives guests the ability to look inside the brain as it is working. Body Builder is an engaging, educational experience that demonstrates Siemens Remote Operation technology. Power City gives guests a hands-on experience relating to Siemens energy and environmental solutions. Additional kiosks are placed throughout the exhibit areas allowing guests to learn more about these Siemens technologies as well as the entire portfolio of Siemens solutions. Above Project Tomorrow, the corporate VIP lounge was also refurbished, and was given the name "Base 21;" it serves as a hospitality and briefing center showcasing the company's story of innovation and technology.

Epilogue: The Wand

Not wanting to spoil the story of Spaceship Earth with details about the infamous wand, I decided to put this section at the end. I apologize to those of you who loved the wand. Personally, I thought the wand was a whimsical way to mark the millennium and denote Epcot as the center of the Millennium Celebration, and initially didn't mind it. However, when the decision was made to keep this ostensibly temporary structure indefinitely, I was dismayed. I felt like I had given up my beloved Spaceship Earth for a short while for use during the Millennium Celebration, and it was given back to me defiled, full of graffiti.

In early 1999, Walt Disney World management was planning the Millennium Celebration, which began on October 1, 1999, and the central park hosting the celebration was Epcot. Taking a cue from the celebration of the 25th anniversary of Walt Disney World in 1997, in which Cinderella Castle was turned into a giant pink birthday cake, the idea was to "accent" Spaceship Earth by constructing a 257-foot-tall structure sporting Sorcerer Mickey's arm holding a wand, and the numerals for the year 2000. This massive addition, the tallest structure in any park at Walt Disney World, was dedicated on September 29, 1999. This fanciful addition for the Millennium Celebration was not liked by everyone, but as a temporary addition for the 15-month Millennium Celebration, it was tolerated. Much of the dislike stemmed from the diminution of the park's iconic Spaceship Earth; the towering wand made the geosphere seem much smaller.

Unfortunately, the decision was made not to remove the wand at the end of the Millennium Celebration, but rather to turn the wand into a "new and lasting beacon to a magical Disney world," according to a press release. A five-month undertaking from January to May of 2001 removed the "2000" and replaced it with the word "Epcot" in a nondescript font heretofore unassociated with the park.

As time wore on, many fans had lost hope that the wand would ever come down. In November of 2005, Siemens AG was announced as the new sponsor of Spaceship Earth. This rekindled hope that money would become available for the removal of the wand. Finally, on July 5, 2007, Epcot Vice President Jim MacPhee vaulted to stardom among the Disney community by announcing that the wand would be removed in time for the 25th Anniversary of Epcot on October 1, 2007. On July 9, the attraction closed and the removal of the wand began. Although a careful choreography was required for the removal to ensure that the outer skeleton of Spaceship Earth was not damaged, the process was completed in less than seven weeks, and Spaceship Earth was returned to its righteous glory on August 24 with the last pieces of the detritus removed.

Much Ado About Hoop-Dee-Doo

Greg Ehrbar

It's near impossible, even for Disney, to manufacture a phenomenon. Sure, success is always the goal (unless you're Max Bialystock) and every effort is made to assure meeting that goal. But as it's been said, if everybody knew how to guarantee a hit every time, they would.

But entertainment doesn't work that way—success is an elusive thing. And sometimes when a mammoth megahit comes along, it simply happens.

Such is the case with an unpretentious, goofy dinner show called the *Hoop-Dee-Doo Musical Revue*. It is unlikely to ever play on Broadway but it doesn't ever have to. It's the longest currently running musical in the history of American Theater.

People still anxiously journey to the far reaches of *Disney's Fort Wilderness* Resort & Campground to line up at the Pioneer Hall box office for standby tickets, in hopes that the long list of tickets, purchased very far in advance, might somehow yield a last-minute availability.

Those who have been fortunate enough to acquire tickets are seated inside in a western dance hall straight out of a classic Hollywood musical. Some are new to the show, some are avid fans—to the point of attending in homemade costumes to resemble their favorite *Hoop-Dee-Doo* Cast Members.

What follows is what seems to be a cornball country vaudeville show, performed in segments surrounding an all-you-can-eat banquet of comfort foods like fried chicken and barbecued ribs. The bulk of the show takes place as the dinner is completed, with strawberry shortcake served by host and hostesses who actually dance off the stage.

The seeming simplicity of the show masks a razor-sharp precision, staggering professionalism and brilliance of multi-level comedy that can only come from a gifted cast on stage, a dedicated dining staff and a creative team whose expertise reaches decades back to the golden age of film and television.

The song itself has a history of its own. *Hoop Dee Doo* was written by Milton DeLugg, a musical fixture in the pioneering days of television as the conductor of The Tonight Show in the fifties and sixties and The Gong Show in the seventies. Still active today, DeLugg continues to direct the music for the Macy's Thanksgiving Day Parade.

Delugg shares the song credit for *Hoop-Dee-Doo* with a close friend he met at Paramount Pictures, composer Frank Loesser (best known for musicals like Guys and Dolls and Hans Christian Andersen). Originally, superstar Perry Como was approached to record "Hoop Dee Doo" as a novel change of pace from his usual ballad style.

Como's first reaction to the song was, "I hate it. It makes me sick." But he relented, recorded and watched the song become a top hit in 1950, crediting DeLugg all the way. And for over 35 years now, this song has been performed several times nightly in front of a live *Walt Disney World* audience as the theme of the *Hoop-Dee-Doo Musical Revue*.

The show itself grew out of an operational need at the campground. Pioneer Hall, then called Fort Wilderness Dining Hall, was a large, informal area where Guests had quick meals, played games and watched movies. A live country-western group called the Star Spangled Washboard Band was hired to play in 1973.

Broadway veteran Larry Billman was asked to write and direct a show for the Hall. Billman, whose 40-year Disney career began with the fabled touring show, Disney on Parade, partnered with another seasoned pro: scenarist and songwriter Tom Adair. In addition to his vast TV and film credits, Disney fans have Adair to thank for his *Sleeping Beauty* lyrics as well as Annette Funicello's first hit record, *How Will I Know My Love?*

Choreographer Forrest Bahruth, just finishing enhancements for the Golden Horseshoe Revue and fresh from a TV career with the likes of Elvis Presley and Tom Jones, was able to bring a keen perspective to the new project as a contrast to the long-running Disneyland saloon show. The *Hoop-Dee-Doo Musical Revue* would be, from the start, a different kind of western musical comedy.

From there it almost became a Mickey Rooney/Judy Garland movie in real life. The first performers were cast from the All-American Musical Comedy Workshop, a group of college students whom Disney selected from schools across the country. They were green but they were game for anything and the working environment was generous and accepting of new ideas.

The Original Dolly

> *"Marilyn Magness was a marvelous energy force to behold," Larry remembers. "Sometimes she made her entrance swinging from the balcony on a rope!"*
>
> *"She would run across the stage, jump up, grab one of the rails, swing herself up over the balcony, run all the way around the balcony come back around the other side and slither down," laughs Forrest. "We finally had to say, 'Marilyn you can't do that.' It's a safety issue. But Marilyn was brimming with talent. It was almost hard to hold her down because she had so much energy. She still does. She's absolutely brilliant."*

Like Molly Brown, Marilyn ain't down yet. She swung all the way to the top echelon as Creative Director of Parks and Resorts Entertainment, making shows, parades and spectacular events happen at Disney Parks worldwide. She was instrumental in bringing Park Guests into the parades, a technique perfected at the *Hoop-Dee-Doo Musical Revue*.

> *"We were this ragtag group of college kids back then, who had no agenda to prove and nobody looking over our shoulders, with this great groundbreaking opportunity. There was a great sense of freedom, laughter and fun. We weren't driven by the fear of failure. It was just, 'let's see what we can create.' That was a big difference."*

The Original Male "Swing"

Ted King was the first hired to play all the male roles in the *Hoop-Dee-Doo Musical Revue* and become part of a highly unusual entertainment phenomenon.

> *"I learned the leading man role, the dancer role and the comic role, and did them all that summer," Ted says. "At first I thought, 'Why did I get cursed with this gig?' but by the end of the summer, I was having the most fun of anybody.*

> *"On Mondays and Tuesdays, I was Jim Handy, on Thursdays I was Johnny Ringo, the dancer, and on Fridays and Saturdays I would be Six Bits, the comedian. I was 20 years old and I was having the time of my life.*
>
> *"And it wasn't just about performing. We met Imagineers, composers and designers in those workshops. It was an amazing summer. "*

The *Hoop-Dee-Doo Musical Revue* became a smash success but had to be recast when the students returned to their campuses that fall. A new cast was selected and the show went on for another year before Ted was among those invited back to Florida to rejoin the show. Eventually he relocated to California to perform at Disneyland as, among other things, one of the Kids of the Kingdom. "When I went out to Disneyland it was a different feel because it was 'the one,'" he comments. "It's the original."

Ted took to heart the inspiration he gained from the college summer program. His career blossomed from performing into the creation of major attractions for theme parks all over the world. But the *Hoop-Dee-Doo Musical Revue* is very special to him. "They did an anniversary night at Pioneer Hall, and they had 60 or 75 former cast members," he says. "I was the only guy in the room who was there on opening night, so that was kind of fun."

Why? Why? Why?

Why has the *Hoop-Dee-Doo Musical Revue* endured? Why do some little kids actually come dressed as their favorite *Hoop-Dee-Doo* characters? Is it because this show is just for folks who still mourn the cancellation of Hee Haw? No. Not by a long shot.

Consider, if you will, Sandra Joseph of Miami, Florida, a sophisticated education administrator from the Northeast who takes regular Broadway trips to see the latest shows. Her husband, Harley, is a electrical engineer and a very imposing figure at 5 foot eleven and 235 pounds. They both loved the show.

"It was terrific, very creative," Sandra says. "The cast was extremely believable. Even the waitresses and waiters danced on stage. And they use unlikely people for likely parts."

One of these parts cast Harley in a very surprising role. We won't spoil it for those who have not seen the show, but suffice to say that he made quite an impression on the audience. "The applause was deafening when Harley came on stage," Sandra says.

When the Josephs boarded the watercraft back to their Disney Resort, everyone on the boat applauded Harley. The next morning at breakfast, everyone in the restaurant stood and cheered when he entered. "My public," he said with a grin.

The Current Director

In his five years as Show Director, Alan Bruun has discovered a key to what makes the *Hoop-Dee-Doo Revue* so compelling to so many: romantic tension.

> *"You've got those three love relationships, all of which play out at different speeds in different ways," he explains, "Maybe tonight's the night that Jim Handy is going to finally commit and pop the question to Flora. Maybe Six Bits and Dolly will stop cracking jokes long enough to realize how they feel about each other, and so on.*
>
> *"Jim and Flora are soul mates, Claire and Johnny are heart mates, Dolly and Six Bits are primates. We've got this sort of worldly microcosm, which all good theatre is."*

Zounds! Who knew the *Hoop-Dee-Doo Musical Revue* was so deep? And while we're being pithy, let's close with what has become our hallowed custom here at the highly dignified and erudite "*Hoop-Dee-Doo* Actors's Stu-Dee-Doo."

So we now ask the accomplished Ms. Marilyn "Dolly" Magness those famous questions created by the renowned French interviewer, Bernard Pivot:

Marilyn, what is your favorite word?
"Fun."
What is your least favorite word?
"Stress."
What turns you on creatively, spirtually or emotionally?
"Laughter."
What turns you off?
"Anger."
What sound or noise do you love?
"Music."
What sound or noise do you hate?
"Traffic."
What profession other than your own would you like to attempt?
"Teaching."
What profession would you not like to do?
"I don't know!"

And since heaven does indeed exist, Marilyn, what would you like to hear God say when you arrive at the pearly gates?
"Good job in the Hoop-Dee-Doo Musical Revue, I liked the show."

Acknowledgments from the author: Special thanks to Bob Hughes for his research assistance for this article.

***Greg Ehrbar,** a two-time Grammy-nominated writer/producer, has hundreds of network television and radio, stage, recordings, books and advertising projects to his credit. Celebrating his 25th year with the Walt Disney Company, Greg's contributions have been seen by countless millions worldwide. He is the co-author (with Tim Hollis) of Mouse Tracks: The Story of Walt Disney Records, one of the essayists for The Cartoon Music Book, and the editor of Disney Legend Jimmy Johnson's never-before-published 1975 memoir, Inside the Whimsy Works: My 37 Years with Walt Disney Productions.*

The 65th Year for Mickey, the Very First Visit for Kids

Greg Ehrbar

When people find out that I work for Disney, a variety of questions come up. One of the most common is: "What's it like to work there? " It's a lot like working in the wonderful land of Oz. A cross between the MGM's Oz (magical, colorful and "most of it beautiful!") and the Oz depicted in Broadway's *Wicked* (imaginative, magical and, well, complicated). And after 25 years there, it's never lost the luster that first entranced me as a young person.

Disney experiences, in one form or another, can strike an emotional chord in people almost beyond comprehension. At no other time in my life did I ever see this manifest itself more than in 1988, when Mickey Mouse celebrated his 60th birthday at Walt Disney World Resort.

The Walt Disney Company celebrated it in some very high-profile ways, including a glitzy network TV special and the first unveiling of *Mickey's Birthdayland* in the Magic Kingdom Park. But there was another component to the celebration that may have had a greater impact, at least to some children to whom Walt Disney World Resort might as well have been in Alpha Centauri.

As part of Mickey's birthday, underprivileged children from around the U.S. were invited for a Walt Disney World vacation. They stayed at Disney's Caribbean Beach Resort and were given personal tours of Magic Kingdom Park and Epcot (the only two Parks of this era).

Groups of children in varying numbers were chosen from the designated U.S. cities. I don't know the details of their selection, but undoubtedly Walt Disney World Community Relations worked with the government and social agencies to make selections.

The press coverage of their visit was low-key compared to the surrounding Mickey's 60th events, somewhat on an individual community level depending on the place from which they hailed. One of the things the public doesn't know is how Disney Cast Members can mobilize as a unit to carry off staggering, immense events such as these. Hundreds of Disney Cast Members pitch in to assist, usually on their own time. I was just one of them.

Some of us were able to choose the city to host, and most selected their hometowns. I got the idea, however, that it might be especially nice to host kids who came as far as possible from Disneyland Resort in California and Walt Disney World in Florida. Smack in the middle of the United States. I figured the further they lived from the Parks, the more like Dorothy they might be.

My fellow Cast Member and I were assigned to assist another Cast Member in hosting 50 children from Cleveland, Ohio. They were a diverse group from all over the city, ranging in age from about 7 to 12.

One could only imagine what a change this was for these kids from their lives back home. Yet here they were in a self-contained fantasy "world" of Disney Characters, attractions and shows.

The trick was how to get them around to experience as much of this "Oz" as possible in a few days. We had to plan around a schedule of meals, a handful of photo shoots and a parade that would see us sashaying down *Main Street U.S.A.* like celebrities, waving at crowds and smiling for cameras.

The kids loved it, but they made it clear after a while that they were here for the rides more than anything. All they knew of Walt Disney World attractions, if anything at all, were *Space Mountain*, Dumbo the Flying Elephant and the Mad Tea Party. We wanted them to learn that there was a lot more and we could make it happen for them.

I got up on a bench. "You want to see lots of great stuff and maybe go on some things twice?" I said. "YAAAAAAY!" they shouted. I felt like Willy Wonka addressing a crowd of Charlie Buckets.

Using years of skill at navigating the Parks, we carefully ushered them from adventure to adventure and I gently but determinedly ran interference like it was the Super Bowl.

Three mental pictures are indelibly inscribed in my head, all these years later. The first is funny: one night at Epcot, after being given "glow" jewelry, some of the kids bit into their hoops and rings. It was non-toxic, of course, but we were quite a sight at night, leading an entourage of glow-faced kids. (If it had been Wonka Gum instead of plastic jewelry, we might have been leading a pack of blueberries through Epcot.

The second image is haunting. There was one small, very pale boy named Andrew who was terrified of going into the Pirates of the

Caribbean attraction. He had no idea what it would be like, but he was petrified. We had no intention of forcing him to ride but he became very intrigued as we approached the attraction. I assured him that, if he really wanted to ride – and it would be okay if he did not – we would be by his side and warn him of any unexpected occurrences.

I'll never forget Andrew, small head in tiny hands as we began our voyage, insisting that he wanted to continue. By the time we completed our journey, his head was high as he said that he enjoyed Pirates of the Caribbean most of all.

The third memorable moment came when we had to say goodbye. The entire group met for the last time at the Resort hotel, with the kids lined up for their trip back to the life they had been able to lay aside for a few days.

As we looked into the eyes of these boys and girls, the words of a Sherman Brothers song played in my mind: "We knew we'd never meet again and yet 'twas clear to see / I'd always be a part of them, and them a part of me."

Maybe it's possible that this visit never left them. These young people had begun their lives in an environment limited to the few miles surrounding their homes.

Now they had seen how incredible things could be. A world of make-believe, perhaps, but a tangible reality of dreams realized. Perhaps if life treated them roughly in the future, they might have these memories to keep them going, maybe to better lives.

If nothing else, these might realize more possibilities ahead for them. And we hosted just one of many groups. Lots of Disney Cast Members had hosted a lot of underprivileged kids for Mickey's 60th birthday.

I'm not saying that, as "underprivileged," these kids were denied any love or happiness in their home lives. They just had missed out, one way or another, on some of the things we often take for granted. It would also be simplistic to assume that "great, big benevolent Disney" could come along and magically transform their lives forever as the sky filled with a smiling sun and birds tweeted.

But when you peel away the big business and major marketing side of Disney, and focus on how it can impact a receptive individual's imagination, especially that of a child, you tap the core of a Disney that has captured the public fancy for so long.

I'd like to think we made a difference to these kids. After all, everyday life could never have really seemed quite the same for Dorothy when she got back from Oz, could it?

Walt Disney's EPCOT and the Heart of Our Cities

Sam Gennawey

What City Planning is:

- An aide to the man in the street to visualize his city properly planned;
- A practical, sensible way of providing a place for everything with everything in its place;
- An instrument for uniting citizens to work for the city's future;
- An efficient means of avoiding duplication and waste in public improvements.

—John Nolen's Comprehensive Plan for San Diego, 1926

The future ain't what it used to be.
— Yogi Berra

Pioneering real estate developer James Rouse, speaking in 1963 at Harvard, said, "If you think about Disneyland and think about its performance in relationship to its purpose, its meaning to people – more than that, its meaning to the process of development – you will find it the outstanding piece of urban design in the United States." Rouse said that Walt Disney "took an area of activity – the amusement park – and lifted it to a standard so high in its performance, in its respect for people, in its functioning for people, that it really does become a brand new thing."

Walt was no stranger creating meaningful and functional places. His animated characters seem to live and breathe in believable worlds. He guided the design and development of his animation and movie studio in Burbank as well as Disneyland in Anaheim. His team explored opportunities that ranged from an indoor experience in downtown St. Louis to a mountain village retreat surrounded by wilderness in Mineral King located in the Sierra Nevada Mountains of California. They also developed all sorts of ideas for projects on undeveloped land.

At Disneyland, Walt could control what his guests saw as they strolled through his park but he could not control the tacky urban blight that was growing up around the perimeter. Walt was not satisfied. So, like everything else he had ever done, he knew he could do it better and he took out a blank sheet of paper. He wanted to go the next step and take everything that he had learned and transform the urban experience into one of more meaning, comfort, and convenience.

And why not? Even Ray Bradbury felt Walt could save the world. When Bradbury asked him to run for Mayor, Walt said, "Ray, don't be silly…why should I run for Mayor when I'm already King?"

Given complete control, what kind of city could Walt Disney have created?
That was a question I just had to explore. As an urban planner, I wanted to learn about Walt's influences and the underlying design principles that would guide the development of his city. With that knowledge, I could better understand what life in EPCOT would have been like and if the concept would have worked.

My professional experience has taught me that the built environment comes alive and has meaning when it is created through a combination of clearly understood policies and the use of fundamental design patterns properly applied.

When I speak of EPCOT, I am not talking about the permanent World's Fair that is at Walt Disney World today. What I am talking about is the city that Walt described to us just before he died. Where people would know that E.P.C.O.T. is an acronym for the Experimental Prototype City Of Tomorrow. His dream of a city with 20,000 residents, which would be built on virgin land and packed with new ideas in planning, design, construction, and governance.

I started by devouring every book I could find on the subject of EPCOT. Two of the best are Steve Mannheim's *Walt Disney and the Quest for Community* (2002) and Chad Emerson's *Project Future* (2010). I have read the Disney biographies and listened to Walt's own words through interviews. The man was like a sponge. He soaked up the best ideas from wherever he could find them and then used his special gift to take those ideas, tie them together, and produce something that is far more valuable then the sum of the parts.

Early on I learned that Walt Disney did not like sequels. He was always looking over the horizon at the next opportunity. However, after the huge success of the *Three Little Pigs,* theater owners were clamoring for a follow-up. Walt hesitated. He proclaimed, "You can't top pigs, with pigs." Nevertheless, he could be practical when necessary and he had ambitious plans for the Studio. He could certainly use the money for those ideas. Therefore, he relented.

Thirty years later, Walt would find himself in the same place. He wanted to build his city of tomorrow and he knew that another theme park could help fund the project. To see if Disneyland-style entertainment would work on the East Coast, he worked his way into four pavilions at the 1964-1965 New York World's Fair. You would think another Disney park would be a no-lose proposition but the failure of Freedomland in the Bronx, a theme park laid out in the shape of the map of the United States and created by CV Wood who was the first Vice President and General Manager for Disneyland, made Walt pause. He wanted to be sure.

The Disney pavilions were a smash hit and were ranked as four of the five most popular at the Fair. Walt also benefited from the huge investments in ride systems, Audio-Animatronics, and other technologies paid for by his sponsors.

With Walt's curiosity about the feasibility of an East Coast Disneyland satisfied, the theme park would become the cash generator that he needed to fund his city. All he needed was enough land so he could avoid a replay of what happened in Anaheim. He always regretted not being able to buy more land around Disneyland he vowed that next time he find enough for all of his dreams.

Walt passed away before his most ambitious dream could be realized. Near retirement, Roy Disney decided to stay and make sense of Walt's ideas. Roy and his team wanted to create something that would make his brother proud. Roy knew the first phase would include an updated East Coast version of Disneyland, resort hotels, campgrounds, and the infrastructure to support long-term development. When the time came to build EPCOT, the plan for a city was scrapped in favor of the theme park.

So where did the idea of building a city come from?

It may have started with the success of Disneyland, which brought an avalanche of offers from other communities looking for an economic boost. His organization looked at projects in Niagara Falls, St. Louis, and his boyhood home of Marceline Missouri. As early as December 1959, Walt was in discussions with billionaire John MacArthur to build a "Community of Tomorrow" in Palm Beach, Florida that would feature a 400-acre theme park and a town of 70,000. According to Harrison "Buzz" Price, Walt and Roy Disney's go-to guy for feasibility studies, this is when Walt started to obsess about building a city.

Harrison "Buzz" Price was asked by Walt Disney to do the analysis for the perfect location for Disneyland. He went on to advise Walt on virtually every project until Walt's death in 1966. Buzz's influence on the theme park business is so profound, he was the first recipient of the Lifetime Achievement Award from the Themed Entertainment Association.

By the early 1960s, Walt's frustration with the area surrounding Disneyland and comments from people such as James Rouse and Ray Bradbury must have stirred his imagination. Plus, building a city is not the sequel to Disneyland but something new. This must have really excited Walt.

At the beginning of my research, the best information resources available to me were the 1966 film *EPCOT* featuring Walt Disney, the model of "Progress City" featured upstairs at the *Carousel of Progress* in Disneyland, and various books.

EPCOT was filmed on October 27, 1966. Marty Sklar drafted the script. The film begins with a history of Disneyland and the economic benefits to the surrounding community. Then Walt outlines his vision for his experimental city. Walt and the announcer describe the features, advantages, and benefits of EPCOT. Finally, Walt gave a call to action to the film's target audience of Florida politicians and private industry. Sadly, Walt would pass away two months after he recorded the film.

Another resource was the incredibly detailed model of Progress City at Disneyland. The model was the post show for the *Carousel of Progress* and it was Walt's vision for EPCOT. It was located on the second level of the show building.

The first three acts of the *Carousel of Progress* takes the audience from the turn of the last century to the 1920s and 1940s. The final act finds an audio-animatronics Father and Mother celebrating Christmas. The scene is set sometime in the near future, maybe five years, just beyond the show's installation date of 1967. They talk about the good life in Progress City. Outside of their floor to ceiling windows, off in the distance, is the EPCOT skyline.

As the giant turntable makes one last turn, guests step on stage and ride a speedramp to the second level. At the top of the ramp was the most massive, detailed model of Progress City one could imagine. It measured 6,900-square feet and contained more than 4,500 buildings and 2,450 moving vehicles. Filled with little details, it was complete with monorails, trains, motorways, and *PeopleMover*s. It had an amusement park and its own tiki restaurant. As day turned to night, everything would light up.

While walking through the viewing area, we hear Father and Mother from the last act narrate a four-minute tour of the model. Spotlights point out various community features and they tell us how life in Progress City is convenient and rewarding.

"Today, a small portion of the model can be seen as you ride the Tomorrowland Transit Authority *PeopleMover* in the Magic Kingdom at Walt Disney World. Much of the detail has been removed and none of the vehicles move anymore.

My real eureka moment came when I was on a tour of the Disney Archives. I met Dave Smith when he was the Chief Archivist at Disney. I asked him if Walt was reading any urban planning books at the time of his death. He suggested I drop him a note and he replied almost immediately and said, "Actually, on checking in his office inventory, he had only one book on the subject, *The Heart of Our Cities* by Victor Gruen."

Victor Gruen (1903-1980) published *The Heart of Our Cities* in 1964. Gruen was born in Vienna, Austria. He was trained at the Vienna Academy of Fine Arts and was very active politically prior to World War II. Gruen left Austria when it was annexed by Germany in 1938. He found his way to the United States and landed in Los Angeles in 1941. He opened Victor Gruen Associates in 1951 and firm continues to practice today.

Gruen designed Northfield Mall near Detroit in 1954. This was the first suburban open-air shopping mall. It was as revolutionary to urban design as Disneyland would prove to be a year later. By 1956, he had put a roof over his shopping mall and opened the Southdale Center in Edina, Minnesota.

Gruen would become known as the father of the modern shopping mall. This is a moniker that he would come to loath. He was striving for something much more important than just a shopping mall. He grew tired of the cheap imitations of his work that destroyed communities instead of healing them. These experiences and more would lead Gruen to rethink the way urban centers could be formed.

Walt and Gruen redefined the public's expectations for functional urban space. Mark Howard Moss said, "Both Gruen and Disney were in the dream business." They knew how to create vibrant urban spaces that had the key ingredients of quality, variety, and surprise. Each man would influence the other.

Gruen believed that there was an underlying cellular nature to a properly built community. If the basic unit of life is a cell, and millions of cells can come together to create an organism, he reasoned that an urban structure based on cells (clusters of mixed-use development) would be the healthiest system. The benefit of a cellular urban organization is that it can be scaled as small as a home or as large as the size of a metropolis.

In *The Heart of Our Cities*, Gruen mentions Disneyland and finds the park to be an important urban space and an excellent example of cellular urban organization. He states that the park has become, "a social center, a center of national and international tourism". Nevertheless, he is critical of what happened to the area surrounding the park.

By the 1960s, Walt was also concerned about the area just outside of Disneyland's gates. It was becoming a hodgepodge of motels, restaurants, and other tourist serving enterprises. The look was chaotic and threatening. Gruen studied these "forces that threaten and destroy the city" and how we they produce the anti-city. Gruen argues that Disneyland was a great start but more land use regulations would be needed. Anaheim's *Laissez-faire* attitude was destroying Walt's strong urban center. It would not be until 2001 that a cohesive vision for the area would be implemented through the Anaheim Resort Specific Plan.

Gruen learned from Walt's experience and tried to find a solution for his next big project. In 1960, a group of local executives called the Washington Metropolitan Board of Trade made a bid with the Bureau International des Expositions (BIE) to host a World's Fair in 1964. The Fair would be in the Washington DC metro area at a location ten miles east near Largo, Maryland. They were competing with New York and Los Angeles.

The Washington DC executives hired Gruen to draft an innovative site plan based on his cellular urban organization. The main Fair buildings would have been at the center of a large property surrounded by an ample greenbelt buffer. "Its most remarkable feature," according to architectural critic Ada Louise Huxtable was, "it is in effect a re-usable plan." Gruen had proposed to build a prototype community for 100,000 based on his cellular organization and using the Fair's infrastructure.

The Washington DC team would ultimately lose to Robert Moses and the City of New York due to their superior financial potential. However, Walt Disney would take full advantage of the New York opportunity and the rest, as they say, is another story.

In May 1960, Ada Louise Huxtable wrote an article for Horizon Magazine called *Out of a Fair*. She reviewed the proposed Washington DC post-fair plan and noted that the vision for the post-fair community "promises comfort, convenience, and calculated visual pleasure instead of the customary catch-as-catch-can arrangement of commercial and national exhibits".

Gruen's major innovation would have been the community's cellular layout. It featured a strong urban center with adjacent land uses that became less intense and dense as you move away from the center. It would follow a gradient that today would be known as an Urban Transect. The Transect is borrowed from naturalists who describe the characteristics and changes in an ecosystem over a gradient. Urban planners use the same concept of a gradient and apply it to the built environment. The Urban Transect measures a community from the most rural to the most urban.

After the Fair, the central core of the fairgrounds would be converted into a huge regional commercial center with shopping, hotels, and offices. The proposal included "clusters of buildings on platforms in a park", which would allow for trucks and other services to be hidden below. The main public areas would be under a climate-controlled roof or dome to protect the pedestrians from the brutal weather.

Surrounding the commercial core would be a ring of high-density residential units. Beyond those homes would be another ring that would blend neighborhood services with lower density attached residential units. Outside of this core are still lower density attached residential units connected by greenways. Finally, the entire development would be "surrounded by parking and transportation facilities ringed, in turn, by an outer area of open land." He compared this urban form to a medieval castle and city.

Huxtable writes that the post fair plan "is a scheme that would be applicable for any city where sufficient open land is available, and its expert attack on modern planning problems is a challenge to municipal governments everywhere."

Could Walt have seen Huxtable's article in May 1960 or know about Gruen's post-Fair plans? One thing we know for certain, according to the Disney Archives, is that Walt was familiar with Gruen's *The Heart of Our Cities*.

The Heart of Our Cities opens with Gruen on a trans-Atlantic cruise. He was reflecting upon the fate of our cities. Gruen noticed that a cruise ship is a city with everything planned with an emphasis on function, comfort, and convenience.

As Gruen suggests, "One of the primary purposes for a city is to bring together many people so that, through direct communication with each other, they may exchange goods and ideas without undue loss of energy and time." Walt wanted to take this idea one step further. At EPCOT guests would be invited to participate in his experimental community and to take the lessons learned back home with them.

Gruen said a city that is functioning properly gives one "free choice" to be "sociable" or to be private. To express your "human gregariousness" while meeting others or "the chance to disappear." This is the freedom granted to everyone visiting the theme parks. How else can you explain people wearing silly hats?

To illustrate the cellular concept, Gruen compares a city to the human body. In a human, a healthy heart is one that shows high cardiac output. For a city, the central business district is the heart and it must demonstrate "high vitality". Vitality is measured by the ability of primary functions to perform successfully and without strain.

A healthy city is one with an "infinite variety whose buildings and structures form, between them, spaces of differing size and character, narrow or broad, serene or dynamic, modest or monumental, contrasting with each other by virtue of varied treatment of pavement, landscaping, and lighting."

The only way to achieve "high vitality" is to ensure that the secondary or "utilitarian" functions are also working well. These utilitarian functions include sewer systems, the telecommunications networks, our the power supply, and our the transportation systems.

In EPCOT, the central business district would be oriented toward the needs and scale of the pedestrian and feature a signature hotel, convention facilities, shops, restaurants, and Disney-style attractions. All public areas would be highly detailed and heavily themed. New Orleans Square in Disneyland may have set the standard for design. Like the theme parks, all secondary functions were going to be hidden from the public's view.

Two ways to objectively measure the success of urban spaces is to use what Gruen described as "Appearance" and "Atmosphere". Appearance is the "sum total of the physical and psychological influence of an environment on human beings." Atmosphere is the "small-grained variety and diversity" that elevates a space from acceptable to exceptional.

To measure Appearance, note the "degree [you] feel enabled to live undisturbed, unmolested, and free of interference." As you move through a space, pay attention to how comfortable you are, how you feel, and are you being inspired.

Atmosphere is about function. As noted author Jane Jacobs said, the "main purpose is to enliven the streets with variety and detail." She adds, "The whole point is to make the streets more surprising, more compact, more variegated and busier than before – not less so." Atmosphere does not come about because of showy architectural statements. Architect Mies van der Rohe said, "God is in the details" and for many, this is what is referred to as the "Disney difference".

EPCOT was going to be built on undeveloped land so Walt was able to avoid one hurdle facing modern cities, which was incompatible adjacent land uses. For example, Main Street USA represents an idyllic town around the turn of the last century. Everything is clean and in its place. The reality was cities at that time were rather brutal places. People used to live next door to stockyards and factories.

So in 1916 the City of New York enacted the first zoning code with the objective to create a separation between incompatible uses. Often the unintended consequence of these land use regulations is to create lifeless cities where the uses are so widespread that they are connected only by getting into your car and driving from one pod to another. Walt and Victor Gruen knew this was sapping the vitality out of our city centers.

At EPCOT, the industrial areas would be located in their own pod and connected by the monorail. Walt and Gruen were strong advocates for separating all mechanical and utilitarian functions away from the public realm. As he had done with other projects, Gruen proposed placing the Fair's truck traffic and utilities underground and building the show buildings on the second level. Walt would propose the same idea for EPCOT and it would finally be tested at the Magic Kingdom.

Using Disney nomenclature, Walt called the public realm "onstage" where Appearance and Atmosphere would create a seamless show.

Hidden "backstage" are the utilitarian functions, away from the guests.

Gruen was frustrated by the lack of progress in the development of new public transportation technologies. He commented that millions of people go to Disneyland to ride a monorail that is being promoted as the transportation system of the future but the technology had been around since the 1890s. Solving the mobility problem is where Walt would make major improvements upon Gruen's design. Transportation systems are one of Walt's passions and specialties. For EPCOT, he proposed to use monorails, *PeopleMovers*, and electric vehicles to move people around.

How we move people and goods around has a huge influence on the design and function of our cities. A vibrant urban space must have the right balance between pedestrian spaces, buildings, private open spaces, access, and the appropriate transportation systems. Many downtowns suffer because the balance is out of whack and too much land is given over to the private automobile and not enough land is dedicated to people.

Gruen's solution was to align transportation technologies along a *scale of gradation of movement*. At each increment, there are certain transportation systems that can enhance the pedestrian experience or make you feel miserable. If the match is done right, the environment will "promise comfort, convenience, and calculated visual pleasure." You will enjoy a positive experience. If the match is not right, the environment will feel unsafe and you will be on edge. You might say it is the difference between walking in a theme park and walking through the parking lot on the way to the theme park.

In reviewing drawings of EPCOT, I used Gruen's *scale of gradation of movement* and I learned a great deal about what life in the city would have been like. In Gruen's book, he provides many suggestions on how to mix uses, preserve the integrity of the public realm, and hide the vital services that keep the community alive.

Another breakthrough in my research came when I interviewed Harrison "Buzz" Price. Buzz worked on feasibility studies for the project. He was able to provide firsthand confirmation on project details and the application of these urban design principles.

Buzz said it all begins at the center. At the heart of EPCOT would be a world-class resort hotel with conference facilities, office buildings, combined with the transportation center. This combination would create a critical mass of activity that would energize the edge uses.

Starting from the hotel and transportation center, and radiating out toward the edge, is what Gruen calls a Pedshed. A Pedshed is the "desirable walking distance" that a lazy walker, on a one-purpose trip without interruption, will walk. If the walker can sit, shop or eat, it distracts them and they can go longer distances. The length of a Pedshed is determined by Appearance and Atmosphere, as well as climate and topography.

EPCOT would have a large Pedshed because of the highly attractive and completely weather-protected environment. A typical guest would easily walk up to one mile or 20 minutes with these conditions. Imagine a network of storefronts like New Orleans Square in Disneyland or the international pavilions at Epcot under one roof to distract the guests.

The theme parks are within the next gradient of the scale. A guest will walk up to a half-mile or ten minutes if you provide a highly attractive environment where the sidewalks are protected from sunshine and rain.

Next, we have the conditions found in many cities. If the central business district is attractive but not protected from the weather and people are exposed to the elements this limits the desirable walking range to less than a quarter of a mile or five minutes of walking. Degrade the environment even further with unattractive spaces like parking lots, garages, or a traffic-congested street, and you limit your range to only 600 feet or two minutes of walking.

Within the Pedshed, Gruen suggested slow moving people carriers like moving sidewalks. Walt's solution to extend the Pedshed and enhance the experience was to use horse-trolleys, fire trucks, the omnibus, and other vehicles.

The common perception was EPCOT would be a city under a dome. This seemed very ambitious and would be very expensive. According to Buzz Price, the actual architecture was going to be much more conventional and predictable. At the center, the transportation center and hotel would be connected to the themed retail and dining districts by a covered pedestrian boulevard. Each highly detailed facade disguises an ordinary industrial building. Once again, think of New Orleans Square in Disneyland.

Once guests pass through the retail areas they will come to another pedestrian boulevard, which connects to the high-density residential apartments. The apartments are typical structures but residents would have been given a choice of views. They could look down at the indoor pedestrian boulevard or outside to a greenbelt that separates the central city from the low-density neighborhoods.

Gruen struggled with a way to move people between one to two miles and that is the next link in the *scale of gradation of movement*. For many, this is too far to walk but it is an inefficient trip in a car. He recommended electric mini-buses and taxis. Instead, Walt would use his *PeopleMover* to connect the hotel complex and transit center to the residential areas. As a planner, a transit system on a fixed rail connecting activity nodes with virtually no headway is a dream. Another benefit would be the overhead *PeopleMover* tracks could define the edges of the themed retail districts.

For trips of two to five miles you need different transportation technologies. Gruen liked fixed rail systems and larger buses. Walt preferred the monorail. His system would run north to south to include the Magic Kingdom, EPCOT, the Industrial district, the gateway transportation center, and the jetport. The monorail is perfectly suited for this challenge.

Gruen continues with recommendations for longer distances. During the planning for EPCOT, the focus was on automobiles, buses, and airplanes. Motorized traffic would have been diverted below EPCOT, out of view of the residents and visitors.

Continental and intercontinental visitors would typically arrive by airplane. One of the most unusual ideas proposed for EPCOT was Walt's proposal for a radial jetport. This unique configuration for the terminal and runways promised greater efficiency in moving planes in and out of the terminals.

Interestingly, Walt Disney World was on the leading edge of air transportation technology with its STOLport. STOL is an acronym for Short Take-Off and Landings. Walt Disney World's STOLport was part of a regional network. For a short while, Shawnee Airlines operated a 19-seat de Havilland DHC-6 Twin Otter aircraft with service between Walt Disney World and the Orlando International Airport. The runway still exists today but it is no longer used as an airport.

One sharp contrast between Gruen and Walt was the outer core of residential units. Gruen stated that "the space-devouring detached single home was not considered as suitable" and he was an advocate of clustered attached homes that shared common open space. Walt was not convinced and showed suburban-style single-family residential units. Buzz Price confided that, "Walt wanted a place for his friends to live."

The Gruen plan for his post-fair city contained enough detail to convince the Washington DC executives to back his proposal. He did a lot of work on the development of data tables that help determine appropriate residential densities from the core to the outer edges of the community.

So I come back to my initial question; would EPCOT have worked?

During my conversation with Buzz, I asked him if the project would have worked. After all, nobody else knew as much about the EPCOT project. He was in the room with Walt. Without hesitation he said, "Absolutely yes." Buzz added, "Walt would obsess over a problem." He reminded me that EPCOT was not revolutionary but evolutionary. Walt was going to use true and tried architectural technologies, creatively blend the land uses, arrange them in a way where the hotel and day guests are coming from one direction and they would meet the residents coming from another direction. Everyone would interact in a beautiful, comfortable, and inspiring public setting.

Buzz concluded by saying that, "EPCOT would have been more famous than Walt Disney World".

***Sam Gennawey** has combined his passion for the theme parks with his career as an urban planner and community engagement specialist. He has won numerous awards for his collaborative planning process that has lead to long-range visions for communities and the implementation of dozens of comprehensive plans for which he has been the principal author. He has demonstrated that if you can dream, you can do it, even in the real world.*

Joe & Carl: Two Men Who Built the World

Didier Ghez

October 1970.

Less than a year before Grand Opening.

Roy O. Disney had turned beet red.

"The life of our company is at stake and you people from J.B. Allen are telling me that you can't open this project… on October 1st 1971? I can't believe this!" Known for his even-temper, Roy was so upset that he stormed out and slammed the door. The door almost came off of its hinges.

Yet Walt Disney World opened successfully on October 1, 1971 thanks to the talent and passion of a handful of Disney executives including, among others: Card Walker, Joe Fowler, Joe Potter, Dick Nunis, Orlando Ferrante, Bob Mathieson, Phil Smith, John Curry, and Carl Bongirno. This story focuses on two of them: Joe Fowler and Carl Bongirno, who helped build Walt Disney World and whose combined careers span from the early days of the Disneyland project (Fowler) to the creation of Disneyland Paris (Bongirno).

The younger of those two men, Carl Bongirno, was born in Pueblo, Colorado on August 9, 1937.[1] Carl's parents were struggling financially and at eleven he got a job as a baker's helper, getting up at four or five o'clock in the morning and working ten to twelve hour shifts when school wasn't in session. At sixteen he was hired as a "bagger" and "checker" at Safeway grocery store, then worked in construction, driving a crane in-between school years. Having attended the University of Denver, he graduated with a B.S./B.A. in accounting and management and joined Arthur Andersen in Denver where he spent about three years as an accountant.

As luck would have it, the Celebrity Sports Center, launched in 1960 and owned and operated by the Disney Company, was located in Denver. Carl, who did not want to remain an accountant all his life, had started to look around, saw future career opportunities in the Disney venture, applied and was soon hired as its chief accountant and controller. Mel Melton, then assistant treasurer at Disney's corporate headquarters spotted him. In 1965, just eleven months after Carl had joined the Celebrity Sports Center, Mel was named President of WED (which would later become Walt Disney Imagineering) and asked Carl to join him as WED's treasurer, based in California. Carl jumped at the opportunity.

Unfortunately tensions developed between the two men and in 1969 Carl decided that it was time for him to leave the company. This was not to be. The director of finance from Disneyland had decided to join another studio and offered Carl his job at Disneyland. Carl stayed with Disney.

In 1970 he would receive a fateful call from Roy O. Disney.

"About a year before we opened Walt Disney World, in October of 1970, I got this call from Roy, who said, 'Carl we are having a big powwow down in Florida. I want you there. I am very concerned about the construction management company team we have down there. I want to get to the bottom of this. If we aren't going to open this theme park on October 1st, 1971 we are going to bankrupt this company. We have got commitments to participants, bankers, and stockholders. I am concerned that things aren't going too well,'" remembers Bongirno.

"I was down there for the meeting. It was held in a doublewide trailer. We must have had 50 guys in that room made up of our general contractor at the time, J.B. Allen, who was also involved in the building of Disneyland, and all of our people: Roy O. Disney, Donn Tatum, Card Walker, Dick Nunis, myself, and Joe Fowler."

J.B. Allen, also known as the Allen Contracting Co., had been hired by Disney on April 11, 1969 to serve as general contractor for the Disney World project.[2]

Bongirno continues:

"Roy had J.B. Allen give a presentation with Joe Fowler on the situation on the site and how things were going and problems that they were having and so-forth and so-on. It was a fairly lengthy meeting—a couple of hours.

"At the end of the meeting Roy said, 'J.B. Allen that was very good. Thank you very much for a very detailed analysis and briefing. I appreciate it very much. I just have one question and I want a truthful answer. Will this project open on October 1st, 1971?' As people were responding non-verbally, Roy is looking around the room. All the J.B. Allen guys are shaking their heads no, back and forth, left to right, right to left. All the Disney guys are shaking their heads yes. We were brought up that if you have an objective you accomplish it. Will we open? Yes we will open. I don't

know what we are going to have to do but we are going to open. The J.B. Allen guys are saying no. Roy Disney—I was sitting a couple of seats away from him—turns beet red. Beet red. I mean all the blood in his body rushed to his head. He jolts up onto his feet and pounds the table. He says, 'Goddamn. Son of a bitch. The life of our company is at stake and you people from J.B. Allen are telling me that you can't open this project on October 1st, 1971 after a two-hour presentation. I can't believe this!' He went on in a tirade for a minute or so. Then he stormed out of the trailer and slammed the door. I thought it was going to come off of its hinges.

"I was staying in the company cottages. Roy was in one, Card Walker was in one, Donn Tatum was in one, and I was in one. About two hours later I got a call from Card. He said, 'Carl, I'm glad I caught you. Why don't you come over? Donn and I want to talk to you.' So I went over to his cottage, which I think was next door, or two doors over. He started of by saying he had just finished a meeting with Roy. Roy was extremely upset and he made the decision to kick J.B. Allen off the project. We were going to run it ourselves. He said, 'I'm sure glad you are here in Florida to be Joe Fowler's number two guy.' [Laughs] I was on a business trip. I was intending to eventually move to Florida but not for about a year. So I didn't say anything. I think Card thought I was already located in Florida. He knew I was going there but he didn't know that I hadn't moved yet. He said, 'I want you and Phil Smith to sit down with J.B. Allen and negotiate their departure. And then work with Joe Fowler in getting this place open on time.'

"Phil Smith was our attorney. He was actually the first person on the Disney property. He lived in one of the old houses there on one of the properties we bought. He was our first hire in Florida. The second one was a young man by the name of Jim McManus. While I was still in Imagineering he had relocated to set up the first office on

the site, to be the spearhead to start the development of Walt Disney World.

"In any event, I went back to my cottage and I called my wife, Carol. She said, 'How are things going?' I said, 'Oh, wonderful. I am now living in Florida and I hope you can join me as soon as possible. Put the house up for sale. As soon as you do I will come back and I will fly you and the children back to Florida. We are now residents of Florida.' And as usual, my wife, in her inimitable way said, 'No problem, I'll put it up for sale tomorrow and we'll try to sell as soon as we can and join you.' So that was my move to Orlando.

"Phil Smith and I negotiated the departure of J.B. Allen. It was quite an exciting experience getting Walt Disney World opened. Through the opening, as the chief financial guy on the site, I worked very closely with Joe Fowler."

Joe Fowler, the "Can Do" Admiral, was born in Lewiston, Maine on July 9, 1894, during the presidency of Grover Cleveland. During his life he got to know Harry Truman, Dwight Eisenhower and Lyndon Johnson, and once roomed with Edward, Prince of Wales, on a British gunship steaming up the Yangtze River.[3]

Fowler graduated from the U.S. Naval Academy in 1917, and served two years in World War I. He later graduated from Massachusetts Institute of Technology with a Master's Degree in Naval Architecture in 1921.

Following this graduation, he supervised construction of the U.S.S. Panay and five sister ships in Shanghai, China from 1925 to 1929. His '"29 children in the Navy"' as he fondly called the warships he was in charge of designing and building, included the two biggest aircraft carriers of World War II, the Lexington and the Saratoga. Fowler served four years in World War II, and was in command of the San Francisco Naval Shipyard in 1946 and 1947. He retired voluntarily from the Navy as Rear Admiral, U.S.N. in 1948, after 32 years of service.

From 1948 to 1951 he had his own office as consulting engineer, but in 1951 he returned to active duty at the request of the Secretary of Defense. He established Federal Cataloguing and Standardization programs, then accepted an appointment by President Harry S. Truman in 1952 as Civilian Director of the Federal Supply Management Agency.

After finishing this assignment, Fowler joined Walt Disney in April 1954 as administrator of construction at Disneyland and built the park in 15 months. "Walt said to me a couple of days after I was hired, 'Now look, I will try to have the ideas, and you make the engineering realities of them,'" remembered Fowler.[4]

After having overseen the construction of Disneyland Fowler later managed its operations and Walt even cast him as technical advisor of the live-action movie *20,000 Leagues Under the Sea.*

In the mid-'60s Fowler was heavily involved in the Disney World site selection and in the initial discussions with key American companies regarding the EPCOT project.

By 1965 most of the land had been bought and Joe could start building. It was the Admiral who got the digging started early at the site.

> *"I called a West Palm Beach engineering firm, Gee & Jenson, and told them I was an admiral from Maine with offices in New York and California and I needed them to build some rivers and lakes for me," recalled Fowler. "This was three weeks before the news was in the papers, so I also had to tell them that I couldn't tell them who they would be working for. They were pretty nice about this and agreed to start work anyway."*

Once this was under way, the Admiral piped a general aboard. The General would be in charge of getting some lights and water into the woods, and many, many other things.[5]

> *"The General's [Joe Potter] primary responsibility was to assemble industry and to negotiate with them for coming into the Disney World, coupled with the fact that he had the responsibility for all the preparations of the site outside the Park itself, with regard to drainage and the preparation of the various and sundry areas," explained Fowler.*[6]

MIT graduate, combat engineer in World War II who helped plan the Normandy invasion, governor of the Panama Canal Zone for four years, right hand of the demanding Robert Moses, U.S. Army Maj. Gen. (Ret.) William Everett Potter, who picked up the nickname "Joe" during his West Point days, was hired by Disney in 1965. Walt had met him while Potter was serving as Robert Moses' right arm on the New York World's Fair.

> *"I'd met several [Disney people before Walt]," remembers Potter. "Jack Sayers,*[7] *for instance, and Joe Fowler, who was in charge of building those things. I'd been familiar with them. I'd met Roy too. I had been working with the 'working level' people, because he only came back there two or three times to my knowledge. One day I was asked whether I'd be interested in joining the organization, not by Walt, but by Jack Sayers. I said, 'Yes.'*
>
> *"Prior to that time I had met with Walt and the staff, downtown in a hotel. Walt at that time had this project called the Hall of Presidents on which we had a presentation. It was one of the things that Walt really wanted to do. When we got Illinois in the Fair, Illinois came in because Lincoln came from Illinois. They wouldn't put up the money for the whole show, but they did want Lincoln. That's when I first got to know Walt. The people in Illinois were extremely money-conscious and the man they had in charge was a Lincoln historian who had his own idea about things. Prior to the second year of the Fair, money became an obsession, and the company was going to need another half-million dollars in order to continue Lincoln in the Fair. Cost of operation.*

> *"At this meeting it was indicated that the company would put up $250,000 and would the Fair put up $250,000? I said, 'Yes,' in fear and trembling, because I had to go back to Moses. The Fair was not in very good shape financially. Mr. Moses approved it. I think that Walt thought that was a pretty good decision made on the spur of the moment and maybe I was the kind of guy that could do the same with him. I think that's why they asked me to come."*[8]

Another story reveals the nature of the relationship between Walt and the General: once, during the early Florida days, Walt called the General "Everett" and the General snapped back, "Yes, Elias," and after that they got along pretty well, agreeing to never again call each other by his middle name. It was also about this time that the General began to get a feel for his new employer. It didn't take long to realize that Walt was a beginner of things, not a finisher. He and Moses were alike in that respect.[9]

If Potter would build what was invisible to the guests, Fowler and Bongirno were tasked with building what the visitors would see and enjoy on a day to day basis. Unfortunately, by the time their task would be complete, Walt would be gone.

> *"Walt didn't live long enough to see us break ground in Disney World, but he used to travel all over the property with me in a jeep," remembered Fowler. "He loved it. I remember he wanted to see how Disney World would look from the top of the Contemporary Hotel. So we got the biggest damned utility crane in Florida, and the two of us got into the bucket and they hoisted us straight up to where the lounge at the top of the Contemporary would be. I was so damn busy hanging on, hoping to get down, and he was so enthusiastic: 'Oh, Joe, look at this! This is going to be great!' He could visualize it all. I could see enough to realize that everything [in the plans] was properly located. Oh my, he was a wonderful man."* [10]

The task of building "the World" was Herculean. At one point during the Florida project, Joe held three posts, simultaneously, including

Senior Vice President, Engineering and Construction for Walt Disney Productions; Chairman of the Board of WED, and Director of Construction for Disney's Buena Vista Construction Company, which had taken over from J.B. Allen. Thankfully Fowler's health and optimism were unshakable.

> *"An old friend of the Admiral was Bob Mathieson, Executive Vice President Parks at Walt Disney World in 1993. One of Mathieson's favorite Admiral Fowler stories is [that] Fowler, then 94, fell and broke his hip while attending the wedding of a relative in the Northeast. The admitting nurse asked Fowler if he had ever been in a hospital before. 'He said, 'Yes, I remember it well. It was World War I. I had my appendix out.' She choked a bit on that.' Fowler was both impish and accurate. He has enjoyed remarkable health throughout his life. Those who saw him work long hours in the stifling swamp that was to become the Magic Kingdom said he never missed a day. 'I don't remember him ever having even a cold,' Mathieson said. 'And he didn't seem to ever show fatigue, no matter how long the day was.'"*[11]

A photographer illustrates the other pillar of Fowler's success through the following story:

> *"I knew Fowler was putting together what we were already calling 'the ninth largest navy in the world' over near Tampa. He was assembling a small fleet of mini-subs, Indian war canoes, steamboats, keel boats, kayaks and paddleboats. Most were being trucked over the same day. I was trying to set up a picture as the caravan drove east on I-4. I told Fowler what I needed, the critical timing involved, the truck schedules, photo locations... the whole setup, and asked what he thought of the idea. It was incredibly complicated, calling for lots of different things to happen at just the right time. Could it be arranged?*
>
> *"He sat quietly for a minute, then said, 'I'll tell you what I think of it,' and he reached into a briefcase, pulled out*

> *something that looked like an old bumper sticker, held it up and smiled. It read, 'Can Do.' From that point on, I always thought of him that way, as the guy who could get any job done in that place."*[12]

Fowler and Bongirno's "can do" spirit was critical as each day brought its share of challenges and as the challenges pilled up.

Bongiorno recalls:

> *"The biggest challenge was that we had a raw piece of land and we had no services that could be provided to us. The power company wasn't sufficient to handle our needs. The local telephone company couldn't provide our needs. When I sent Jim McManus to be the second person on the site after Phil Smith was there, it took him I forget how many weeks to get a telephone set up on the periphery of the property in the trailer he had rented. It was just ridiculous.*
>
> *"Also we had to do a tremendous amount of preparation work with canals and levees so that we would control water coming on to the property and coming off of the property, so that we did it right ecologically, so that we maintained the ecological balance of what it was before we were there, to keep it the same after we did the development. So the first major thrust was to develop all those canals and levees and then to plan and build the entire infrastructure that was necessary to support that project: including our own power plant; our own water treatment; telephone company; and the whole gambit.*
>
> *"As a matter of fact, before we had opened Roy had called me one day and he wanted the board of directors to come down and he was wondering if I would host them and give them a tour of the property. This is just a few months before we opened, maybe two months before we opened. As we were kind of wrapping up the tour one of the board members named Bagnall,*[13] *when we were walking out of*

the power plant put his arm around me. We are walking out of the power plant over to the maintenance building and he said, "Carl, you know it hadn't really occurred to me, I have been with this project from the very beginning, but we basically built all the requirements of a small city here." I said, "Yes, you are right." This is exactly what we had done. It was like a light turned on. We built all the requirements of a city right here on this piece of property. And we did and that was quite a remarkable comment by Mr. Bagnall.[14]

"[Another] one of the biggest challenges was getting the land prepared and dredging all of that dirt to develop all those beautiful lakes and lagoons and building it up to elevate the location for the theme park so that we could have all of the utilities and the wherewithal to move merchandise and food and beverages and so forth under ground instead of having to do that above ground. That was quite an undertaking. I had forgotten the millions of yards of dirt that we excavated and then stacked up on that site for the theme park.

"At Disneyland one of our biggest problems was that our employees dressed in Frontierland costumes were walking through Tomorrowland to get to their job. That always bothered all of us that we were detracting from the theme of lands by having employees walking through with costumes that were not specific to that land. The other biggest problem we were moving hot dog buns and hamburger buns and other products on the surface and mingling with the guests. It was just a nightmare. So that is the reason we did the utilidoors [at Walt Disney World]. If we had a problem with the utilities at Disneyland we would have to close the land and dig up the earth and get down to the pipe that busted and fix it and then try to get the land opened as soon as possible. We could be closed a couple of days until we fixed the problem. Those utilidoors [at Walt Disney World] were an extremely integral part of what we did in phase one."

Joe Fowler adds: "We built the so-called underground so that all of the service operation for the Disney World would be conducted underground rather than through the streets, as I had to do in Disneyland when the trucks would break the corners of the buildings, plaza and signs. Our repairs day-by-day were quite heavy."[15]

Joe Potter, father of the utilidoor concept never forgot the challenges hinted at by Carl Bongirmo: "I think I brought the idea of utilidoors to this outfit. Normally, in a development you bury the utilities, and then, when you want to dig to repair a sewer line, you dig up the telephone line, too. Up in Alaska[16] *we had utilidoors all over the place. A utilidoor is a ditch or a tunnel in which your utilities go, and early in the game I employed three consultants to give us advice on what they thought we should do with the utilities, and one of the things they recommended, which I also recommended, was the use of the utilidoors.*

"But if you go in the basement and go underneath the castle you will notice there's a terrific slope there and that's deep. When we were digging down there we had a series of very heavy rains and it looked like we'd never get out of that lake that we were keeping pumped underneath what is now the castle. It was a terrific job and old Joe Fowler, I think, took on a couple of years while he was getting the contractor to get those pilings in so we could get the castle going as well as the other things that go with it."[17]

In later years Imagineers would come to remember sticky mud as the nightmare that haunted them during the building of Disneyland Paris. As far as Disney World was concerned water, water again and again, was the main foe. In an interview he granted in 1973 to Bob Thomas, Fowler explained the issues in detail:

"You know, Florida has been noted for its areas where unexpectedly there'll be a sink [hole]. So we engineered the thing thoroughly and tested it out. We went to the extent of drill testing every area where we'd have buildings, or

the monorail, or weights superimposed on the earth, which was damned expensive. I suppose we spent three or four million dollars just testing. But we couldn't afford to do otherwise.

"We introduced new equipment, because we found that the ordinary equipment which would handle 35 yards was damn expensive and we introduced great big pieces of equipment that had never been used [there] before. It was used in the quarries of Illinois, which would take 55 yards, and double-ended. That saved us a lot of money.

"You see, in the ordinary construction, in West Palm Beach, for example, if you had an area, you just spread the area out and built on the earth and realized that you were going to get a certain sinkage and not go to the expense of digging out the root mat. As far as compacting, which we did with all of our areas, getting the compaction to 95% hadn't been heard of in Florida. And the contractors couldn't understand it, but we insisted upon it. The result is that Disney World is built to last against any sinking, or hurricanes or whatnot.

"In building the Monorail for example, in drill-testing for all my pylons, in some places I'd strike solid rock at forty-five feet, other places I wouldn't strike anything down to 170 feet and I'd have to put in a spread footing of three or four pylons in place of the one, before I got to the pilot cap which would support the pylon itself.

"When we built the lagoon, we had to take out an enormous amount of root mat. Root mat is a composition that is fifty percent roots and fifty percent muck. It's so dense that contrary to the ordinary root that's buried, which decays, these roots are just as good as maybe 100/150 years ago when they were buried, because no oxygen could get to them. The material that we took out, this so-called root mat, is not worth a damn. You couldn't use it for fill, because subsequently it would rot, you see, and your earth

would collapse to that extent. So we had to dig all this damn stuff out and pile it.

"We piled it all up in the different areas and we were too damn busy to follow through some of our ideas. One of our ideas was we thought we might grind it up and make mulch out of it, which may be done someday. But now the roots were exposed and eventually we could burn them and recycle the bark. You have to be very careful because there's a lot of peat in that material and we were afraid if we started a fire that way without taking the roots and separating them, we might get that big pile burning and you never would be able to get the damned thing out, because peat burns in a ball. Oh, we had a lot of problems. [Walt] loved these problems!

"Then, of course, when we decided to pump the lake and get rid of all of the... There was a brownish, brackish water... to get rid of all that debris and make the water clear, he was fascinated with that. His idea was the one that we followed in draining the lake.

"We built the channel which unites the lake and lagoon and then we had to build a subway under that; we had a hell of a time trying to keep the water [out]."[18]

But even someone as exceptional as Fowler could not be everywhere and be aware of all the issues. After all, it was no less than 10,000 workers from 87 subcontractors that had to be supervised.

"Joe had a military jeep, and I'd go down there and [he] would get me into the jeep, and we'd go around in the mud." remembered Ed Morgan.[19] *"They'd bring tractors in to drag us out of the mud, and then we'd proceed from station to station. Joe would ask a foreman questions, then he'd say, 'Can do boys. Keep up the good work!' And we'd go to someplace else. I'm looking at this, and things seemed pretty strange to me. So while Joe's talking to these guys, I'm watching them, and I'm finding out that*

there're cranes picking up steel and they are putting it in one place, and a little while later another crane would come and put it back where it was. They were just making work for themselves. I didn't know what to do. I thought it was ridiculous. We're having a hard time making open, and this stuff is going on. So I finally decided to tell Joe, and Joe looked at me and he didn't want to accept it."

According to David Koenig in his book *Realityland*, Disney World therefore needed one more dynamo, since "by May 1971 it became increasingly clear to [Card] Walker and [Donn] Tatum that maybe J.B. Allen was right: at the rate construction was crawling, very little would be completed by October 1."[20] They sent Dick Nunis.

"You have to credit two people. Joe Fowler, the Admiral, who created all the levels of contractors, of suppliers. He planned the invasion. Nunis took them across the channel. They made a great team," once said Sandy Quinn, the first Disney World marketing executive.[21]

Ironically Nunis soon became "General Nunis," when he hung a caricature of himself in his office as General Patton wearing a hard hat.

Here is how Nunis remembers those frantic days:

"I was flying back to California with Donn Tatum and Card Walker after a visit to the site—I think it was in May or June. One of them said, 'Dick, what do you think? Can we get open by October 1?' I said, 'Frankly, from what I've seen, under the present circumstances I don't think so.' The asked me if there was any way we could make it. 'Only if we throw all the resources of the company into it,' I said.

"They called me into the office on Monday morning and said, 'If we turn the total energies of the company in one direction, Dick, would you be willing to go down and get it open?'

> *"I left Disneyland with their total backing. There was no time to worry about budgets. They told me I could get anyone I called for. I called the Disneyland heads in before I left and told them, 'It's your baby. When I call, don't say when. It means yesterday.'*
>
> *"From then on, we literally stripped the other divisions. The Studio. Design. Disneyland. They began to call us the 'Nunis Raiders.'*
>
> *"We had a couple hundred key management people and experts on the site now. There was no discussion of changing the date. We had to open. Roy Disney, Donn Tatum, Card Walker, all of them were here. We had acquired some houses at Bay Hill for them. Decisions were made quickly. On the spot. No memos.*
>
> *"I carried a tape recorder and dictated all day long as I went around the project. Secretaries typed the memos at night and sent them out the next day."*[22]

Joe Fowler remained heavily involved, of course:

> *"Dick had a real responsibility. He had to make sure things dovetailed into his operation. Dick and his people were a tremendous amount of help. I used them. I used them without their realizing it. I had them working for me.*
>
> *"Everyone realized what was at stake. I had one powerful asset. Roy Disney. He lived beside me. Between the two of us, we made a lot of decisions that nobody knew about."*[23]

And the pace increased, again. The last days before the opening sped by in a blur. Roy O. Disney was seen helping unload a truck. Dick Nunis supervised the laying down of lawn in front of the Contemporary Hotel, at night, a few hours before the Grand Opening.

That same night Carl Bongirno was busy in Fantasyland:

"The biggest problem just as we were getting close to opening day was the pouring of the concrete in Fantasyland. That was the last land to receive concrete. As a matter of fact, at four or five o'clock in the morning—when we were scheduled to open at 9:00 a.m.—they were pouring concrete in Fantasyland and I was there watching them. We actually had a helicopter come in to create air movement to dry that concrete so it would be dry by the time the guests started coming in and started walking on it. It was a close call. It was very tight."

On October 1, 1971, the park opened on time.

Bongirno spent the next ten years in Florida as Vice President of Finance, a responsibility to which was added that of Vice President of General Services in 1973. In 1979 he moved back to California when Card Walker named him President of WED, a position he held until his retirement in 1987 and which allowed him to supervise the creation of EPCOT, of Tokyo Disneyland and the early days of the Disneyland Paris project.

Joe Fowler retired from Disney in 1978 and created an engineering consulting company in Orlando with his former colleague Joe Potter who had retired in 1974. A few months before his death at age 99, on December 3, 1993, the *Orlando Sentinel* wrote a portrait of the Admiral, which read:

"Joe Fowler, who was riding bicycles when the Wright brothers were still making them, pedals a three-wheeler these days. He likes to joke that he rode a tricycle as a kid in the 1890s and he's riding one again, figuring this one will be his last.

Then again, he quickly adds, he plans to be around for a long time. When Disney executives told him they expected to throw a blowout 100th birthday party, the 98-year-old retired Admiral gave his trademark, two-word reply: 'Can do.'"[24]

It was the only “can do” the Admiral was unable to fulfill… Walt and Roy were waiting for him.

Acknowledgments from the author: This essay would not have been written without the help of Becky Cline, Michael Crawford, Mike Grygo, Jim Korkis, Ed Ovalle, and Todd James Pierce.

***Didier Ghez** has conducted Disney research since he was a teenager in the mid ‘80s. His articles about the parks, animation, and vintage international Disneyana, as well as his many interviews with Disney artists, have appeared in such magazines as Persistence of Vision, Tomart’s Disneyana Update, Animation Journal, Animation Magazine, StoryboarD, and Fantasyline. He is the co-author of the art book Disneyland Paris - From Sketch to Reality, runs the Disney History blog (http://disneybooks.blogspot.com), the Disney Books Network website (http://www.pizarro.net/didier), and serves as managing editor of the Walt’s People book series.*

Disney Brings Sports to the World

Adam Goswick

Pregame

Disney is a huge name in the entertainment industry. We all know that. They make a habit of releasing blockbuster movies, introduce stars that become sensations among young music fans, and attract hundreds of millions of guests to their theme parks each year.

But movies, music, games, and attractions aren't everything that people care about. Spectator sports are a huge form of entertainment. How many fans sit down to watch their favorite football team on Saturdays, Sundays, Monday evenings, and even some Thursdays?

Baseball games are still a great family outing. Soccer may be a sport growing in popularity in the United States. These are just three popular sports we are familiar with. We could talk about basketball, hockey (in its field and ice varieties), track and field, weightlifting, wrestling, and many others.

So what would happen if Disney got involved in sports? The result would have to be huge, right? Well, Disney has gotten into sports, and one of the results required over 200 acres of land in central Florida. Disney's Wide World of Sports is a huge sports complex at the Walt Disney World Resort, and we're about to take a look at how it became reality.

Building the Field(s) for Dreams

The complex's heritage goes all the way back to April 29, 1961 - pretty far back for a facility that's not been open for fifteen years. This is when ABC aired its first episode of *Wide World of Sports*. At this point in time, Disney had a relationship with ABC thanks to Disneyland, though they were far from the time when they would take ownership of the broadcast company. *Wide World of Sports* enjoyed a successful run. It delivered the first broadcasts of many famous sporting events, such as Wimbledon, the Daytona 500, the Indianapolis 500, the Little League World Series, and others.

But Disney itself didn't have an official presence in sports until much later. In 1992, Disney stepped into the rink when the National Hockey League (NHL) awarded Disney its own franchise. The Mighty Ducks of Anaheim, named after Disney's popular movie franchise, is still a notable franchise in the NHL – and the movies are still worth a viewing, also!

Bolstering Disney's presence in the sports scene was their purchase of the American Broadcasting Company, or ABC to the rest of us. When Disney bought Capital Cities/ABC in the mid-1990s, they also picked up a sports-focused cable television network: ESPN. ABC acquired an 80% share of ESPN in 1984, so Disney picked up ownership of the network with the purchase of ABC. ESPN comes back into our story later, so this is an important acquisition.

This also meant that Disney now owned the network responsible for the *Wide World of Sports* TV program. So, when Disney began building a sports complex in August 1995 at Walt Disney World, what name could be more fitting than the name that was originally known for bringing sports entertainment into the home? The new home for sports at Walt Disney World would be Disney's Wide World of Sports.

Disney's Wide World of Sports was slated to open in May 1997. The plan was to create a facility that could house tournaments, multi-sport events (Disney Olympics, anyone?), training sites, competition areas, and many others. Obviously, we know today that the Wide World of Sports does this and more.

The facility was designed to play host to at least 30 individual and team sports, including everything from baseball to martial arts. Among the facilities Disney planned for were a professional ballpark (and a baseball quadraplex to boot), a tennis center with multiple courts, a track-and-field arena, and many others.

But if you're just not interested in competing at the Wide World of Sports, you could also enjoy some atmosphere. The Wide World of Sports originally opened with an All Star Café: a sports themed restaurant owned by some of the biggest names in professional sports. We'll circle around and talk more about the restaurant in just a bit.

Moving to Game Plan B

Not even a year after the Wide World of Sports complex opened, Jim McKay (the original host of ABC's *Wide World of Sports*) announced the TV series was to be cancelled after more than a 35 year run. Since 1997, ABC only used the program as a name for their weekend sports programming.

Disney's Wide World of Sports, however, would retain the name it was christened with for years to come. The fact that the complex's namesake was no more wouldn't have much of an effect on the Wide World of Sports. In fact, Disney would add and change a few items.

The Jostens Center, for example, was announced in March 2007 during the complex's 10th anniversary. The Jostens Center, an arena 45,000 square feet in size, opened about a year and half after it was announced. It features 1,200 seats surrounding six college-sized basketball courts, volleyball courts, and roller hockey rinks.

Another change to the Wide World of Sports was the somewhat closing of the All Star Café. The restaurant at the Wide World of Sports was actually the last remaining Official All Star Café in 2007, but it was changed to a general restaurant. It would actually remain like this for a few years, but once again (in the name of chronology) we'll have to leave it and come back.

The next big phase of the Wide World of Sports started on May 13, 2008 when Disney revealed their plans to re-brand the Wide World of Sports using the ESPN brand. Interestingly, the "Wide World of Sports" name is still intact more than a decade after its namesake left the airwaves. The official new name of the Wide World of Sports would be the ESPN Wide World of Sports Complex.

As the official rebranding approached, bits and pieces of the ESPN name started to come out. One of the most interesting additions was the ESPN Innovation Lab, which opened in October 2009. Think of it as the Future World for sports technology. Here you will find some of the most cutting edge ideas in the sports industry. Unfortunately, the Lab is not open to the public, so you won't be able to experience it up close. You will, however, be able to experience the results of the Innovation Lab. ESPN is already using technology created here to conduct virtual interviews with "holograms" of athletes any number of miles away from the ESPN studio. ESPN also tested 3D technology here, and you'll soon have the chance to experience live 3D broadcasts of your favorite sports (if you aren't already).

The rebranding wouldn't be complete until February 2010, and Disney unveiled it in style. The unveiling was also part of Disney's annual ESPN: The Weekend event, which meant the stars would be coming down to witness the re-launch of the Complex. Among the well-known talents that man the fort at ESPN were some of today's biggest stars in the athletic world, including Olympic gold medalist Shawn Johnson.

With that, we're pretty current on our Wide World of Sports history. Now, why don't we delve into some of the venues at the Wide World of Sports so perhaps you can plan a visit the next time you're at Walt Disney World?

Get On Your Gear and Hit the Field!

The ESPN theming brought new life to a facility that was already pretty lively, and there are more than a few ballparks and arenas at the ESPN Wide World of Sports Complex. In fact, you could spend a day here enjoying some competition, taking in the atmosphere, and grubbing at a new sports grill.

One of the oldest venues at the Wide World of Sports is Champion Stadium. This is the big-league experience at Walt Disney World, as the stadium offers a great baseball experience. If you plan your trip at the right time, you can watch the Atlanta Braves work at their spring training sessions. It also hosted Major League Baseball games in 2007 and 2008 with the Tampa Bay Rays playing as the home team. As grand as it is, though, Champion Stadium isn't the only place for baseball at the Wide World of Sports. There are actually four other baseball diamonds here at the Baseball Quadraplex, which also has 10,000 square feet of batting practice tunnels and a practice infield. The Softball Diamondplex features six fields that can be used for fast-pitch, slow-pitch, or little league ball games. If you are a baseball fan (or have a baseball fan in your family), the Wide World of Sports has it.

You'll find plenty of other playing surfaces at the Wide World of Sports. Very near all of baseball diamonds, for example is the Tennis Complex. Here you will find 10 different clay tennis courts, along with Center Court Stadium (which is big enough to sit 1,000 fans). The Hess Sports Fields add to the sports the Complex can accommodate. The fields themselves can accommodate dozens of sports, including soccer and football. The National Football League's Tampa Bay Buccaneers held the training camp at the Hess Sports Fields until a few years ago. Also contributing to the Complex's outdoor playing surfaces is a Track and Field Complex and Cross Country course designed to the exact specifications of the International Amateur Athletic Federation. The Track and Field Complex is able to sit hundreds of spectators.

The Wide World of Sports is home to the Milk House, a huge multi-sport facility. The 70,000 square foot behemoth is the site of the annual Old Spice Classic. It can seat 5,000 people with rows as high as 35 feet off the ground. The Milk House also features a state-of-the-art weight room. This is undoubtedly the big brother of the Jostens Center, which we explored earlier. The Milk House is able to accommodate large indoor events, while the Jostens Center can compliment it with other indoor events.

One of the venues that came with the ESPN branding was the ESPN Wide World of Sports Grill, the current iteration of what was the All Star Café. The Grill is open for dinner Thursday through Monday, and it can be reserved for special events.

If you consider yourself a gamer of other sorts, perhaps you should check out the Mecca of PlayStation gaming: the PlayStation Pavilion. Located at the Wide World of Sports Grill, this area allows you to experience the PlayStation 3, one of today's most advanced gaming systems. You'll be able to play a number of different games from Sony and third-party developers, and you can do so on a 40-inch HDTV. Actually, there are sixteen HDTVs set up in the PlayStation Pavilion, each with its own PS3. That's not even the best part: as of right now, you can enjoy all of this for free! You don't even need to pay admission to the Complex to enjoy the PlayStation Pavilion.

These venues make up the main parts of the ESPN Wide World of Sports. All together, they can accommodate 60 different sports. Basically, if you or a member of your family competes in a sport, there's a pretty good chance the ESPN Wide World of Sports Complex can host it. Oh, and let's not forget that we're still on Walt Disney World property, so you can visit a gift store for all of your game day memorabilia!

One thing, though: the Complex isn't really available for a family pick-up game of flag football, so don't go expecting to be able to walk onto the field. You can go check out some of the competition, though. There is an admission charge to get into the Complex, so check out their web site for ticket information.

If you are competing, be sure to keep your eye on the ball, but be mindful of the cameras, too! The ESPN Wide World of Sports Complex is wired with a number of cameras and high-tech video monitors so you'll be able to see highlights of all the big plays happening across the Complex. Also, don't forget to set your DVRs, because the top plays of the day are sent from the on-site video production center to ESPN media outlets, and you never know what can happen from there!

The ESPN Wide World of Sports may be one of the more overlooked parts of Walt Disney World. It offers much more than marathons, cheerleading competitions, and football or baseball games – although those are very important to the Complex. The Wide World of Sports may be a great way to spend some time on your next vacation.

Plus, it is a huge testament to how well Disney blends with the world of sports. Sports are huge sources of entertainment, and this whole Complex is the perfect example of what happens when an entertainment giant like Disney gets involved in what they know best.

Adam Goswick's *Disney fandom started during his childhood with animated classics like The Lion King, and he has been a regular visitor to Walt Disney World since his first trip on his 16th birthday. As a Pittsburgh native, he also enjoys rooting for his favorite hometown teams. He currently resides in Western Pennsylvania with his wife Denise and their dog Abby.*

Whatever Happened to Beastly Kingdom?

Scott and Carol Holmes

To quote Michael Eisner as he welcomed guests on April 22, 1998: "Welcome to a kingdom of animals, animals real, ancient, and imagined. A kingdom ruled by lions, dinosaurs and dragons; a kingdom of balance, harmony, and survival; a kingdom we enter to share in the wonder, gaze at the beauty, thrill at the drama, and learn. The guests found lots of real animals, and some monstrous animatronic versions of creatures from the past in the Countdown to Extinction, (now renamed Dinosaur,) but where were the creatures conceived in myths and legends? Parking in the Unicorn section of the parking lot and buying your ticket under a statue of a dragon's head that was also featured as the center silhouette in the Animal Kingdom logo were not enough.

The dragon fountain close to Camp Minnie-Mickey still remains but the fire breathing cave, reputed to be the home of the dragons according to the Discovery River Boat captains is no longer featured. There used to be some partially melted suits of armor left over from the brave knights slain by the dragon with wisps of smoke still hanging around them. The cave remained even after it was turned off, visible in its dormant state from both the Camp Minnie-Mickey Bridge and the boats for many years. Early presentations stressed the coming "Beastly Kingdom" where it would be divided into realms of good and realms of evil. Its denizens would be derived from fairy tales and story books.

The dark side was to be dominated by a burned-out hulk of an abandoned castle called "Dragon's Tower." A glittering treasure was to be guarded by a miserly, fire breathing dragon. The speaking part of the attraction was scores of bats, talking as they hung upside down. The storyline was that the bats were asking for help in attempting to steal the dragon's fabulous treasure. An inverted coaster would take guests on a wild ride as the dragon gave chase. The climax of the ride would be when the master of the castle revealed himself in all of his fire breathing glory, while the guests would barely escape without being the dragon's not hot meal. With the tall castle and the coaster trains constantly running in and out of the castle, this would have been the dominating "wienie" for Beastly Kingdom.

The good realm was to be dominated by a large maze named "Quest of the Unicorn." A leisurely adventure takes guests on a journey through the maze populated by medieval creatures based in mythology. An interactive search to find the location of the hidden unicorn's stable. This would easily have been the largest of the Beastly Kingdom attractions. The creative ability of Disney artists to compose a population of never-were characters would have guaranteed a stunning attraction.

Another attraction was conceptually named *Fantasia* Gardens. A musical boat ride would take guests through the various scenes from the movie *Fantasia*. The hippo ballerinas represent daytime and waltzing crocodiles the nighttime are all accompanied by the "Dance of the Hours." The centaurs, fauns, and even Pegasus from

Beethoven's "Pastoral--Symphony No. 6" were to be dancing around Mount Olympus. This would have been a natural marketing tie in for the upcoming *Fantasia*: 2000, already in production.

According to internal Disney surveys performed five years before Animal Kingdom opened its doors, the Beastly Kingdom area of the park would have been responsible for the majority of the return visits. With an immersive experience of imaginary animals, beautiful place-making, and roller coaster, who wouldn't want to come back again and again? Even though people know how the Disney movies end, the storytelling is so superb people watch them over and over. It was expected to be the same with Beastly Kingdom.

So what happened? Did cost overrun doom the planned attraction? Was it something that was planned to breathe new life after attendance matured? In reality it was all and more than just these two factors that tanked the planned fantasy kingdom. There were two other classes of animals to consider besides imaginary ones. Disney's Animal Kingdom's mission was to immerse guests in a voyage of discovery of all animals, including the live ones and the extinct ones. The name of the new park was Animal Kingdom. It would make sense that those guests' expectations were to see some live animals in the park. Heavy emphasis on the African and Asian sections burned through a reported $800 million dollars. So why did the live animals cost so much? After all, Michael Eisner said in the April 21, 1995 press conference, "The park is base on mankind's enduring love for animals and celebrating all animals that ever or never existed."

Marty Sklar had a vision of Disney using its storytelling skills to stimulate a higher level of conservation awareness. He recognized that they didn't have enough animal expertise in house so in 1991 Imagineers started showing up at meetings of the American Zoo and Aquarium Association. While this tipped their hand towards future planning, they wanted to bring on board an advisory council to help keep them moving forward in the right direction. The 11 member Advisory Board was born. Rick Barongi, Disney's animal specialist convened the first meeting during January of 1993. The members were encouraged to speak up and set some lofty goals. Karen Allen, of Conservation International said, "Every venue must have a conservation message. Your ethics have got to be impeccable, beyond reproach in terms of animal acquisition and access to information about how you run things."

Michael Hutchins, representing the American Zoo and Aquarium Association said, "What can Disney do for conservation? Disney can make it a household word… Disney can make the emotional connection, the first step to intellectual commitment." At another time he said, "The Imagineers weren't animal professionals. They had no idea about some of the implications of their designs. Disney was to create fun. We, (the Advisory Board,) helped them strike a balance between fun and education, between fun and conservation. Terry Maple, from Zoo Atlanta, said, "The Disney Company, with its resources and ideas, would do things the zoo world couldn't do…As long as Disney stays close to the truth of living animals in nature---if part of their story is always living creatures and how they're faring---they could turn the tide of conservation." These were lofty goals indeed. Rick Barongi summed it up, "We are not just displaying animals for entertainment. We have a real commitment to conservation and education."

Moving over 400 million cubic yards of earth to create landscape took a lot of time and dollars. The basically flat landscape required years of planning and work to morph into the undulating landscape guests enjoy today. Before the final landscaping could be started over 60 miles of underground utilities had to be completed. One million square feet of rockwork needed to be finished. At the high point during the construction process, over 2,600 construction workers donned their hardhats and went to work every day. Once the designers requested two growing seasons prior to the animals arrival, the planners began to run wide open to make sure everything could be finished in a timely fashion.

The back-of-house areas for animal husbandry were reviewed by many in the Advisory Group and also their many contacts in the animal industry. Disney built their animal care areas with cutting edge technology and few compromises. Jones and Jones, from Seattle lent their expertise in designing the immersive exhibits. Duane Dietz, Jim Brighton, and Pat Jankowski oversaw the lion's share of the planning. The melding of story and animal living arrangements necessitated reducing some of the different varieties of creatures due to budget limitations. "I would rather remove an entire habitat instead of making compromises across the board," says Rick Barongi. "We lost hyenas and wild dogs on the African safari due to budget." Even through budget constrictions, "No animal will be acquired if it is to the detriment of the wild population of the species," says Barongi. "We have to get our credibility established before we accept wild animals."

This is where they spent the $800 million, as an investment in the future well-being of the animals and also as Disney's conservation legacy. So this left the other two types of nonexistent species to ponder, extinct and never-was. One cannot deny that Disney has mastered the art of cross merchandising with their other media properties. Grossing millions of dollars annually with just movie tie-ins, this swung the deciding vote in favor of the long ago creatures of history. With over $30 million already invested, and well on the way to surpassing the $150 million mark, the film studios were banking on "Dinosaur" being one of Michael Eisner's famed tent poles. He insisted that Disney's Animal Kingdom feature something related to the movie. The movie ended up not being released until 2000 and the "Countdown to Extinction" attraction was updated, (a statue of Aladar replaced the meteor outside the front entrance, and it was renamed after the movie.)

At Walt Disney Imagineering the grumbling began. The original mission of the park was to provide a reason for guests not to leave the property, cruise over to Tampa and visit Busch Gardens, but instead for them to enjoy an enhanced experience good for another day or more at Disney's Animal Kingdom. There would be live animals and wild rides. Well after they spent all that money on the live animals, they had to plan an attraction based on dinosaurs. The money was already a sunk cost for the upcoming movie, so the only thing to do was embrace the challenge. There weren't any dollars left for Beastly Kingdom.

The plan was to feature a large as life animatronic version of Aladar from the "Dinosaur" movie. He was a heroic iguanadon, and the only thing he ate more of than Imagineer's design time was money out of the budget. Even the Discovery River attraction felt the crunch of budget constraints. While the team from WDI anticipated using it as a showcase for the upcoming land, optimistically planned for Phase Two, they could not foresee it was doomed. Remember the cave with the melted armor. That would only be the beginning.

The dragon was planned to poke his head out at the passing boats, roaring and belching a flaming blast of propane. After being rudely awakened, he would quickly fall back asleep. Most of the design work was already done, for he would be an active version of the dragon already developed for the Le Chateau de la Belle au Bois Dormant operating at Disneyland—Paris. But it was not to be; only a loud noise and a flaming blast were left after the dollars dried up. As he resumed his nap, the boat would begin to traverse a frothing section of the river, as the captain would nervously warn the guests that these were the signs of the Kracken, born of Greek Mythology. According to legend, music puts the Kracken to sleep so your intrepid captain plays a tune on a genuine Greek lyre. After the lullaby has its effect, the boat moves on.

Here comes one of the centerpieces of the ride. A unicorn rises out of the mists as the boat moves on. Standing in a grove of trees and appearing to float on the fog, the mythological creature acknowledges the guests and silently disappears as the boat rounds the bend. Designed to give guests just a taste of the upcoming Beastly Kingdom, both the Kracken and the unicorn fell under the budgeteers knife. The Discovery River lite version that opened with the park quickly aroused the ire of the guests. Waiting over an hour for a five minute ride, with nothing to show for it, guest complaints mounted as it quickly became one of the least popular attractions in Disney's Animal Kingdom. Instead of a showcase of what was to come, it quickly became an embarrassment to the Imagineers. They knew how to fix it; the design work was done, they only need some money. But here, like many other areas of the park, Burbank said to do it the cheap way instead of the right way.

Even Phase One was not completed in time for Opening Day. With only the Africa section to handle the expected surge of guests, what to do with them all day was a concern. Without having a full days worth of attractions in the park, how would guests react after they plunked down the cash for a full day's admission. Continuing their track record of doing things the cheap way, Michael Eisner's "temporary" solution was create a temporary land that would be upgraded/replaced later. It had been done before and was therefore acceptable. The timeline for "*Mickey's Birthdayland*" was only ninety days, from the very beginning to opening day.

To WDI this was an abhorrent suggestion. Joe Rohde and rest of the Imagineers were not willing to stand up and say to Eisner "This sucks," so they said that they didn't have time to add this to their task while they were overseeing the building of Disney's Animal Kingdom. Rather than coming up with a new idea, Eisner put the Walt Disney World entertainment division in charge of the project. Following the concepts of "*Mickey's Birthdayland*," and with no budget for even the most inexpensive stock rides, the entertainment division stayed close to home. Reusing the same floats from the "Lion King Celebration" parade as the stage for the "Festival of the Lion King," the entire park section was based on two low budget shows and a character meet and greet. In order to quell the rising minions in WDI, Rohde asked his Imagineers to keep quiet and stay on the ship, because he was convinced that once Phase One was successful, then they would get the okay from Burbank to put in the rest of Discovery River build Beastly Kingdom. And if Burbank's expectations had proven true, it might have happened.

Why, in his wildest dreams Michael Eisner thought that guest counts in all of Walt Disney World's properties would set records in both attendance levels and length of stay is a mystery known only to him. The boost to guest traffic was supposed to increase the revenues for all the hotels, the shops, and the restaurants. Fantastic profits would appear at the bottom of the income statement, but the result was slightly divergent from his expectations. Every time a new Disney park opened at Walt Disney World, Epcot in 1982 and Disney-MGM Studios, (now Disney's Hollywood Studios,) in 1989, the attendance slumped at the old parks as people went to the new park. As time went on, the attendance levels would slowly rise at the existing parks as the guests returned to experience their favorites once again. But no one in Burbank was prepared for the other parks to average a nine percent decrease in attendance, as opposed to the expected five percent decline.

A shift in attendance was expected, so new attractions were implemented in each of the other parks to be concurrent with the opening of Disney's Animal Kingdom. The goal was to entice the guests who had come down to see the new park to stay longer, on property of course, to experience the new attractions in the other parks. But again, reality had the upper hand. There wasn't much done to Magic Kingdom, because the 25th anniversary celebration was still going on. Magic Kingdom's attendance dropped eight percent. Over at Epcot, the new "GM Test Track" attraction didn't open until over a year past the Disney Animal Kingdom opening, and as a result, that park's attendance declined eleven percent. At Disney's MGM Studios, *Fantasmic!* was still over the horizon after the financing for David Copperfield's restaurant dissipated. The earth-shattering meetings in Burbank must have rivaled the California earthquakes in intensity.

Burbank wanted to restore attendance levels at the other Walt Disney World parks immediately, if not sooner. Walt Disney World managers requested some quick appropriations for new attractions, including but not limited to, some parades and shows. Such was the level of panic that the cash infusions were approved immediately. But where did they find the money? Yes, the coffers for Phase Two of Disney's Animal Kingdom were raided. WDI was now set on open revolt, stating the obvious, that now it would be many years before the expansion could take place. While it was admitted this was true, based on guest surveys it was better to put money somewhere the guests liked, rather than the newest park. The new park was taking a beating in guest surveys. The teething problems experienced by the new park were based on the cost-cutting measures of the past.

The vegetation presented in true jungle fashion made it difficult for guests to navigate their way through the park to their destinations. The park is a designed to replicate finding your way through the jungle as this was maybe too realistic. Revamping all the signage became an early requirement. When the park opened, only the African safari was operational. The animal denizens would follow their nature, and during the heat of the hot Florida midday, seek out places in the shade. Usually, there weren't any animals to see on the African safari adventure after 10:00 AM. As word of these phenomena was spread by the hotel staff, guests sometimes had completely filled the park between 7:30 and 8:00 AM. Once the animals disappeared, so did the guests. This new version of the guest experience meant that most of the food establishments were overwhelmed before lunch.

But after lunch it got worse. Many reports of two hour lines for the African safari meant that people came and left early. The queue for "It's Tough to Be a Bug" exceeded an hour, but at least it was inside and air conditioned. This attraction maintained its ridership but the minimal outdoor attraction queues were hot, lines were long, and most guests blasted through the park by lunchtime and went somewhere else. After lunch Disney's Animal Kingdom became a ghost town. And when you don't have guests, you don't sell souvenirs or food.
Walt Disney World upper management tried to brainstorm some quick fixes to the problem. They couldn't do a parade, because the same crooked pathways that confused the guests were not large enough to accommodate both a parade and spectators, especially after dark. The problems they were already having with the small "March of the Art-imals" parade quashed that option. There was no way the animal curators would allow a fireworks show to disturb their charges. Joe Rohde's team suggested expanding the areas of the park that functioned without the animals. Unfortunately, Burbank had already spent that option. It was beginning to look like it would be longer than that promised "five" years before there would be any significant enhancements to Disney Animal Kingdom. But they had a plan.

Universal was spending lots of money to build a new park adjacent to Universal Studios. The name of the park was "Islands of Adventure." With over two billion dollars to invest, the plan was to create attractions far beyond what was available at Walt Disney World. WDI was secretly wishing the best for the new Universal Park because they were counting on the competiveness of Michael Eisner to not let Disney be outdone. He would see what was available across town and begin to throw money at WDI to see what outstanding attractions they could design. Burbank ordered WDI to begin developing a contingency plan after the holidays following Disney's Animal Kingdom's first season. The Imagineers were thrilled at the opportunity to show what they could do when pressed. But again, reality and some of Disney's past actions threw this particular train off the tracks.

When Islands of Adventure first opened, everyone raved about the level of theming and the intensity of the rides. It was the strongest combination ever seen outside of Disney properties. The rides were aimed towards the thrill seeking crowd that went to Busch Gardens while the level of immersive theming proved able to entertain the rest of the family. Burbank wanted major attractions readied for all the Walt Disney World parks. These included "Mission: Space," at Epcot which had suffered the most since the "GM Test Track" delay turned out to be eighteen months. Magic Kingdom was slated to receive "Fire Mountain," designed to feature a never seen before vehicle changing roller coaster themed to tie in with the scheduled 2001 release of the movie "Atlantis." "The Great Movie Ride" at Disney-MGM Studios was to have been rehabbed into Chinese Theater's "Villain Ride" utilizing the then new 3D technology. A lot of laughter and backslapping was heard in the halls of WDI. The long planned Beastly Kingdom land would be added to Disney's Animal Kingdom. Happy day were here again.

But the attendance levels at Islands of Adventure were below expectations. Even with nearly two months of technical rehearsals and the new "Incredible Hulk" roller coaster being featured in a Chrysler commercial, the expected crowds never materialized. With actual attendance achieving only half of the projected numbers, this was one of the more spectacular flops in amusement park history. And over twenty-five percent of these guests came from the Studios Park. Common belief was that the park hadn't been marketed correctly. That it was promoted as just another new section of the Universal Studios Park, and not a standalone park. The entire marketing staff was replaced. Interestingly enough, with the recent opening of "The Wizarding World of Harry Potter," Universal allowed the idea that it was a new park to survive, and is now dealing with the back lash from disappointed guests who find the new area less than what they were promised.

Walt Disney World properties received little to none in drops in attendance. And with that, Burbank's interest in "plussing" the existing Orlando properties declined as well. The new plan was for Beastly Kingdom to be pushed back until 2008. While Joe Rohde and Imagineers were devastated, at least they still had hope for the project. But after Michael Eisner's visit to Islands of Adventure in January of 2000, these hopes were dashed. After a low-profile tour accompanied by some other Disney personnel, he flew back to Burbank and announced that while he thought the new park didn't meet Disney standards, it still was better competition than they had seen before. But somehow "A few of those attractions looked awfully familiar."

The amusement business is full of stories of people adapting others ideas for their own implementation. Dick Kinzel and Rob Decker visited Hard Rock Park during the grand opening celebration. Tony Baxter visited Knott's Berry Farm when he was a Disney employee. Walt Disney himself brought back ideas from parks in Europe. So when the Imagineers that Disney laid off were hired by Universal, many of the ideas they had developed became incorporated at Islands of Adventure. The similarities between "Dueling Dragons" and the not yet built "Dragon's Tower" were striking before the rehab associated with the opening of the "Wizarding World of Harry Potter. Was this coincidence?

After the opening of Disneyland-Paris, then Euro Disney, due to the project completion and ensuing dismal financial performance of the new property, as a cost cutting measure several hundred associates of WDI were laid off. Many of them were based in Orlando and already knew others in the industry by reputation so when Universal began their expansion, why not bring on board someone who was trained and worked at WDI? The park and attraction design business is really a small world after all. And many of the former Imagineers had poured their total efforts for years into designing Disney's Animal Kingdom. They enthusiastically put forth some of their best ideas for Island of Adventure.

Seeing some of the concept art for "Dragon's Tower" that has leaked out over the years, the fact that "Dueling Dragons'" genesis began at WDI is irrefutable. But to the few guests at Islands of Adventure, they rode a state of the art rollercoaster with groundbreaking theming and never looked back. The run down castle with the live Wizard supporting the storyline engaged roller coaster riders as never before seen in amusement parks. To the public, they didn't care where the ideas came from, they just wanted to ride. Soon Islands of Adventure put in another family coaster called the "Flying Unicorn," now renamed "Flight of the Hippogriff." No matter who thought through the concepts of the new ride first, to the guests "I rode this at Universal first" was all that mattered. Perception is reality. But this put Burbank in a difficult spot concerning the Phase Two of Disney's Animal Kingdom.

Michael Eisner's competiveness necessitated a drastic revamp of the proposed "Beastly Kingdom." The centerpiece decrepit castle had to be removed; because he could not stand the thought that some guests might think Walt Disney World was copying Universal Orlando. The same command applied to anything with a unicorn in it, but they did leave it in the parking lot. No maze, no addition of a unicorn to "Discovery River" or "*Fantasia* Gardens." The never built Beastly Kingdom based on the never world of fantasy animals would never be built. But there was no time to hang black bunting in WDI. Burbank was still changing the park, in eyes of the Imagineers, and not for the better. The temporary Camp Minnie-Mickey was evolving to a more permanent area all the time. It had already been expanded with some standard rides guests could experience at their local county fair. Adding new paint and backdrops does not embellish a story line or make it a more immersive experience. The "Lion King Theater" had already been expanded, and on the entertainment side of the corporation, they anticipated years of revenue from sequels to the original. So it would a long time before that "temporary" installation was updated. What would be the end result?

It appears that "Expedition Everest" has replaced the long envisioned Beastly Kingdom. Providing a "weenie" visible from far outside the park, it is the signature attraction for Disney's Animal Kingdom. Does this mean Beastly Kingdom has now become extinct like the dinosaurs? Maybe not, with Disney expanding into China it could be revived in some way syncopated with the local culture, as they won't care about any similarities to "Dragons Challenge" or the "Flight of the Hippogriff." Many present Disney attractions were based on original concepts over a decade old, for at WDI, many old ideas have resurfaced after being dusted off and pointed into a new direction. In the case of Beastly Kingdom, it has become as legendary as the animals upon which it was to have been based. Here's to resurrections, Disney lovers, for here we can all believe in make believe.

Scott and Carol Holmes *have written many history related amusement park articles for both the print and electronic media. They currently provide content for News Plus Notes, www.newsplusnotes.com. They have been traveling to Walt Disney World for more than four decades.*

Magic of the Night:
The Evolution of Walt Disney World's Nighttime Fireworks Displays

Debra Martin Koma

I've loved fireworks since I was a little girl -- the flashes of color and light bursting repeatedly in the sky, the reverberations I felt in my chest from the fireworks that were exploding overhead. It was quite a feeling. Not to overuse a word heard all too often in Disney circles, but there has always been something "magical" about fireworks to me.

It shouldn't come as a surprise to you, then, to learn that the first Disney fireworks I saw in person took my breath away.

It was the end of the day on my first trip to Walt Disney World 16 years ago, and we were in Epcot. It was about 9 p.m. and both my 2-1/2-year-old son and my husband were tired and cranky and ready to head back to the hotel.

"But, but, but..." I spluttered, as my husband started to drag me toward the park exit. "We'll miss the fireworks!"

Just then a shell burst overhead, slicing the sky with a flash of light and color and putting World Showcase in the distance in silhouette. Then there was another, and another, and I gasped at the brilliance, but my husband had had it. He resolutely pushed our son's stroller away from World Showcase Lagoon and toward the turnstiles. I remember glancing over my shoulder as I ran quickly after him, thinking to myself that I would have to come back and see that show some day. That was only the start of my romance with Walt Disney World's nighttime "spectaculars." I have since seen the shows grow and evolve in ways that never fail to surprise me.

Fireworks may have been invented by the 12th century Chinese, and in fact, China is the largest manufacturer and exporter of fireworks in the world – but the Walt Disney Company is, not surprisingly, the largest consumer of fireworks in the United States, and, according to some sources, in the world.

Long before I ever set foot in Walt Disney World in 1994, the Disney Company was building its reputation as a premier provider of pyrotechnic entertainment. It started a few years after Disneyland in Anaheim, California, opened, and Walt Disney commissioned a special fireworks display to conclude each evening. Called *Fantasy in the Sky*, the program soon became a sentimental favorite with park visitors. When Walt Disney World opened in 1971, it was a given that Florida's Magic Kingdom would replicate the fireworks display that had been running at Disneyland since 1958. *FitS* (as it came to be abbreviated) was subsequently staged at Walt Disney World almost nightly for 32 years, illuminating Cinderella Castle with more than 200 shells in about five to seven minutes.

But while *FitS* continued to garner "oohs" and "aahs" from its appreciative viewers, Disney, never content to rest on its laurels, was toying with other fireworks display concepts at its other theme parks.

About a year after Walt Disney World opened its third theme park, then called Disney-MGM Studios, in 1989, it introduced its own Hollywood-themed fireworks show. *Sorcery In the Sky*, with narration by Vincent Price, employed lights and fireworks set against a medley of familiar movie themes, but the show was fairly traditional by the standards of the times. In 1992, Disneyland introduced *Fantasmic!* – a true evening show, complete with full story, that included fireworks as just one element. It wasn't long before it was announced that a similar show would be developed for Walt Disney World, and in October 1998 *Fantasmic!* debuted in the Florida theme park.

Fantasmic! at the Studios differs from its California counterpart in that it is held in its own dedicated 6900-seat amphitheater – there's room for an additional 3000 standing spectators. This 25-minute show not only uses fireworks, lights, lasers and water animation, but it features 50 performers who tell the story of Mickey Mouse battling evil in a dream that includes images from myriad Disney classic films projected on water screens. With its popularity and permanent location, it appears that *Fantasmic!* will be the nighttime show for what is now known as Disney's Hollywood Studios for some time to come.

The evolutionary path of the nighttime spectaculars over at Epcot is a little more circuitous than the path followed by fireworks at the Studios or Magic Kingdom.

Shortly after Epcot opened in October 1982, guests who stayed until the end of the day were rewarded with the *Carnival de Lumiere*. The show, staged on the park's World Showcase Lagoon, incorporated both water and music elements into the fireworks display, but it could only be viewed from limited areas. These obstructed viewing opportunities destined this show to a short run, and not quite a year later *A New World Fantasy* debuted. This show broke some new ground, coupling synthesized classical music with the previous show's rear projection screens set atop floating barges.

Apparently still not satisfied with the result, Epcot developed yet another show, which premiered in June 1984, *Laserphonic Fantasy*. While the soundtrack for this show was essentially the same as that of *New World Fantasy, Laserphonic Fantasy* added lasers projected from barges and around the lagoon, said to be the first use of laser graphics on a screen formed by sprayed water.

Finally, on January 30, 1988, Epcot introduced *IllumiNations*, a show that assimilated the elements that had been tested in the park's previous attempts: lasers, lights, and pyrotechnics, all set to a soundtrack of classical and familiar music performed by a real orchestra. The 14-minute program made much of its surroundings — the country pavilions of Epcot's World Showcase — by lighting up each country (with the exceptions of Morocco and Norway) in sync with changes in the music. (In case you're a bit slow, as I was when I first heard the word, that's how the show derives its name -- each NATION is ILLUMINATED, hence *IllumiNations*!) Along with the innovative use of technology, *IllumiNations* was a different sort of nighttime show for another reason — fireworks weren't used until later in the program, rather than from the start.

Except for the holidays, when a special version with seasonal music was performed, this *IllumiNations* was not really tampered with until September 1996. At that time, as Walt Disney World was celebrating its 25th anniversary, a new edition of *IllumiNations* was introduced, dubbed *IllumiNations25*. This new program updated some of the show's effects, as well as its music, concluding with the film The Lion King's soaring anthem, "Circle of Life." A few months later, in the spring of 1997, *IllumiNations25* reverted to a more classical score, again looking to such composers as Ravel, Tchaikovsky and Mussorgsky to supply the musical backdrop for its pyrotechnic and laser demonstrations.

This was all well and good for the end of the 20th century, but with a new millennium looming, Epcot's *IllumiNations* was due for an "extreme makeover." Expounding on the precedents set by the original incarnations of *IllumiNations,* show director Don Dorsey added more and better show elements, more and better pyrotechnics, all perfectly synchronized to a whole new, specially composed score, to come up with *IllumiNations 2000: Reflections of Earth.*

One of the biggest changes to this 13-minute version of *IllumiNations,* which officially debuted October 1, 1999, was the addition of a giant steel-ribbed "Earth Globe" that rotated on a 350-ton floating island housing six computer processors, 258 strobe lights and an infrared guidance system. Using more than 180,000 light emitting diodes (LED's), the globe, 28 feet in diameter, showed geographic landmarks like the Himalayas and Mount Rushmore, along with images of noteworthy people from around the world -- Martin Luther King, Mother Teresa, Albert Einstein, and more.

With a few minor changes, and the deletion of the "2000" from the show's title, this version of *IllumiNations* is the one currently being performed nightly at Epcot. What's truly impressive about this show, in my opinion, is the thought and care that went into crafting its story, making it so much more than just a simple fireworks display.

The show begins with a firestorm — an explosion generated on an appropriately named "inferno barge" that blasts propane flames from 37 nozzles. After the initial shock of this scene, dubbed *Chaos*, a certain calm and *Order* is restored, as symbolized by the gentle appearance of the Earth Globe gliding to the center of the lagoon. The globe begins to display civilization as we know it today, and lasers and colorful fountains give way to fireworks, both in the lagoon itself and in the skies above. Finally, we reach a point of *Meaning*, with more dazzling fireworks in a brief moment than many displays feature in an entire program.

Although the globe dominates the visuals at eye level, the real star of the show, in my opinion, continues to be the fireworks, which are masterfully synchronized to the rousing score composed by Gavin Greenaway. About 2800 shells are exploded every night, launching from 34 different locations around the World Showcase Lagoon. It's all coordinated by 67 computers set in 40 locations.

There is a slightly different display offered on the Fourth of July and New Year's Eve, and at the December holidays a special "tag" is tacked on to the show featuring the song *Let There be Peace on Earth* along with an additional few minutes of fireworks. And in any incarnation *IllumiNations: Reflections of Earth* remains my personal favorite nighttime spectacular at Walt Disney World... ever.

But that's not to say that I don't enjoy the fireworks displays put on at the other theme parks — I am at heart a fireworks junkie. Which brings me back to Walt Disney World's Magic Kingdom, and the most recent addition to the Walt Disney World nighttime fireworks landscape.

As I mentioned earlier, the Magic Kingdom was quite content with its *Fantasy in the Sky* program. For 32 years, the show, with its holiday variants, entertained. But with the advent of shows like *Fantasmic!* and *IllumiNations: Reflections of Earth*, and even *Believe... There's Magic in the Stars* out in Disneyland, it was inevitable that *Fantasy in the Sky* would eventually give way to a new and improved Magic Kingdom fireworks show. It's clear the current trend is to tie a cohesive storyline to the fireworks to blend it into something that will not only entertain, but will evoke emotion and a desire to see the show again and again.

On October 8, 2003, the Magic Kingdom introduced a new show that does just that — *Wishes: A Magical Gathering of Disney Dreams*. *Wishes* is 12 minutes of breath-taking, perfectly timed explosions, featuring 683 individual pieces of pyrotechnics, launched from a number of different locations. Some of these pyrotechnic effects had never been seen before in a Disney theme park. In fact, several effects were developed especially for the show, such as a "wishing star" that soars approximately 100 feet above Cinderella Castle. The program begins with a sweet child's voice breaking the quiet of the evening and continues with a story that spotlights the age-old and highly relatable theme of wishes coming true. Classic Disney songs have been reworked into a musical score that features vocal appearances by a number of notable Disney characters, including Jiminy Cricket, Snow White, Cinderella, Peter Pan, and Ariel (*The Little Mermaid*). Clearly, it's a far cry from the original *Fantasy in the Sky* fireworks.

Wishes became an instant fan favorite, masterminded by creator/ show director Steven Davison, whose credits include *Believe... There's Magic in the Stars* at Disneyland; music director Steve Skorija (composer of one of my personal favorite Disney themes, from the *SpectroMagic* parade); fireworks designer Eric Tucker, (*IllumiNations: Reflections of Earth*); and composer/arranger Gregory Smith, whose work includes *IllumiNations 25* at Epcot.

The basic platform for *Wishes* is now well-established, but Disney has tinkered with it occasionally for special occasions. At Halloween, for instance, the program takes on a "not-so-scary" theme, featuring music from the movie *The Nightmare before Christmas*. The storyline highlights Disney villains and lots of orange and green hues shining on the castle for a show known as *Happy Hallo-Wishes*. And as the Christmas season approaches, the program is converted into *Holiday Wishes*, with an appropriately themed storyline and special fireworks launched around the perimeter of the park.

On a limited number of occasions, the Magic Kingdom has also shown *Magic, Music and Mayhem*. This fireworks display, similar in nature to *Wishes*, was shown during the theme park's limited run *Mickey's Pirate and Princess Parties* and also in a revamped version as part of *2010's Summer Nightastic!* This program was well-received, but the emotional connection that audiences feel with *Wishes* guaranteed its return and continuation.

In the years since my first Walt Disney World vacation in 1994, I have seen lots of changes at the Florida theme parks, and not all of them have been what I would call improvements. In this one area, however — in its fireworks and what it calls its "nighttime spectaculars" — I believe Walt Disney World will always excel. I can't wait to see what they come up with next!

***Debra Martin Koma** is a freelance writer who has written about food, travel and lifestyle for a number of local and national publications. She fell in love with Walt Disney World on her first visit there in 1994.*

For the last 14 years, she has written about her passion for all things Disney for the readers of AllEars.Net, an unofficial Disney vacation planning website, and AllEars®, the site's affiliated weekly electronic newsletter. Deb is also co-author (along with Deb Wills) of PassPorter's Open Mouse for Walt Disney World and the Disney Cruise Line, a guidebook designed for vacationers with special travel requirements, from special diets to mobility issues.

Meeting Mickey:
Remembering Mickey's Toontown Fair

Jim Korkis

Where do Mickey Mouse, Minnie, Donald Duck, Goofy and Pluto live and relax when they are not entertaining audiences on stage and on film?

Since one of the concepts that made these Disney cartoon characters different from the characters at other animation studios was Walt Disney's conceit that his world beloved characters were actually actors who were just performing in humorous, outrageous film stories, this was a legitimate question for their many fans over the years.

At the Magic Kingdom in Walt Disney World, that location was *Mickey's Toontown Fair*.

At that location, everyday was a special day because the County Fair was going on and some famous toon celebrities had come to visit and join in the festivities. While some Disney fans considered the area just a small interactive playground for young children, there were plenty of playful details to entertain adults and many imaginative references to the classic Disney animated cartoons.

The Thirties and the Forties are considered the Golden Age of the Disney animated short cartoons and this land was a tribute to that simpler era. It was also a tribute to what Walt Disney referred to as the "Plausible Impossible". Basically, that term meant that in Disney cartoons no matter how impossible and exaggerated the action, there was always a foundation of logic.

For instance, a character could run so fast they he would build up so much momentum that he could literally still run on the air after he ran off the edge of a cliff....until he recognized he was standing on thin air and then would fall unless he could quickly scramble back fast enough to get to grab hold of the edge. Of course, in real life, this defies all the basic principles of gravity but in the world of Disney cartoons, it made sense...and some still well loved cartoon classics.

That same principle applies in *Mickey's Toontown Fair* from everything to a stove that can produce volcano heat to a shark that is so large and powerful it can take a huge eight foot high bite out of a massive boat. While impossible and deadly in the real world, it seems logical and fun in the world of cartoons.

Mickey's Toontown Fair went through a fascinating twenty year evolution to become the wonderful photo opportunity location most remembered by Walt Disney World guests. It all began in 1988.

Over the decades, earlier birthday celebrations for Mickey Mouse were truly memorable occasions. In 1988 for Mickey's 60th, there were special parties around the world, his own television special (where while fooling around with the Sorcerer's Hat Mickey gets lost and has to be found by Roger Rabbit), a special magazine (with a "faux" collector's cel) entitled *Mickey is Sixty* devoted specifically to the occasion in addition to countless general magazine coverage, appearance on a float in the Rose Parade, the "Party Mickey" hot air balloon that traveled the country, new merchandise and much, much more including his very own land at the Magic Kingdom at Walt Disney World.

A year earlier in 1987, there was concerns in the Disney kingdom. The biggest guest complaint at the Magic Kingdom was that guests often couldn't find Mickey Mouse in person and snap a souvenir photograph or get an autograph. In addition, Team Disney saw that when Epcot opened, there was a huge drop in attendance the previous year at the Magic Kingdom since guests were saving their hard earned money and vacation trip for a year so they could enjoy both parks.

In 1989, not only was the Disney MGM Studios going to open but also the delayed Pleasure Island and Typhoon Lagoon so it was expected there would be another drop in attendance in 1988 if there wasn't something new but temporary (to push the urge of "come soon or miss it") to see. And, of course, there would be a huge promotional push for Mickey's 60th birthday and something was needed at the Magic Kingdom to capitalize on it.

Michael Eisner and Frank Wells gave the immediate green light to creating a special land at the Magic Kingdom to celebrate Mickey's special 60th birthday, *Mickey's Birthdayland*. It was planned to only be there for eighteen months and there was only three months for it to go through the design process. The area allocated included some backstage land near Fantasyland but in addition, the Grand Prix Raceway (now known as the Tomorrowland Indy Speedway), had to have its track moved and shortened in order to allow for construction of the location.

Mickey's Birthdayland would solve the problems of having something major to encourage guests not to postpone their visit to the Magic Kingdom, something to help showcase the 60th birthday celebration and most importantly, some place that was guaranteed to provide guests with a chance to meet Mickey Mouse.

Brightly colored circus tents seemed very much in keeping with the party spirit and would be easy to erect quickly for the temporary location. Steve Hansen was the show writer and the director for the first new land added to the Magic Kingdom. It was also the smallest land at the Magic Kingdom covering roughly three acres.

Instead of having guests trudge through the park to get to the out of the way spot at the top of the park at the conjuncture of Fantasyland transitioning into Tomorrowland, a new train station stop was created. The train that circled the park was re-named "*Mickey's Birthdayland* Express" and was decorated for Mickey's surprise party. Ron Schneider, the original actor who portrayed the walk around character of Dreamfinder at Epcot, wrote and recorded the song for the train as it passed little scenes along the way showing the rest of the Disney characters on their way to the big event.

The Three Little Pigs in their house of straw were on a raft in a nearby waterway. The Mad Hatter's Tea Party was abandoned in the woods with a sign declaring "Gone to Mickey's Party". Pinocchio and friends were by Stromboli's wagon stopping for a moment for a puppet show. All of these were two dimensional cut outs since the time and budget did not permit three dimensional figures.

Cindy Williams (of the then popular television program *Laverne & Shirley*) and First Lady Nancy Reagan were on hand to open *Mickey's Birthdayland.* On June 18, 1988 Cindy cut the ribbon officially dedicating the area.

Where did the Disney toons live? Duckburg! Yes, a town with a population according to the prominent sign of "bill'ions and still growing. A town that's everything it's quacked up to be!" With streets named Tailfeather Trail, Quackfaster Circle, Cornhusker Lane and of course "Barks & Nash" (after famed Donald Duck comic book writer and artist Carl Barks and the original voice of Donald Duck, Clarence Nash), it was just ducky with its quickly done two dimensional storefront facades.

Only Mickey's house would be a solid structure that guests could enter and it was much different from the country cottage in *Mickey's*

Toontown Fair. This original home had straight exterior architectural lines (rather than the curvy "toony" architecture of the one in *Mickey's Toontown Fair*) and a different layout of the interior rooms. Outside the house was parked Mickey's balloon-tired red car as another photo opportunity.

Why Duckburg, the famed hometown of Donald Duck, Uncle Scrooge and all their friends? First, the animated syndicated television series *Duck Tales* featuring the adventures of Uncle Scrooge and the nephews in Duckburg had premiered to great success beginning in September 1987. Second, show writer Steve Hansen was unfamiliar with any city associated with Mickey Mouse other than Burbank or Hollywood. (In the comic books, there had been an attempt to call Mickey's hometown, Mouseville, but it never caught on just like a later attempt to call it Mouseton, as in "Houston".)

However, Hansen was a fan of Carl Barks' work on the Disney ducks and was familiar with that mythology. Third, the popular film *Who Framed Roger Rabbit* that would make Toontown the official home for all toons, a concept that was quickly embraced by the general public, would not debut until June 22, 1988 after the land was built. That film's success was so instantaneous and overwhelming that Roger Rabbit soon was shoehorned into *Mickey's Birthdayland.*

In keeping with the history that Carl Barks had created for Duckburg, there was a statue of Cornelius Coot, the founder of Duckburg. He was Donald Duck's great-great-grandfather and supposedly scared off Spanish soliders who were attacking Ft. Duckburg by popping corn to fool them into thinking reinforcements had arrived and were firing off their guns.

Coot also piped mountain water into the area that allowed corn crops to flourish. So that is why Coot is proudly holding out an ear of corn and why the first statue was in a water fountain. The statue was an accurate recreation of the one that first appeared in the comic book story "Statuesque Spendthrifts" by Carl Barks in Walt Disney's Comics and Stories #138. That statue remained when the area became Toontown Fair where Coot was retroactively also made the founder of the Toontown Fair especially since his corn crop fit in nicely with the fair story of exhibiting prize produce.

Mickey's Birthdayland included a children's playground and a topiary/shrub maze. Nearby was Grandma Duck's petting farm filled with goats, pigs, ducks, miniature horses and chickens presented by Friskies. The star of the farm was Minnie Moo the cow, who had the iconic three black circle Mickey Mouse head silhouette on one side of her white body. (Just like the cow, Mickey Moo, at the Big Thunder Ranch at Disneyland.) She was later moved along with the other animals to the ranch at Fort Wilderness and died in the summer of 2001.

The buildings now used as the WACKY radio station (that's why the rowdy rooster announcer is Red Barns…he does his show in a red country barn) and queue entrance for *Goofy's Barnstormer* were part of Grandma Duck's Farm. WACKY radio ("All Country, All the Toon") is playing on the radio inside Minnie's Country Cottage with some amusing announcements and commentary that were generally ignored as background noise by guests visiting the house.

Donald Duck had a boat, the S.S. Donald, but it was only a façade like ones for the Duckburg News (founded 1928), Scrooge McDuck's Bank, Daisy Duck's Millinery, Goofy's Clip Joint barber shop, HD&L Toys (Huey, Dewey and Louie), Duck County School and more. It wasn't until *Mickey's Toontown Fair* that the boat became three dimensional and was renamed the "Miss Daisy" in honor of Donald's girlfriend Daisy who also modeled for the figurehead.

However, most guests rushed to the Birthday Party Tent. After watching Disney cartoons in the pre-show area, guests could see a show called *Minnie's Surprise Party*. Management wanted it called *Mickey's Party* but Hansen fought for the title because he had based it on the classic 1939 cartoon where Minnie surprised Mickey with a party and a birthday cake and wanted to retain those elements including a cake cooked by Goofy in an oven with a "volcano heat" dial (a gag that still survives on the ovens of Mickey and Minnie's kitchens in *Mickey's Toontown Fair*). Reportedly, in the beginning, the show would run over two dozen times in a single day.

After the show, guests would proceed to Mickey's dressing room and visit with the birthday boy to get an autograph or a photo. Multiple dressing rooms guaranteed that guests would not be disappointed and that the line would move quickly even with just a small number of guests being allowed to visit at a time.

The area was so popular that instead of closing after eighteen months, it remained open until April 22, 1990 and only closed at that time so the area could be re-themed as *Mickey's Starland* that opened on May 26, 1990, since the birthday theme was no longer appropriate and the place was, after all, the home of all the Disney cartoon stars.

The Duckburg facades were updated, looking very similar to the ones that would later grace Disney Afternoon Avenue near Videopolis at Disneyland in 1991.

The song on the train was modified and it was no longer *Mickey's Birthdayland Express*. *Minnie's Surprise Party* live action show was replaced by *Mickey's Magical TV World* that featured characters from the Disney Afternoon syndicated animated television series. The stage show was continually changed each year to showcase the new television shows.

It premiered with the Gummi Bears who were replaced in 1991 by Darkwing Duck. The *Duck Tales* characters were later replaced by characters from *Goof Troop*. Even the forgettable Bonkers (Disney's attempt to create a Roger Rabbit character they completely owned) popped up. A live host, with the unisex name of "C.J." (so that it could be used by either a male or a female), and a rapping computer narrator named D.U.D.E. were also included.

The area continued to be unbelievably popular so on the West Coast, Disneyland decided to re-create it. At one time, there were plans for an elaborate Hollywoodland to be developed behind Main Street that would have featured Roger Rabbit and his friends along with attractions devoted to the movie *Dick Tracy*. However, the expense of opening EuroDisney among other things resulted in scaling back those plans and the continued success of *Mickey's Starland* demonstrated that a smaller vision could be effective so Disneyland's *Toontown* was born.

The Imagineering storyline was that Mickey and his friends always lived in that area even before Disneyland was built, and in fact that was one of the reasons Anaheim was chosen for Walt's theme park. However, by 1993, it was time to tear down the wall separating the two sections and welcome guests to come and visit. So January 24, 1993, *Toontown* located near *it's a small world* and Videopolis opened at Disneyland and as expected was enthusiastically embraced by the guests.

Back on the East Coast, to update the area for Walt Disney World's 25th anniversary in 1996, *Mickey's Starland* became the more elaborate *Mickey's Toontown Fair* (opening October 1, 1996), taking inspiration and some design elements from Disneyland's *Toontown.* While Mickey and the gang lived in *Toontown* in Disneyland, this land would be their vacation home and one of the reasons they were all taking a vacation was it was the time of year for the big local country Fair and traditionally Mickey was one of the judges. In fact, the sign at the entrance shows a proudly smiling Mickey in his judge outfit which guests can later see hung carefully in Mickey's bedroom.

Guests know it is only a temporary event because of all the banners that decorate the more permanent structures like the train station and of course, the tents that have been erected just for the fair. There's even a makeshift farmer's market set up with the goods displayed on carts and wagons and a pedestal bath tub.

The brooms from *Fantasia* are on vacation as guests could see on the trash cans where in keeping with the country theme the brooms are wearing straw hats and bandanas as they keep the area clean.

Mickey's Toontown Fair was a leisurely respite from the relentless activity in the rest of the Magic Kingdom and a particular favorite section for young children. Disney filled the area to overflowing with visual and verbal humor and it all began at the entrance.

When someone travels on vacation, traditionally they do so by car. That is why Pete's Service Station is at the entrance of this land. It would be the first place someone might want to stop after a long trip or before they take a long trip. It is a chance to use the restrooms, fill up on gas, check the tires, get directions and more.

There is a stereotype that such out of the way rural service stations are crooked and will overcharge or not take care of a car correctly so that is why a Disney scoundrel, the infamous Pete, is running the place. He's been causing problems for Mickey Mouse since the first Mickey cartoon *Steamboat Willie* in 1928.

Obviously, Pete doesn't know what he is doing because if you look at the drinking fountains near the restrooms, they are connected to cans of Pete's Oil and everyone knows that oil and water don't mix. Also, sneaky Pete has dropped the restroom key into the gas pump to help keep customers around longer and hopefully charge them more until it is fished out.

By the way, Pete selling "Gulp" gas is a sly reference to "Gulf" oil who was a long time Disney sponsor and even published a handful of Disney related giveaway magazines with comics and stories and two record albums of Disney songs that were available at their gas stations.

Pete was a customer of a service station in *Mickey's Service Station* (1935) but evidently thought it was a good enough business to take it over from Mickey, Donald and Goofy. Throughout *Mickey's Toontown Fair*, there are subtle allusions to the classic Mickey Mouse cartoons of the Thirties. These are not necessarily direct re-creations from the specific cartoons but playful references to remind guests.

Nearby, Cornelius Coot County Bounty tent attracts attention almost immediately with its large cartoony banners tempting guests to enter. Goofy is bringing a bushel of corn, Donald Duck a prize acorn and Daisy Duck some award worthy baked goods and all of them hope to win a blue ribbon for their efforts just like at any local fair.

Although this is primarily a merchandise location, the tent is themed to the story of a county fair. This is where the toons bring their homegrown or homemade treasures to be awarded ribbons for being the best.

Inside, some of the Disney characters' entries for the big judging competition including Toby Tortoise's turtleneck sweater and Clarabelle Cow's bell bottom jeans with cowbells are displayed with the awards they have won. Underneath these exhibits is a plethora of Disney merchandise from plush toys to books to pins for guests to purchase.

Expanding the original concept of the area, the interior of the tent is also the entrance to the Hall of Fame where guests can meet some of their favorite Disney characters and not just Mickey Mouse. Over the years, those character meetings have changed as to what characters from Disney villains to Mickey's friends are available to interact with guests. In 2010, there was a room dedicated to Tinker Bell and her fairy friends and another for the Disney princesses.

In front of the tent is Cornelius Coot Commons with the familiar statue of the enterprising old farmer. "Cornelius Coot, who turned his corn crop into loot" states the plaque on the statue. It was one of the most prominent remnants of earlier incarnations of the area.

The centerpiece of this land is a chance to visit the four room interior of Mickey's Country House. There is a bedroom, living room, game room and kitchen. Both the living room and game room feature a strong Sports theme while the kitchen is undergoing a disastrous remodel for a contest by Mickey's friends Donald Duck and Goofy.

Inside this bright yellow house everything is "mouse-ified" from the design of items with the famous three circle icon like checkers, chairs, and plants as well as references to Mickey's favorite food, a variety of cheeses.

Unlike Mickey's house in *Mickey's Birthdayland*, the Disney Imagineers designed the house with curves and the animated "stretch and squash" architecture that echoes one of the major principles of

Disney cartoon animation. During construction, both Mickey's and Minnie's houses provided some difficulties for builders who were used to straight, level lines rather than the toony curves. It was the same problem faced with building these houses in Disneyland's *Toontown* where the designs originated.

Of course, Mickey isn't at home at the moment because he is out in the Judge's Tent next door participating in the fair.

This walk through tour gives a clever glimpse into the lifestyle of the world's most famous mouse and is filled with a seemingly endless selection of humorous details. Mickey's bedroom has an open closet filled with the exact same pressed black, white and red suits that Mickey always wears and there is a drawer overflowing with the famous four fingered white gloves. A huge pair of glasses on the bed suggests that the Mouse's eyes may have finally succumbed to age. The room is filled with pictures and memorabilia that would logically be in Mickey's house including photos of Mickey as a baby, posing with Santa and as a Boy Scout.

Just outside the bedroom by his telephone is mail including a package from Peter Pan with the notation "use no hooks", referring to Peter's nemesis Captain Hook. A letter from Buzz Lightyear has the return address "Infinity and Beyond" and another from Ariel the Little Mermaid was sent from "Under the Sea".

The living room has recently been abandoned because Mickey lost track of the time and had to rush to his appointment in the Judge's tent but it is evident by the remains that Mickey and his friends were just watching a sports competition between Duckburg University and Goofy Tech. Pennants, pompoms and popcorn are scattered around and the television is still broadcasting news of the big game.

Mickey must love sports because he has an entire game room filled with activities and once again, some clever often unseen pieces of humor like a real rubber dart hitting a picture of Donald Duck's rear end as he is golfing. Trophies and memorabilia fill the room and a scoreboard shows that Mickey is winning a ping pong game.

Directly across from this room is Mickey's kitchen but it is completely unusable because Donald and Goofy have entered the Toontown Fair Kitchen Remodeling Competition and have left the work unfinished. There is a dangerously tipping stack of paint cans in the sink, makeshift wiring hung from the top, tools and blueprints scattered around, paint splattered on the wall and the cabinets and more. There are even red hidden Mickeys in the wallpaper. In fact, the entire house is filled with hidden Mickeys scattered among the more obvious decorative Mickeys.

The blueprints are from the Chinny Chin Chin Construction Company with General Contractor Practical Pig, a reference to the Three Little Pigs, and the plans include a garbage disposal that is merely a pig under a sink among other amusing possibilities that rewarded a careful view by a guest.

On Mickey's stove there is a heating dial that indicates "volcano heat" and that is a reference to the cartoon *Mickey's Surprise Party* (1939) where Goofy uses that setting to quickly bake Mickey's birthday cake.

Outside is Pluto's doghouse with bone shaped wind chimes. This house may seem a little plain and unused because Pluto probably stays inside with Mickey most of the time. In fact a pet gate screen to Mickey's bedroom shows the silhouette of Pluto bursting through to join his master.

While it might surprise some people that Mickey Mouse is quite a gardener, the classic Mickey cartoon *Mickey's Garden* (1935) reveals he has had some previous experience, especially with oversized items. Mickey's Mousekosh overalls hang nearby awaiting Mickey when he finishes his duties in the Judge's Tent.

His cactus garden has grown into the shapes of his toon friends. His pumpkins (the "Pumpkin Pie Are Squared" variety) are huge thanks to the special growth mixture, Super Toon Plant Food, that Mickey borrowed from Minnie who lives next door. There is a healthy crop of tomatoes, too, labeled "Hollywooden Vine Tomatoes" of the species "Maximus Ketchupicus".

After exiting Mickey's backyard garden, guests are given an opportunity to return back into *Mickey's Toontown Fair* through Mickey's garage or to go to the Judge's Tent for a chance to have a private meeting with Mickey himself. In the Judge's Tent, a video pre-show about Mickey's exploits entertain guests who are waiting to meet the Big Cheese.

The Toontown Hysterical Film Society has set up an old sheet and projector to entertain the Guests. Now showing is Mickey's "History of the Fair," but some of the upcoming programs listed include "The Art of Crop Dusting" by Goofy and Minnie's film "Paint Yourself Silly."

Like his house, Mickey's garage is filled with wonderful details that will bring a smile. There is a "Last Aid" kit rather than a "First Aid" kit for emergencies. Craftmouse tools. Books with clever titles: "Build a Staircase in 3 Easy Steps" "Repairing Electrical and Bermuda Shorts" "How to Toon Up Your Car," "Replace Your Wheels Without Tiring," and "The Auto-Biography of Susie the Blue Coupe - It's Not the Years, It's the Mileage." That last book title is a reference to a Disney cartoon short, *Susie the Little Blue Coupe* from 1952, which helped inspire the character designs for the Disney-Pixar film *Cars*.

On an upper shelf is Mickey's mailbox from his original house in *Mickey's Birthdayland* while another shelf has cans of Mohave Oil, the oil company whose tanker truck has run into trouble at Catastrophe Canyon at Disney's Hollywood Studios.

A picture can be worth a thousand words. On the wall of Mickey's garage is a framed picture of Mickey fishing with Pluto. It is from the cartoon called *The Simple Things* (1953), the last of the regular series of Mickey Mouse theatrical shorts. In fact, Mickey wouldn't appear in another theatrically released film until *Mickey's Christmas Carol* thirty years later. Up above in the rafters are framed posters of some of Mickey's classic cartoons *Mickey's Good Deed* (1932) and *Mickey's Nightmare* (1932). *Mickey's Good Deed* is the story of an impoverished Mickey and his dog Pluto and how their friendship is put to the test and survives at Christmastime while *Mickey's Nightmare* is a dream where Mickey marries Minnie with a frightening outcome.

That house next door painted pink and lavender and covered with hearts is obviously the country home of Mickey's long time girlfriend, Minnie Mouse.

In Minnie's Country House is a living room filled with pictures and mementos of her family and friends, especially her boyfriend Mickey Mouse. Then guests get a chance to go through the craft room, her office and finally her kitchen. Her back porch is filled with items related to her love of gardening.

Starting in the living room, it is evident that this is a well kept and very feminine location. Minnie obviously takes pride in being a great housekeeper with everything in its proper place.

In a corner of her living room is a huge radio tuned to W-A-C-K-Y radio ("All Country, All the Toon") that is broadcasting from across the street.

In Minnie's living room on the fireplace mantle is a picture in a blue frame with pink hearts of an elderly mouse supposedly Minnie's grandfather with a cane and a newspaper ("The Cheese Report"). That picture was actually based on a specialty drawing done by Mickey Mouse comic strip artist Floyd Gottfredson in 1948 for a never published magazine article on how comic strip characters might look when they are old and gray. It was supposed to be what Mickey would look like when he was sixty years old but some clever Imagineer adapted it for use here.

Those other pictures on the fireplace look suspiciously like they were borrowed from the comic strip by Gottfredson as well by the distinctive drawing style and the pictures decorating the walls are stills and scenes from some of the animated cartoons that starred Mickey and Minnie. However, the captions reveal that these are actually Minnie's many relatives and ancestors who bear a striking physical resemblance to Mickey and Minnie.

Between the chair and the couch on a blue table is a picture in a pink frame of Mickey sitting in a chair and petting Pluto. Many Disney fans mistakenly think that is one of the John Hench's famous Mickey

Mouse birthday portraits. It is actually an alternative Mickey Mouse 50th birthday portrait by artist Paul Wenzel, who did the sketch of Walt Disney on the classic eight cent postage stamp released in 1968. The official John Hench 50th portrait of Mickey had a more suburban Mickey standing in front of Epcot. This classic alternative was done for publicity where a more classic Mickey was required and is the only time that an additional birthday portrait was done besides the official John Hench versions.

Minnie's cabinet displays some of her Disney collectibles including her award winning sculpture of Donald's ship, the Miss Daisy. Just around the corner to the right is Minnie's craft studio.

Minnie is very artistic and dabbles in pottery, sewing and even painting. Her homemade quilt on the wall has won a blue ribbon. Currently on her easel is a painting detailing the crash of Goofy and his plane into the water tower across the street that Minnie must have observed through the large window that brings in so much light into her studio.

On the wall hangs a portrait of Donald Duck in a style that mimics the classic painting "Blue Boy" by Gainsborough. That is actually a recreation of one of sixteen parody paintings of Donald Duck done in the style of the classic paintings of Degas, Gaughin, Whistler, Rembrandt and more by Disney artists that appeared in *LIFE* magazine (April 16, 1945). Minnie won another blue ribbon award for this portrait.

On the floor is a toon version of Norman Rockwell's *Triple Self Portrait* that was earlier parodied by Disney artist Charles Boyer for a still charming poster featuring Walt and another featuring Mickey Mouse.

Like the Martha Stewart of the Toon World, Minnie is editor of *Minnie's Cartoon Country Living* Magazine. As you walk through her office, guests can check the latest messages on her answering machine, read notes and memorabilia on her bulletin board and see covers of past issues of *Minnie's Cartoon Country Living* Magazine decorating the hallway.

Minnie's kitchen is very interactive. Guests can bake a "quick-rising" cake at the touch of a button on her oven, or pop up a fresh batch of noisy microwave popcorn. Trying to grab one of Minnie's cookies set out on a plate becomes a challenge since it is merely an old magician illusion designed to spark some chuckles. The spice rack has Thyme, Good Thyme, Bad Thyme and Out of Thyme…just another example of the many charming details that are in plain sight but often ignored by guests rushing through the house.

Opening the door to Minnie's "Westingmouse" refrigerator is a blast of icy cold air revealing all the different cheese products inside including Cheese Chip ice cream!

Finally, there is a sunroom porch with some examples of potted plants Minnie has grown including Dandylions that have the floral faces of a lion, Tulips that literally have two lips, and tigerlilies with the faces of a tiger and many more examples of punny plants.

Interestingly, there is no bedroom in Minnie's house but it has been suggested that since she knew that visitors were dropping by that the bedroom was not on the tour since she wanted to keep that private. Another significant difference with Mickey's house is that Minnie has a loveseat and chairs that guests can actually sit on. Originally, this physical location of the house was the spot where Mickey's Hollywood Theater was in *Mickey's Birthdayland* and *Mickey's Starland.*

In Minnie's well kept outdoor garden is a delicate pink gazebo where Minnie sometimes greets her guests.

Exiting Minnie's house, is the Toontown train station. Guests can only board the Walt Disney World Railroad on Main Street, Frontierland and only since 1988, the Toontown Station. Unlike the other more elaborate train stations, this is merely a metallic queue line. There is a temporary banner announcing the fair, another indication that this is a special, out of the ordinary day. There is a small water tower on the other side of the tracks so this is the only location that the train can take on water if needed as it sometimes does.

Between Minnie's house and Donald's boat across the street is the small child friendly Toon Park with a tiny playhouse, tunnels, small slides and more for the little ones to burn off some steam. Over the years, this area has gone through changes as well, once including character shaped topiaries.

In *Mickey's Starland*, Donald Duck had a boat, the S.S. Donald, but it was only a façade like the storefronts.

It wasn't until *Mickey's Toontown Fair* that the boat became three dimensional and was renamed the "Miss Daisy" in honor of Donald's girlfriend Daisy Duck who also modeled for the figurehead. Not only is Donald's sailor suit hung out to dry on the rigging above the ship, but a careful look from a distance at the ship itself reveals that is resembles Donald himself with the yellow cabin as a beak (the porthole serving as an eye), the roof being a blue sailor cap, etc.

This is an interactive water play area where pint sized sailors can wade through the water, actually blue tinted Saf Dek padding, surrounding the boat, splash on the lily pads and dodge sprays of water that jet up unexpectedly.

The mysterious hole in the side of the ship is explained by a picture inside Mickey's Country House that shows a massive shark gleefully taking a large bite out of the boat while Mickey, Donald and Goofy were out fishing which is why the boat is probably dry docked across the street for repairs.

Inside the ship is a detailed explorer map created by Ludwig Von Drake that is filled with duck related puns including the Quackatoa Volcano and Mount Quackmore. The map also reveals that the town of Duckburg is now 23 miles away!

There are also two hanging ropes. The one on the right will ring a loud bell if pulled firmly. The one on the left will squirt water on whoever just went out the gaping hole in the side of the boat. Guests can also spin the Captain's wheel.

A few steps away from the ship there is a makeshift Farmer's Market set up with souvenirs and an opportunity to get a piece of fresh fruit or a cold drink. Merchandise is displayed on carts and wagons with even an old fashioned pedestal bath tub being re-purposed into a merchandise cart.

This open air structure reinforces that like most Farmer's Markets this is just a temporary event and once the fair is over, it will be abandoned until the next weekend or special occasion. Notice that the design of the structure is very similar to the farmer's market at *Disney's Hollywood Studios* that was inspired by the famous Farmer's Market in Southern California.

Overhead the screams and laughter alert guests that they are near Goofy's Barnstormer with odd aircraft quickly swooping and twisting and turning as if they were out of control. Barnstorming was a popular form of entertainment in the 1920s where stunt pilots thrilled audiences with heart stopping maneuvers in high flying bi-planes. Barnstormers also toured local farms selling tickets to the citizens for a short airplane flight usually during the season of harvest fairs.

In *Mickey's Birthdayland*, this area was Grandma Duck's petting farm. Those buildings are now used as the W-A-C-K-Y radio station and the queue entrance for Goofy's Barnstormer. The real chickens were relocated along with the other animals to the Ft. Wilderness Campground and were replaced by audio-animatronics ones from the *World of Motion* attraction at Epcot that closed in 1996 to make room for *Test Track*. By the chickens is even a "chicken exit" for those who don't wish to ride the attraction and have "chickened out". These lively birds cluck loudly whenever the plane crashes through the barn.

Goofy took over the area of Grandma Duck's farm but his Wise Acres Farm isn't as successful since his squash has actually been squashed by his big shoes, his bell peppers are in the shape of bells, there is a crop of popcorn and the Goofy scarecrow seems to attract crows. Wandering through the queue line through the crops, guests discover that in order to pay his bills, Goofy has tried to supplement his lack of farming income by making some changes.

He has attempted a business of crop dusting (although his own 1920s bi-plane has crashed into a nearby water tower) and opened an aviation school known as Fido's Fearless Flight School with more experienced canine instructors like Bold Yeller and Amelia Airdale. Goofy's misadventures with flying bring to mind the classic cartoon *Goofy's Glider* (1940).

Goofy's also quite the inventor as well and is working on a Multiflex Octoplane powered by a chipmunk (from the blueprints, it is apparently Dale) running on a hamster wheel and guests can test this new contraption in a wild flight pattern that lasts less than a minute and ends up crashing through the barn. Obviously, guests have been retracing Goofy's erratic flight pattern as can be seen by the hole his distinctive silhouette made on the side of the barn. However, unlike Goofy, guests land safely back at the beginning.

Goofy's Barnstormer was designed by the same outside company, Vekoma, that designed the Rock -n- Rollercoaster at Disney MGM Studios while the Disney Imagineers added the appropriate theming. This attraction mirrors Gadget's Go Coaster at Disneyland's Toontown as a mild roller coaster primarily scaled for children.

Finishing that journey returns guests back to the traditional entrance where they notice that the storyline of Pete's Service Station has expanded. Across the street from the station is Pete's Paint & Body Shop, where "Head" Painter Pete and his crew can give a child's face a "Toon Up" with face painting while they sit in bucket seats. The colorful paint cans and elaborate machinery add to the fun and the theme of a automotive shop where cars are painted.

There is also Pete's Impound Lot where he "impounds a lot" for stroller parking. Pete's even growing a bumper crop of car bumpers just as other residents were taking pride in their gardens.

For an area originally created to last at most eighteen months, this land of toon fun thrived for two decades bringing smiles and laughter to countless guests. Many have fond memories of the different evolutions of the area and it was always a welcome alternative for young children frightened by the traditional Fantasyland dark rides with their scary themes and velvety black interiors.

In September 2009, the Disney Company announced that *Mickey's Toontown Fair* would be replaced with an expansion of Fantasyland. The stated intent was to construct individual areas like a small castle, cottage or chateau where guests could dance with Cinderella, celebrate the 16th birthday of *Sleeping Beauty's* Princess Aurora or perform a role in a story with *Beauty and the Beast's* Belle.

There will be a new restaurant themed to the film *Beauty and the Beast* as well in this enchanted Fantasyland forest expansion. In addition, the popular Dumbo ride will be relocated to a newly themed circus grounds area and will double in size with Goofy's Barnstormer reportedly re-themed to the circus storyline. Eventually, there will be a new Pixie Hollow for Tinker Bell and the other fairies to meet with guests.

Whether any elements, like Mickey and Minnie's homes, from *Mickey's Toontown Fair* will survive at a different location or be incorporated in this new expansion is unclear.

Like some other Magic Kingdom favorites including the *20,000 Leagues Under the Sea* attraction or *Mr. Toad's Wild Ride* or even the Plaza Swan Boats that once floated in the waters near Cinderella's Castle, *Mickey's Toontown Fair* may one day just be another vaguely remembered footnote in the development of Disney's first Florida theme park.

By the end of 2010, *Mickey's Toontown Fair* was still very much alive with the sounds of laughter and colorful details for guests of all ages to enjoy as behind the scenes construction preparation had already begun that would eventually evict the toons from their lovely little country homes and usher in a new storyline for this location.

Jim Korkis *is an internationally respected Disney Historian and the author of the recent book, The Vault of Walt. For over three* *decades, he has written hundreds of articles and done hundreds of presentations about Disney history. He has received acclaim for his personal research and insightful interviews that help document previously unexplored areas of Disney history.*

For Your Pleasure:
The Mythology and Reality of Pleasure Island

Jim Korkis

"Fun for all and all for fun!" was the motto of Merriweather Adam Pleasure (1873-1941?) reputed founder of Pleasure Island.

Originally opened as Lake Buena Vista Village, a "restful shopping atmosphere similar to a New England seaside village" according to Disney publicity, on March 22, 1975, the shopping area at the end of Hotel Plaza Boulevard was later known as Walt Disney World Village. In 1989, it underwent another name change becoming the Disney Village Marketplace with the addition of a nighttime entertainment area called Pleasure Island to the west end of that quiet and quaint location.

Shortly before the opening of Epcot Center in 1982, President of the Outdoor Recreation Division Dick Nunis originally announced that the land to the west of the Walt Disney World Village would be developed into a New Orleans themed resort and shopping location inspired by the New Orleans Square section of Disneyland. The Empress Lilly riverboat restaurant that had opened in May 1977 would serve as the architectural icon with a story of a stern wheeler that had docked at that well known port to unload goods from its journey down the Mississippi River. However, the cost of building Epcot Center and the transition to new corporate leadership in 1984 scuttled those plans.

At a press conference July 21, 1986 on the Empress Lilly, CEO Michael Eisner announced to the world that a new concept in Disney nighttime entertainment would be opening instead at that very same location. It would be an entire island of themed nightclubs and stores called Pleasure Island.

Eisner told the press that he had decided that it was pretty quiet on Disney property after dark except for the fireworks at the Magic Kingdom and Epcot. So he had decided there was needed an after-dark entertainment location for guests, Orlando residents and conventions. Disney's Pleasure Island was the answer with construction to begin in August.

It would be a six-acre island that was scheduled to open Spring 1988 and would be "a place to go when the sun goes down… in a nice Disney way" according to Eisner.

Attending the press conference with a model of the Pleasure Island layout was Madame Zenobia (portrayed by actress Anita Goodwin), who Eisner said would be the hostess of the Adventurers Club and "who will read your palm and tell your future and consult with our studio execs about what pictures we will make."

Also there in full beard, pipe and a brimmed sailor cap looking a bit like Popeye's scruffy father was Captain Spike (portrayed by Craig McNair Wilson who had directed improvisational shows for Epcot's World Showcase) who would run the waterfront club, Madison's

Dive, and tell salty stories about his love of a mermaid inspired by Madison the mermaid from the Disney hit film *Splash*, a particular favorite of Eisner's

The Disney "nightclub district" got its own team: Rick Rothschild (show producer), Chris Carradine (architect), Joe Rohde (art director), John Kavelin (designer), Craig McNair Wilson (writer and director of improvisation) and then later many others including Tony Anselmo (designed and directed the interior effort for Mannequins), Tom Sherohman (the original director at the Comedy Warehouse) and Roger Cox, (director and writer for Adventurers Club).

However, this was not to be the infamous Pleasure Island of the Disney animated classic, Pinocchio, where naughty little boys drank beer, smoked cigars, shot pool and turned into jackasses. Walt Disney Imagineering created an extensive and convoluted storyline to explain the history of the shopping and dining district. When the area opened in 1989, many of the cast members who were trained to work there knew the basic story thanks to the original official training manual but over the years, the more elaborate elements were quickly forgotten and never shared with the newly hired employees.

According to the story, the Empress Lilly, originally christened the "Floating Arts Palace," was a paddlewheel vessel that plied the mighty Mississippi River for twenty-five years. Boat fancier Merriweather Adam Pleasure purchased it in 1911.

In 1911, the Mississippi sidewheeler steamed into Lake Buena Vista and dropped anchor. An adventuresome Pittsburgh entrepreneur, Pleasure saw that on this island he could create a one-man dominion like Edison's Menlo Park or William Randolph Hearst's San Simeon.

Pleasure was an inventor, industrialist and bon vivant. He envisioned a manufacturing center, research lab and development facility, as well as a social gathering spot for the famous and well-to-do.

His motto was "Fun for all, and all for fun!" Pleasure was known to all as "The Grand Funmeister" after being called that name by the

U.S. Secretary of Agriculture in 1927. (A "Grand Funmeister" icon of a yellow half moon face with an open smiling mouth decorated Pleasure Island in its earliest days.)

The boat was to serve as home, guest house and entertainment center while construction began on the island. Living on the boat with his Italian wife, Isabella; his sons, Stewart and Henry; and his daughter, Merriam, Pleasure built his Island empire and founded a canvas manufacturing and sail fabricating industry. The Florida climate favored his business, and though the merchant sailing industry was in its twilight, pleasure yachting and the need for canvas for tents during World War I assured his immediate success.

The business was known as Pleasure Canvas and Sailmaking LTD. The first buildings went up in 1912.

The Pleasure family soon outgrew their showboat home. In 1918, they moved to a Bermuda-style mansion overlooking Lake Buena Vista. The Pleasure Family Home (now Portobello Yacht Club, serving Italian food because Isabella was Italian) was designed so that Isabella Pleasure could host hundreds of tea socials, garden parties and croquet tournaments, featuring fine food and uninhibited conversation. As Mrs. Pleasure often said, "If you don't have something nice to say about someone, come sit next to me!"

"Lilly Plaza," the area directly in front of the docked paddlewheeler, was officially christened in 1922. Originally a turnaround for the limousines of guests visiting the Pleasure family houseboat, the plaza was remodeled for the July 4, 1937 debut of the 118 member Pleasure Island Philharmonic Concert Band (PIPCB) conducted by Maestro Don G. O'Vanni. The PIPCB concerts on this site always ended with a piece Mrs. Pleasure commissioned, the haunting "Fugue for Triangle, Piccolo and Steampowered Riverboat Whistle."

Aware of the westering circumnavigations of Irving Johnson and the youthful crews of his Yankee Clipper, Merriweather Pleasure commissioned the yacht Dominoe (named for his then-favorite pastime and yes, this was the official spelling with the additional "e" on the early Imagineering documents) in 1929, which brilliantly foresaw the awesome J-boat formula.

With his 18-year-old daughter, Merriam, he embarked on a series of eastward 'round-the-world voyages. He turned the business over to his two sons: "Awkward Stewart" Pleasure who pursued the sporting life and Henry who was known as "The Mad Genius of Lake Buena Vista" and succeeded in creating a Cellular Automaton (sort of an early version of a computerized robot that was later discovered at Videopolis East by the Imagineers).

Merriweather and his daughter returned from their many expeditions with a vast treasure of adventure and discovery. The trophies eventually overwhelmed Pleasure's comfortable Bermuda-style house and Mrs. Pleasure threatened to eject her husband from the house unless he found a place for the books and artifacts collected on his journeys.

An imposing building on the opposite side of the island was designed to house Pleasure's huge personal library and archeological trophy collection. Pleasure reportedly won the plans for the building in a game of dominoes. (A domino design is still evident on the outside of the building.)

The building became the headquarters for the Adventurers Club in 1932. The Adventurers were Pleasure's zany band of globe-trotting friends, yachting cronies and hangers-on who all swapped tall tales. Exotic souvenirs of the members' outlandish expeditions and riotous adventures were displayed on the walls.

Merriam Pleasure is listed on a plaque in the Main Salon as part of the "Founder's Circle" in addition to Otis Wren, Pamelia Perkins, Hathaway Browne and Col. Critchcow Suchbench. Merriweather Pleasure is listed on that same plaque as the sole "Founder."

It was also in 1932 that Merriweather Pleasure created the "Adventurer's Creed" which was framed in the Zebra Mezzanine. "We climb the highest mountains, just to get a better view. We plumb the deepest oceans 'cuz we're daring, through and through. We cross the scorching desert, martinis in our hand. We ski the polar ice cap in tuxedo, looking grand. We're reckless, brave and loyal and valiant to the end. If you come in here a stranger, you'll exit as a friend."

The Pleasure Perfect Upholstery shop (now the shop Changing Attitudes selling apparel and accessories) had six full-time seamstresses working to refurbish the interiors of the custom yachts in the Pleasure Island dry dock. In 1934 the shop was responsible for stuffing the head of a rare Mongolian Yakoose for the Adventurers Club. This profitable sideline ended in 1943 when a war-time shortage of kapok put taxidermy on the endangered species list.

Between journeys, Pleasure returned to his beloved island and devoted himself to a quest for reusable energy and the conversion of some of his factories to mysterious laboratories that included the construction of an experimental flying vessel as well as broadcasting messages to outer space (now the home of the club XZFR Rockin' Rollerdome).

Unfortunately, the Funmeister's good fortune ran out in 1941. The "Dominoe" was presumably lost with Merriweather, Merriam, and all hands, having been reported pitch poled in a howling summer storm while attempting a circumnavigation of Antarctica in December 1941. After Pleasure vanished at sea, the Adventurers Club was closed and sealed.

Mrs. Pleasure died in 1949 resulting in the disbanding of the Pleasure Thespian Players and the closing of the Power Station (now the Comedy Warehouse) where they performed elaborate Central Florida historical pageants including the seminal "Song of the Seminole."

The canvas business continued to be successful for more than a decade until Henry's poor business decisions and Stewart's lavish lifestyle forced Pleasure Canvas and Sailmaking into bankruptcy in 1955. As a note of finality, Hurricane Connie inflicted near-total destruction two weeks before the creditors' sale leaving the island an un-saleable shambles.

This was the same hurricane that transformed Placid Palms Resort into Typhoon Lagoon. Many of the contents of the various Pleasure

Island buildings were strewn across Lake Buena Vista by the winds of change and some debris ended up at Typhoon Lagoon.

The once bustling harbor community became a ghost town. But in 1987, Disney Imagineers re-discovered the island. Some buildings were renovated and some, like the Adventurers Club that had survived disaster, were reopened.

The legacy of "America's First Family of Fun" was revived and according to "Jasper W. Linedozer", the self-proclaimed semi-official Pleasure Island historian who wrote the pseudo-historical plaques on the island, "along the streets of this reawakened Island you can sometimes catch a glimpse of a portly, but strangely ethereal man, dressed in a yachting cap and natty plus-fours. Or perhaps you'll be sitting in a restaurant booth or a cozy corner of a nightclub when you hear a voice murmur quietly, 'Fun for all—and all for fun!'"

The actual history devised by the Imagineers continues for many, many more highly detailed pages connecting every building on Pleasure Island to the legacy of Merriweather Pleasure including the AMC Theaters at the far west side.

According to the long missing original plaque: "Pleasure had the building refitted in 1938 as a laboratory for testing 'thermomagnetics'—a process designed to harness the earth's magnetic force. The success of the experiment was proven in 1940 when the facility blew sky high with no visible, provable use of combustibles. Pleasure commanded that the ruined super structure and outbuildings remain as testimony to 'the awesome power of the planet'. Rebuilt jointly by American Multi-Cinemas, Inc. and the Walt Disney Company. Opened in 1988."

There were two real life inspirations for Disney's Pleasure Island. Imagineer Chris Caradine was impressed with Granville Island in Vancouver. There, a manufacturing village that had fallen on hard times had its buildings transformed into restaurants, theaters and shops in the Seventies and became a popular destination for both the residents and tourists. Some of the colorful artistic signage there was also adapted for the Disney version.

The second inspiration was the Church Street Station area in downtown Orlando. By 1985, it had become the fourth most popular tourist attraction in the state of Florida, right behind Walt Disney World, Sea World and Busch Gardens. Its colorfully themed clubs like Rosie O'Grady's Good Time Emporium, the Cheyenne Saloon and Opera House, Phineas Phogg's Dance Club and Lili Marlene's Aviator's Pub and Restaurant along with the Church Street Station Exchange, a three story shopping emporium featuring dozens of shops and restaurants, were a favorite nighttime spot for both locals and tourists.

"At some point, we dug out an aerial photo of WDW Shopping Village and noticed a little peninsula at the far end adjacent to the Lilly Belle restaurant and how easy it would be to make it an island," remembered Craig McNair Wilson, an Imagineering consultant who worked on the project.

Originally a peninsula, Disney dug a trench separating it from the Disney Marketplace. The trench that makes Pleasure Island an island is technically a water quality drainage feature. In most locations, Disney digs aesthetically pleasing ponds to hold water and allow sediment and heavy metals to settle out before discharging to canals and rivers. At Pleasure Island, the theme of an island makes that pond more like a small waterway isolating the island from the mainland with three footbridges at different locations providing access for guests to the area.

"We began to riff and created the mythology and back story of Merriweather Adam Pleasure," continued Wilson. "We all improvised it and it grew and grew…at one point, the full mythology was way too long and Marty Sklar called me into his office and asked me to rewrite it in one voice and make it pithy, brief, and fun. The now famous Pleasure Island plaques were excerpted from that document: The Final, Ultimate, Semi-Official History of Pleasure Island."

When the Island opened, there were twenty-seven plaques placed at the entrance of the island and on the individual buildings by the Pleasure Island "Histerical" Society to explain the mythology of the island in elaborate detail. Unfortunately, these dark black out-of-the-way plaques were difficult to find and read at night, especially after guests had too liberally enjoyed the alcoholic offerings in the clubs. As a result, neither guests nor cast members discovered the complete history of the island or fully understood the complicated connections that they did discover.

The clubs that eventually opened were considerably different than the original plans. Madison's Dive was soon cancelled with some of its special effects like a sinking ship in a bottle moving to the Adventurers Club. A planned Jazz Club transformed into a Country and Western location when Eisner saw the popularity of a similar venue at Church Street Station in Downtown Orlando. A proposed magic club very reminiscent of the famous Magic Castle club in Los Angeles was never built and again, some of its elements were incorporated into the Adventurers Club.

"We wanted a T.G.I. Fridays open twenty-four hours where the Portobello Yacht Club is today," recalled Wilson. "We presented Marty (Sklar) with a menu of fifty food, entertainment, and retail ideas for Downtown Disney and West End. There were a few Disney attractions in the mix that various teams had been playing with, including 'Do It Yourself Disney' that eventually evolved into DisneyQuest. The list included House of Blues, T.G.I. Fridays, a 1940s era Hollywood Canteen (dance and supper club), All That Java (coffee and jazz club), Villains (aka Villains Volt, an 'underground' haunted night club themed on classic Disney Villains), and 100 Acres (from the stories of Winnie the Pooh) which would have been a nighttime day care for kids while adults shopped and dined. I was very excited about a twenty-four hour diner inspired by Orlando's Bubble Room, but completely decorated and stuffed with antique Disney memorabilia. From the outside it would be a classic, stainless steel American diner with flashing neon signs. Inside, you would find hearty dishes with the best Disneyana we could find, buy and borrow including authentic Disney movie props. The name would have been 'W. Elias's' as a tribute to Walter Elias Disney. It would have been located where Planet Hollywood is today."

For a variety of reasons including cost and time since the project was running over deadline and over budget, all of these proposals narrowed down to the clubs and restaurants that actually opened in 1989: Mannequins Dance Palace (with a large rotating floor and overhead mannequins attired in a variety of dance costumes), Neon Armadillo Saloon (a country and Western location inspired by the Cheyenne Saloon and Opera House at Church Street Station that Eisner visited and saw a huge line waiting anxiously to enter) XZFR Rockin' Rollerdrome (a dance club with a skating rink on the upper floors), Videopolis East (a non-alcoholic club catering specifically to people younger than 21), the Fireworks Factory (a restaurant specializing in barbecue to match the "burnt" theme of a stray spark from Pleasure's cigar that had set off fireworks and blackened the interior of the building), the Portobello Yacht Club (an authentic Northern Italian cuisine restaurant), Merriweather's Market (a food court with four distinct sections where everything was cooked to order) the Comedy Warehouse and the Adventurers Club.

In addition, there were many shops unique to the location including Avigators Supply (featuring aviation and clothing merchandise with a winged alligator who was supposed to be another mascot of the Island just as Lagoona Gator was to become the mascot of Typhoon Lagoon opened the same year), YesterEars (selling Disneyana items), Suspended Animation (selling Disney artwork) and Jessica's of Hollywood which opened in 1990 and showcased a giant two-sided neon sign of Jessica Rabbit with sequined dress and swinging leg who sat atop the light purple colored building to entice customers inside to purchase jewelry or nightgowns with her logo. (When the shop closed, the sign was re-positioned on a building near the West Side footbridge and became a symbol of Pleasure Island.)

When Pleasure Island officially opened May 1989, it went through some changes almost immediately as the Disney Company adjusted to running a club district for the first time. Almost a year later, April 1990, an admission gate was placed at the front of Pleasure Island (using redesigned train cars from the closed Ft. Wilderness railroad as ticket booths) so that guests who wanted to visit the area after 7:00 p.m. now had to pay roughly ten dollars for the pleasure.

To encourage guests to visit at night after their day at the Disney theme parks, from 1990 through New Year's Eve 2005, Pleasure

Island celebrated New Year's Eve every night with a street party at the West End Stage at midnight with confetti, professional dancers and musicians, loud blaring music and finishing with a countdown climaxing in a fireworks show.

Over the years most of the restaurant and store venues changed radically. Pleasure Island Jazz Club took over the space of Merriweather's Market in 1993. XZFR became the Rock'N'Roll Beach Club in 1990 because of possible safety issues with the skating rink that was replaced with billiard tables and other games. BET (Black Entertainment Television) Soundstage Club took over the Neon Armadillo location in 1998. 8TRAX (a 70s/80s music club) replaced Videopolis East in 1994. The Fireworks Factory changed to the Wildhorse Saloon (Country and Western club) in 1998 and finally Motion (dancing to top 40 tunes) in 2001. Stores changed as well.

These severe changes from the original concept were indicative of the challenges of operating such a unique venue. In the process, the storyline of Merriweather Pleasure was slowly lost as it did not adapt to these new businesses and guests showed no interest or understanding of the existing mythology.

Major renovations to Pleasure Island were made in March 2006 in an attempt to reverse declining attendance. By this time, there was no longer an evening entry fee to Pleasure Island and as a result, the area was attracting large groups of rowdy local teens who came to just hang out and cause trouble which was considered undesirable for a Disney location.

In late June 2008, Disney announced that the six remaining nightclubs at Pleasure Island would close by September 28, 2008, to make room for additional family-oriented entertainment.

Only two of the original clubs had remained in continuous operation for nearly nineteen years, the Comedy Warehouse and the Adventurers Club. The Comedy Warehouse (with its tiered interior decorated with authentic Disneyana memorbilia on the walls) opened with a scripted show entitled *Forbidden Disney* that poked good natured fun at Disney and the tourist experience. However, within a year, the club transformed into a typical improvisational comedy club where the talented performers solicited suggestions from the patrons to create short humorous sketch comedy.

"*Forbidden Disney*, in its original form, was essentially a mini-musical. Every scene had a song. I wrote all of the original music and the lyrics that went with them. The lyrics to *SuperConcientiousFriendlyDisneyWorldEmployees* (which were brilliant) were done by Kevin Rafferty. Rich Proctor wrote the lyrics to *It's Tough to Be a Fairy in the Eighties* which I set to music. The original *Forbidden Disney* was almost an hour and a half long. Michael Eisner loved the show, and the idea of doing the show. Unfortunately, the Warehouse show definitely polarized the audience. The vast majority found the show to be quite funny, and they admired Disney for having the guts to do it. Others—most notably some WDW people—absolutely hated the show, and were insulted by it. We actually got hate mail from some of these people," sighed Lynn Hart who wrote countless songs for both the Comedy Warehouse and the Adventurers Club including its well-remembered theme song.

For the most part, the Adventurers Club continued to provide the same type of entertainment for almost two decades. It was meant to resemble a 1930s World Explorers' club decorated with many "treasures and artifacts" brought back from far off expeditions. Many of the artifacts were not as inanimate as they seemed and often came to life throughout the evening to entertain the guests. Official club officers and members interacted with the guests the entire evening by telling stories and introducing them to the club's customs and activities.

The announced reason for having an "Open House" for new members to the exclusive club every evening was to help pay off the lease on the building "one drink at a time" at one of the three bars in the building.

A large sign outside the entrance proclaimed: "Welcome to the Adventurers Club! You who crave danger and snicker at fear will find most agreeable company here. Thrill seekers, nomads, high-flyers and low, rovers, explorers and getters of go, from every far corner, you'll meet at this hub. The world is your oyster. The pearl is our club! Tonight!"

Situated toward the top of the winding Hill Street, the odd looking building exterior was decorated with a variety of strange surprises from a crashed plane in the front lawn to monkey skulls on spears and ancient pottery cluttering the entrance.

According to the original plaque describing the building: "Adventurers Club. Founded 1932. This imposing building was designed to house the huge personal library and archaeological trophy collection of Island founder and compulsive explorer Merriweather Adam Pleasure. Pleasure won the plans in a game of dominoes and attributed them throughout his life to noted architects Sir Edwin Luytens, Charles Rennie Mackintsoh, and Eliel Saarinen. The building became the headquarters for the Adventurers Club, Pleasure's zany band of globe-trotting friends. Exotic souvenirs of the members' outlandish expeditions and riotous adventures were displayed on the walls. After Pleasure vanished at sea in 1941 the club was sealed until it was opened to the public for the first time in 1989."

The logo for the Adventurers Club, a globe and compass with overlapping banners, was created by Joe Rohde as an homage to the logo of the *True Life Adventures* film series made by the Disney Company in the Fifties.

The members included Hathaway Browne (daredevil aviator and ladies' man), Otis T. Wren (club treasurer and ichthyologist), Fletcher Hodges (club curator), Pamelia Perkins (club president), Samatha Sterling (explorer), Emil Blehall (from Sandusky, Ohio and contender for the Balderdash Cup), Graves (club butler) and the maid. Over the years, there were a variety of maids including Sugar Snap, Kiki McGee, Gabby Normal and Dusty Cabinets.

The club was also home to some not quite human members as well including Fingers Zambezi (the invisible spirit who played the organ in the library), Colonel Critchlow Suchbench (club glee master and chief of club security who in actuality was a large scale puppet torso nailed to a chair in a balcony on the wall), Babylonia (the great stone goddess whose talking head was nailed on the wall over the restroom entrance), the Yakoose (half moose and half yak who instead of being sent to the taxidermist was mistakenly sent to the upholstery shop), Beezle (the head of a genie who floated mysteriously in a lamp in a cabinet in the Treasure Room) and Arnie and Claude (two talkative masks in the Mask Room).

The festivities each night included shows devoted to honorary member inductions, the Balderdash Cup competition, an episode of the radio cliffhanger *Tales of the Adventurers*, and some odd acitivities in the Treasure Room and Mask Room. These were the primary shows that delighted guests over the years but other shows, especially for holidays or special events, also came and went.

Jim Steinmeyer, legendary designer of magical illusions and theatrical special effects who was working with Imagineering at the time, stated, "I really think that the Adventurers Club is a perfect blend of two personalities: Joe Rohde and Roger Cox. You see Joe's sense of visual fun and old fashioned adventure, and you experience Roger's offbeat humor and loving evocation of these old-fashioned, bigger-than-life personalities. It was a project that fell outside of the usual Disney formula, and worried everyone before it opened. Roger was very un-Disney in his thinking and Joe was always deliberately pushing the envelope."

Larry Hitchcock, who worked on the Pleasure Island project and was responsible for bringing in Roger Cox as the writer concurred, "I agree Roger delivered the text, and Joe the visuals but they pushed and fulfilled each other. Roger's prose painted a picture. Joe's art suggested a story."

Production designer Susan Cowan who was referred to as Rohde's right hand on the project said, "The Adventurers Club remains a favorite project of mine after all these years. As art director, I production designed all the show elements, including the illusions provided by the talented Rock Hall and Monty Lunde of Technifex. I also bought about ninety-five percent of the fifteen hundred plus props. I am sure the finance department at Imagineering will never forget me. Lots of receipts scribbled on brown paper bags because many of the props were bought at my favorite haunt, the Rose Bowl swap meet in Pasadena. By the way, Joe who was the primary art director on the project painted the artwork (for the two paintings) that hung in the library. He and I are rendered in both of the paintings along with Roger Cox, the show director, and Rick Rothschild, Pleasure Island's show producer (and Chris Carradine)."

In January 1990, Chris Oyen was brought in as a show writer and director of both the Adventurers Club and the Comedy Warehouse to maintain, and where necessary, modify the experience so that it was consistent. Oyen was responsible for creating the character of Samantha Sterling, readjusting the performing matrix so that there was a beginning, middle and end to the evening, created and edited the *Adventures Almanac* newsletter and wrote several new show segments. Over the last decade of its operation when Oyen went on to other assignments, several other entertainment directors rotated into the venue supervising the established shows.

When guests entered the club there were on the top floor known as the Zebra Mezzanine because of a zebra designed bar designed by Rohde that was prominetly placed there. The walls were covered in ancient artifacts and yellowing photos all connected with the exploits of the members with captions explaining their significance.

"All the framed photos, throughout Adventurers Club are ninety percent from a huge historic photo library in New York City. I brought in my old, portable, Royal manual typewriter. I still have it. We sat around WDI for days coming up with captions for them. They were typed on newsprint that we had soaked in tea and left in the sun to dry. I think everyone got their name-or some version of it (or a friend's name) in at least one of those captions," remembered Craig McNair Wilson.

A winding staircase (or slightly hidden elevator) led down to the circular Main Salon. This central room of the club was filled with more artifacts and photos as well as the head of a Yakoose (voiced by Tom Sherohman and this distant relative of the audio-animatronics Melvin the Moose from *Country Bear Jamboree* would spring to life unexpectedly to talk to the guests), the Colonel who would help induct new members with the creed and song, Babylonia who would flirt with the patrons, and a replica of the Artemision Bronze statue, commonly known as the "javelin thrower statue" or at the club itself as "Zeus with a Fishing Rod" (with the fishing line entangled in exhibits overhead).

Along the sides of this Main Salon were entrances to four additional rooms: The Mask Room (where the masks on the wall would spring to life like in *The Enchanted Tiki Room*), The Treasure Room (holding the cabinet with the floating head of Beezle the genie along with other assorted treasures), The Rest Room and The Library (where the primary shows were performed).

During the last decade of its existence, the Library shows (generally a half hour or less in length and often featuring music) were performed in the following order on a small raised stage:

Welcome Party
Samantha Sterling and Fletcher Hodges throw a welcome party to officially start the Open House.

Radio Broadcast
Otis T. Wren and Pamelia Perkins lead a version of their weekly old-style radio serial, *Tales of the Adventurers Club*. However, half the cast is missing and must be replaced by audience members. The show was sponsored by the cereal Jinkies with its unforgettable slogan: "Jump Up for Jinkies! We Love 'Em!"

The Balderdash Competition
Hathaway Browne, Otis T. Wren and Emil Bleehall compete to be "Adventurer of the Year" by relating the most outrageous stories that have supposedly happened to them and demonstrate their skill. Bleehall always won with his demonstration of tap dancing pigeons that could be heard on the roof of the building.

The RadioThon
A talent show performed by various members of the cast to attempt to raise $2,000 using a radio telethon to save the club

from losing its lease. Except for the last performance, the club was always saved at the last minute by a check from the House of Wong, a Chinese restaurant.

Samantha's Cabaret

A musical show focusing on the vocal talents of Samantha Sterling.

The Maid's Sing-A-Long

A musical show featuring the maid and audience participation.

The Hoopla

The Adventurers Club evening finale to close the night.

Steinmeyer summed up the continuing appeal of the experience, "To me, the charm of the Adventurers Club was that it was eccentric and unexpected. The humor was unpredicatable and off beat. But it all seemed to make perfect sense, unto itself. That's the comfort of the Adventurers Club, really. You've gone to someone else's party. They've been throwing that party for a long time. They're experts at it. But over the years, it's taken on all of their personalities and quirks. Audiences felt they'd fallen into a rabbit hole and experienced another world."

The final public performance at the Adventurers Club was the night of September 27,2008 to a crowd that overflowed into the street. The premise of the final show was that the Adventurers had failed to raise enough money in their nightly RadioThon to pay their lease, and the members were being immediately evicted. Fortunately, Marcel (a Missing Link character who disappeared during the early years of the club) had become filthy rich due to lucrative investments and had returned to whisk the club members away for a year long safari. They marched out of the club, followed by their fans, and the club was officially closed except for a few special convention events during the following year.

Disney has intimated that in the new Mystic Point section of Hong Kong Disneyland, there might be an Adventurers Club restaurant but no specific details have been announced.

With the closing of the Adventurers Club, the last bit of the Merriwether Adam Pleasure story finally disappeared from Pleasure Island, leaving gutted buildings, boarded up entrances, blocked pathways and a ghost town feel that ironically resembled how the Imagineers supposedly first found the location over twenty years ago.

"Our decision is largely based on guest feedback," said the official Walt Disney World statement in July 2008 explaining why the clubs were closing, "We are seeing more demand for shopping and dining experiences and less demand for clubs. Certainly, we understand that some guests may be disappointed by the closing of Adventurers Club, but we believe it is necessary for implementing our long-term vision for Downtown Disney."

During the last two years since all the clubs closed, only one new venue opened on Pleasure Island, a South and Central American restaurant with a tequila bar called Paradiso 37 in June 2009. It is in the same building next door to the Adventurers Club that used to house Avigators Supply that according to the Pleasure story were Florida stunt pilots befriended by Merriweather and who operated a short lived import/export business and crashed a plane in the front yard of the Adventurers Club.

The logo on the tail of that aircraft is still visible to guests walking briskly through the nearly deserted Hill Street from the Marketplace to the West End: "Explore the Unknown. Discover the Impossible." For a brief period of time, Disney did exactly that in an unusual location known as Pleasure Island.

The Relative Truth About If You Had Wings

Mike Lee

If You Had Wings was the only Disney attraction my paternal grandmother, Vernice Lee, ever claimed to love. She didn't care for Big Thunder Mountain Railroad – having only boarded that runaway train once, she said a second time around would have done her in. She also had no use for The Haunted Mansion, where she found the allusions to mortality off-putting. It's A Small World and the Country Bear Jamboree both agreed with her sensibilities just fine, but neither one spurred her to employ superlatives. No, the only ride that she took the time to praise was a 4.5 minute Omnimover trip through cavernous dark rooms where Eastern Airlines' travel destinations were recreated via dioramas and film projections. In her own words, it was "as close as she could get to heaven without working for it."

To be fair, I only know how she felt about If You Had Wings because I asked. In the course of writing early tributes to the ride in 1989, I drove a hard bargain with family and friends to give up recollections of the recently closed attraction. She could have lied to make me happy, but childhood conversations that she recorded on Kmart cassettes (tapes we found a few years ago) confirmed that this particular ride was truly special to my grandmother long before it closed. Only as a kid that wouldn't have seemed unusual to me, because, really, didn't *everyone* love If You Had Wings?

As it turns out, not everyone. In 20-plus years of trying to keep memories of the ride fresh, I've learned that people who liked it seemed to do so fervently but that many Magic Kingdom visitors thought it was too silly, too low-tech or both. The middle ground was populated by those who just couldn't resist a free ride (back when other rides required an A,B,C,D or E coupon) that was air-conditioned, usually had a short line and featured a "Speed Room" – an early variation on projection-based motion simulators. Then there were those who forged a more magnetic and vaguely spiritual bond with the very idea of the ride, along with its music and message. These are the people who, in e-mails and online comments, tell you that this was their favorite - and you sense that they aren't kidding. For them, my grandmother included, If You Had Wings represented something transcendent.

That's a pretty impressive accolade for a theme park attraction which was essentially an extended commercial for a major corporation and - by virtue of its very floor plan - could have been cast as an afterthought. If You Had Wings was tucked into an awkward space (the current home of Buzz Lightyear's Space Ranger Spin) between Tomorrowland's CircleVision 360 theater and the outer perimeter of the WEDway *PeopleMover* track which, while not put to use until 1975, was already a known physical quantity when Tomorrowland construction began in 1969. The available square footage, therefore, was predetermined. And, as with the surrounding attractions in Tomorrowland, Disney was seeking a sponsor for whatever would come to pass in that location.

Sponsorships had been an integral part of the Disney park experience from the time Disneyland opened in 1955. At that time, "lessees" (as the company once called them) were as varied as The Upjohn Company, Swift, and Kaiser Aluminum who sponsored, respectively, Main Street USA's Pharmacy and Market House and Tomorrowland's Hall of Aluminum Fame. Their financial contributions helped make the construction of the park possible, and their presence in the park's shops and exhibits put their corporate logos and/or services in plain view of millions of visitors every year.

By the time planning for Walt Disney World began, Disneyland had developed a more mature and far-reaching "participation program" for its growing roster of major corporate sponsors. Concurrent with Walt Disney Productions' becoming a partner to Pepsi-Cola, the Ford Motor Company and General Electric for those companies' 1964-1965 New York World's Fair pavilions, they had also in 1964 secured United Airlines as a ten-year sponsor of Disneyland's new (1963) Enchanted Tiki Room attraction.

Six years later, Disney naturally sought a major airline for a similar relationship with Walt Disney World. In 1970, however, United Airlines was coming off a decade of diversification and its first year of multi-million-dollar net losses. Additionally, since WDW was under construction there was no opportunity for a company to merely assume the sponsorship of an "existing" attraction as United had done with the Tiki Room in California. Rather Disney was now seeking the commitment of a company to help underwrite the building of an as-yet-to-be-determined attraction.

Their focus soon turned to Eastern Airlines. In 1970, Eastern was a major nationwide carrier that had dominated air traffic routes along the Atlantic coast since the 1930s and provided flights to Orlando from 60 different cities. A ten-year contract was signed between WDW and Eastern that year. Their sponsorship commitment was $10 million, according to Robert Serling, author of 1980's Eastern Airlines history *From The Captain To The Colonel.*

WED Enterprises (Disney's design & engineering division) set out to develop an attraction that would suit the needs of both the sponsor and the park. Eastern wanted to promote the variety of exotic travel destinations to which it provided service - most of them in the American Southeast and the Caribbean, while Disney needed something to fill that vacant slot in WDW's Tomorrowland and increase the Magic Kingdom's hourly capacity.

This is where one of WED's most versatile artists, Claude Coats, came into play. Coats had been a key contributor to Disney's films and parks since 1937's Snow White and the Seven Dwarfs. His designs, color stylings and backdrops had shown up in many of Disneyland and WDW's key attractions. He pioneered the use of black light in three-dimensional environments, making him a master of the dark ride format. Just prior to WDW's opening, one of his most recent successes was a marriage of creative setbuilding, filmed images and a new ride system that allowed him to point riders' lines of sight in whichever direction he desired at any given point along the track.

The ride was Adventure Thru Inner Space, which WED created for Monsanto. It debuted in 1967 as part of Disneyland's "New Tomorrowland." In near-countless ways it served as the prototype for the ride that WED would soon craft for Eastern, including:

- Both were located in the Tomorrowland sections of their respective parks (and both to the right of the main entrance thoroughfare)
- Both were designed specifically for major corporate sponsors
- Both contained a queue where guests previewed those ahead of them boarding their vehicles and disappearing into an iconic prop (at Disneyland the "Mighty Microscope," at WDW an oversized globe)
- Both incorporated the Omnimover ride system, created by Roger Broggie and Bert Brundage
- Both had blue passengers cars and a clockwise-moving track
- Both relied heavily on projector effects and staggered props
- Both featured a song written for the attraction by longtime Disney composers

The similarities between the two rides were so numerous; few could have experienced both and not marveled at the fundamental common elements. Yet for all the crossover devices, the combinations yielded vastly different experiences. Whereas Adventure Thru Inner Space was cool and scientific (you entered the heart of a snowflake crystal after being "shrunk"), If You Had Wings was bright and a little freaky (with technicolor imagery and frenetic action that bordered on psychedelia). And although Inner Space served as the basic model for the new ride, the planning effort for If You Had Wings remained complex due to aforementioned boundaries set for the building itself.

Coats and his WED co-workers, including engineers Stan Maslak and John Zovich, turned an arguably compromised beginning into 28,000 square feet of remarkable kinetic art built around the simple premise that Eastern Airlines (whose marketing tagline in the early 1970s was "The Wings of Man") could widen your world and take you to all manner of fascinating places.

To convey this through the use of a high-capacity ride, Coats designed a series of both flat and sculpted set pieces depicting Mexico, various Caribbean ports and New Orleans. Those sets would frame out screens for 16mm film projections and comprised the first 2/3 of the experience. The final third consisted of the bullet-shaped Speed Room, with its high-speed 70mm projections surrounding the ride vehicles and the box-shaped Mirror Room, which elicited a sensation of being lifted gently over mountain ranges and rolling desert landscapes. When pieced together with lighting effects, music and the versatility of the Omnimover, the varied elements comprised a compelling and immersive experience.

Many of the films used in the ride were shot in real-life locations. Shooting took place in settings as diverse as Acapulco, Jamaica, New Orleans, California's Imperial Valley and Canada's Laurentian Mountains. Over two dozen staged production shots were put together as well. These ranged from a full-blown Mexican fiesta with authentically costumed dancers to a far more casual round of limbo dancing on a false beach. To work these into the ride, If You Had Wings would ultimately hold 41 16mm projectors, three 70mm projectors (one for the Speed Room and two for the Mirror Room), 40 special lighting effects projectors and one 35mm projector.

Music for the attraction was recorded under the supervision of Norman "Buddy" Baker, who composed the ride's title theme along with lyricist X. Atencio. Baker also adapted a piece of music - the "Airbus" theme - from Eastern Airlines commercials of that same time period. The instrumental he came up with provided the background for both IYHW's Holding Area and Mirror Room scenes. WED's sound department provided additional audio for the attraction. The sounds of foot traffic in the Bahamas and of a jet takeoff were two of the most predominant recordings. Less overt effects, such as fireworks, seagull calls and native Mexican musical instruments were brought in for additional authenticity.

By March of 1972 the blueprints for the ride's interior sets were completed and If You Had Wings was being pieced together in preparation for summer crowds. The show's set pieces were designed in California by WED and installed on site by another division of the company, PICO West. The majority of the sets were constructed of 1/4" plywood with 1" framing. When assembled they often formed simple three-dimensional structures or spaces such as the Aztec pyramid or the New Orleans courtyard. Props and artifacts typical of the locations depicted (Mexican pottery, Caribbean straw goods, fishing gear) were added to the sets as a final measure of third-dimensionality.

The ride opened to the public on June 5, 1972. Eastern Airlines and Walt Disney Productions officials formally unveiled the attraction during a dedication ceremony the following month, on July 2. It was the first new ride in the Magic Kingdom that wasn't simply held over from the previous October's park opening.

If You Had Wings' entrance was its least remarkable feature: an open glass portal framed in dark blue, built into the side of a white concrete building that was defined by the WEDway track running overhead. It had a 30' white pylon sign - identical to those in front of its neighbors, CircleVision 360 and Mission To Mars - featuring an Eastern logo above the ride's name. Otherwise it was of no more interest than the mirror-image entrance to the Space Port shop just across the main Tomorrowland thoroughfare.

Once inside the building, though, guests encountered the more engaging sight of the open holding area. Eastern Airlines described this space as "a spacious, modern airport passenger terminal." This vast room had high ceilings, sparkling white walls and orange carpeting (which changed to blue shortly after opening). At the far side of the room was the Load area, where guests stepped onto a Speedramp and took a seat in one of 102 continuously-moving Omnimover vehicles. These ocean-blue cars trailed off to the north side of the room, where they entered an oversized and elongated globe through a large hole in its side. Attached to the side of the globe for much of the ride's lifespan was a model of an Eastern jet, heading west. The sight of the cars passing into this sphere was exciting and a little ominous, as what lie beyond the darkness of the globe's interior was anyone's guess. A twisting queue area was recessed into the center of the room. Guests passed by large backlit signs for arriving and departing flights, which blinked exotic destinations such as "Bahama's 100,000 Islands" and "The Magic Kingdom." Echoing throughout the holding area was Baker's lush orchestral arrangement. Over this theme, the voice of a man announcing a series of arriving and departing flights could be heard periodically... "Eastern Airlines announces the departure of flight 811, Whisperliner service to the underwater reefs of Bermuda." Initially this was the voice of Orson Welles, who could also be heard in Eastern Airlines' commercials of that time. By the mid-1970s his voice in If You Had Wings had been replaced by that of Disney studio mainstay Peter Renoudet.

When guests reached the end of the queue, they were guided onto the Speedramp by a host or hostess and split into groups, typically 2 adults per vehicle. From here forward they cruised at a rate of two feet per second, steadily approaching the big hole in the globe. Geographically, the hole was situated just south of Florida, throwing guests smack into the middle of the Caribbean – the approximate center of Eastern's more celebrated vacation routes.

The ride began with guests disappearing into darkness. The black walls of the globe's interior came alive with the white silhouettes of seagulls in flight. The persistent whirr of the ride's 16 millimeter film projectors snuck up out of nowhere and the ride's theme was introduced by a gleeful chorus of unseen singers. This simple song became a favorite for many Magic Kingdom visitors — *"If you had wings, you could do many things, you could widen your world, if you had wings... If you had wings, if you had wings, if you had wings, had wings, had wings, had wings..."* It was repetitive to the point of absurdity, making it all the more memorable.

As the ride vehicles spun inside the globe, the seagulls on the wall turned into jet airplanes racing off to exciting destinations. These silhouettes faded into the background as guests approached the first location, Mexico. The cars faced off to the right of the ride's forward motion, and the track began a climb through the room. Spread out before the guests was a vision of old Mexico, brought to life by a series of two-and-three dimensional props, film projections, lighting and sound effects. Rising from a sea of geometric cloud formations was an Aztec pyramid basking in the rays of a blazing stylized sun. In the distance were the cliffs of Acapulco, where a series of divers took the breathtaking plunge every few seconds. Soon the cars swung over to the left. As they did, guests were confronted by a large stone dragon's head, a representation of the Aztec god Quexalcoatl.

To their left, guests faced a panorama of modern Mexico. Flower-laden boats drifted across the shimmering floating gardens of Xochilmilco, carrying dancers and a Mariachi band that blared the ride's theme from their trumpets. In the sky above, projections of pottery and other crafts rose from the horizon and flew through the sky. Further along was a main plaza of Mexico city, where the shadows of festival-goers frolicked in the distance. Closer to guests, through the open arches of a downtown building, dancers in fiesta regalia spun across the floor.

In that scene and those yet come, all sense of motion - beyond that of the actual vehicles - was achieved through the use of film and effects projectors. There were no moving props or animated figures, but the ride was still very "alive" thanks to Coats' gift for staging. His talent gave the ride a strong sense of atmospheric plausibility.

After passing below the dragon's head, the cars descended into a Caribbean seaport. To the right was an ocean liner, inventively dubbed the "Caribbean Cruiser," preparing to set sail. Passengers lined the railings of the boarding deck, waving and throwing streamers. A steel drum band played in their midst. In the harbor below, an armada of smaller watercraft dotted the horizon. The image of a dancing couple was silhouetted against the sail of a sloop. Down in the water, divers groped through the kelp for treasure.

At the water's edge, in a shack marked "Sport Fishing," a tourist posed proudly with his catch (a swordfish of indeterminate proportions) while his wife set up to snap a picture. As the man stood there beaming, the fish hanging next to him grew larger and smaller, evidently illustrating the disparity between what he'd caught and the tales he was going to spin about it. This scene alone could stand as Exhibit A in a case built around Imagineering's likely use of recreational hallucinogenics.

By this point in the ride, If You Had Wings' maddening acoustics could be fully appreciated. Since the first half of the ride took place in one large room divided only by props and set walls, all of the various scenes' musical tracks blended into a nice messy din. That made it hard to pick apart the song lyrics for any given area, but guests would catch bits and pieces. Clarity aside, this music was a key element of the attraction, as integral to the If You Had Wings experience as It's A Small World's signature song is to that world of singing dolls and dancing children.

The cars turned left again and entered a straw market. In a small building decorated with all manner of hand-woven goods was another couple, who tried to make a sale (in time with the music) to passing guests. "Wanna buy a sombrero," the man inquired, "made of real fine straw? His wife sat beside him, eagerly trying to unload a hat. The straw market scene then gave way to Puerto Rico, as the cars swung back to the right and began another slow incline. Through tropical foliage guests viewed a group of young people doing the limbo. Then the battlements of San Juan's Castillo San Felipe del Morro rose around the track. Through its archways guests had aerial views of the seacoast and the fort, with now-familiar seagulls passing by. In another arch was a musical group fronted by a cheerful lady playing the maracas and putting yet another twist on the ride's theme song.

The cars leveled off at the entrance to the fort, wherein another series of arches framed out scenes of the Bahamas. A marching band stormed by with their rendition of the song, and with every other line of music their image gave way to a street traffic traveling in the opposite direction. This motif was repeated in the next several archways, but now the street traffic alternated with a flurry of flamingos rushing down a shallow waterway. In a central arch, a Bahamian traffic cop in white knee socks and shorts had his hands full attempting to regulate this bizarre flow of events. With a whistle perched resolutely in his mouth, he pivoted to the left and right in a thankless pursuit of order.

Off to the right, a view of Jamaica's Dunn's River Falls unfolded beyond jungle vegetation rife with butterflies. Making their way up to the top of the many-tiered waterfall was a large gathering of young people in swimsuits. As they reached various plateaus on their climb, they "danced" across the water in group formations - in reality holding on to each other so as not to slip. Further along was a window looking out across a twilight lagoon in Trinidad, where more flamingos flew by every few seconds.

The next scene was New Orleans' French Quarter during Mardi Gras. In an open courtyard to the left, the shadow of a Dixieland quartet delivered its version of "If You Had Wings" on a vine-covered wall. On the right, the street was blocked-off for the parade that was passing just a little further down. Other Mardi Gras festivities (including the somewhat creepy sight of a lady holding hands with a man wearing a huge zebra head) were viewed through the corner of a nearby building laced with wrought iron balconies. Fireworks burst in the sky ahead, and guests moved toward them on their way into the massive space just around the corner.

This was the Speed Room, also known as the SuperSpeed Tunnel … or as the part of If You Had Wings that no one forgot. Guests moved down the middle of this huge bullet-shaped chamber while 70mm projections of high-speed adventures played out on the walls around them. The ride vehicles tilted backward and large fans added to the sensation of motion created by "you are there" scenes, such as racing in a dune buggy across the desert, water-skiing on a busy lake and flying down a forest path in the engine of a speeding train. The Speed Room, of course, is an effect that went on to uses in other attractions such as Disneyland's *PeopleMover* and Epcot's World of Motion. Now that those two attractions are gone, the only Disney Speed Room left is the original, now a part of Buzz Lightyear's Space Ranger Spin.

After taking in five or six scenes in the Speed Room, guests moved through a small hole at its far end and entered the Mirror Room. The walls of this box-shaped space were covered with slightly concave mirrors, against which the projections of snow-capped mountains and other placid ranges were reflected. Each scene was shot from an ascending angle, which created a gentle, lifting sensation. The holding area's orchestral theme was reprised here, adding to the already serene environment.

The final scene brought back the seagulls, which now breezed across a dark blue sky. Between the birds, an Eastern jet would come shooting past every few moments. The voice of the holding area's announcer came back with these parting words: "You do have wings, you can do all these things, you can widen your world, Eastern... we'll be your wings." Then the cars approached the unload area, where guests gathered their belongings and stepped out to their right onto another moving belt. A final version of the theme song played between here and the exit, where the lyric "If You Had Wings" became "You Do Have Wings." Just before stepping back out into Tomorrowland, guests had the opportunity to stop at an Eastern-staffed reservations desk, where they could make travel arrangements or other inquiries. Pins featuring the Eastern logo flanked by golden wings were given out free to visitors in the first several years of the ride's operation.

That is essentially what If You Had Wings was all about - a loud jaunt through images of happy people goofing around in tourist spots, wedged between a big globe and a tunnel full of racing scenery, set to upbeat music.

Jill Rees, A first-year WDW employee who was on If You Had Wings' opening crew, remembers the initial cast member reaction as being typically mixed just like those of park guests. "We were a little surprised when they finally let us preview it," she said, "since we'd been led to believe this would be a major addition to the park." The Speed Room impressed them, but the rest of the ride was something of a head-scratcher. Eastern Airlines, in a souvenir book produced for its employees in 1972, remarked upon the fact that the ride would be free and suggested that it otherwise would have been an "E-ticket attraction." If, however, one's only association with Omnimover cars in 1972 was the E-ticketed Haunted Mansion, If You Had Wings could reasonably have been viewed as more of a C-ticket curveball. Yet it was the very nature of the curve that made the ride appealing to so many others - especially kids like my brother Brian and me who really needed a free ride like that when we got down to our A-tickets and didn't want to ride the Omnibus over and over. If You Had Wings became like a friend to us and its inescapable weirdness just made it that much more special over time.

For its part, WDW seemed unsure of what to do with their strange new ride or how to promote it. At the time of its opening, the park was still so new that marketing If You Had Wings as an addition would not have made sense … not with submarine rides, a stage full of presidents and jungle river excursions upon which to focus. Beyond that, If You Had Wings was largely overlooked in terms of any post-opening attention from within the company. Pictorial souvenirs produced between 1972 and 1987 only featured a photo of the ride once, in 1986. The attraction was not represented on postcards, view-master reels, 16mm films or even latter-day VHS tapes that offered Magic Kingdom overviews. Even the less interesting Mission To Mars was accorded a higher level of coverage throughout the 1970s and 1980s.

From 1972 to 1987, If You Had Wings underwent very few visible alterations outside of modified Eastern logo placement, updated carpeting and new cast member costumes in the early 1980s. An employee suggestion in 1979 led to the introduction of a waterfall sound effect in the Dunn's River Falls scene, but by and large the attraction was left unchanged for fifteen years. It also remained well-attended - even if the lines didn't compare to those at *Space Mountain* or the StarJets.

Most of the time a ride's successful ability to draw visitors ensures its long-term prospects, in other instances it has no bearing at all. With a sponsor-dominated attraction like If You Had Wings, the solvency of Eastern Airlines became the governing factor in the ride's destiny. When Frank Lorenzo bought Eastern in 1986, the company was in dire financial straits. The following Spring, on the eve of bankruptcy and with Michael Eisner reportedly raising the proposed cost of their continued sponsorship, Eastern declined to renew their status as the official airline of WDW. Disney quickly inked a deal with Delta airlines and made the pragmatic decision to give If You Had Wings a temporary makeover for the summer of 1987 while designing a replacement ride for Delta.

So If You Had Wings closed on the first of June 1987 and reopened five days later as If You Could Fly. The Eastern logo was replaced by a seagull icon. All other references to the airline were removed and the ride's song was switched out – the new one also named for the attraction with lyrics built around the various destinations visited along the way. Everything else remained as it had before. On paper the changes sound minor, but in practice they made for a genuinely different attraction. The juxtaposition of all those familiar sights set to a different soundtrack was perplexing, at best, for anyone who even remotely liked the earlier incarnation. If You Could Fly lacked the flair of the original and invited disappointing comparisons. That didn't last long, however, as this version of the ride hosted its last visitors just eighteen months later on January 4, 1989.

At that time almost everything visually inherent to If You Had Wings and its successor was destroyed and removed from the building's interior as trash. As a Magic Kingdom East 'Operations Host,' I walked through the ride during its demolition; standing inside the globe and looking through holes punched in its side was pointedly sad – as was the sight of so many film reels scattered across the floor. But the ride's moment in time *had* passed; without Eastern its soul had already left the building. By the time Delta Airlines' Dreamflight opened there in June 1989, If You Had Wings was just an echo with another attraction built around its track.

Dreamflight itself has long since passed, of course, and there is now a generation of children who never experienced it just as those born in the late 1980s missed out on If You Had Wings. For as fun as it might have been, for me Dreamflight underscored just how brilliant If You Had Wings was by comparison. If you stripped away nostalgia and personal preferences, there remained the impressive feat of spatial design accomplished by If You Had Wings' creators. Because while it seemed incredibly simple, arranging all of its show elements into an odd-shaped building, having all the film effects hit their targets without projectors cluttering up the scenery and leaving no corner undecorated was a daunting task pulled off admirably. The Caribbean Port Scene alone, which guests only experienced for ten seconds, contained four separate projector and screen positions configured at, above or below the ride track level with one projection shot over the track from behind. What people saw from their vehicles was cohesive, but the configuration of scenery, projector platforms and equipment hidden from view was markedly intricate. Additionally, this scene was one of three within the ride that was also viewed by guests aboard the WEDway *PeopleMover*. They viewed the port segment from a completely different vantage point than guests inside If You Had Wings, yet their angle worked on its own merits and showcased the never-ending stream of Omnimover vehicles snaking through the port and straw market scenes.

It's a testament to Coats and his team that later groups of Disney personnel working on replacements for If You Had Wings weren't able to duplicate his successful use of the full available space. Viewpoints from the *PeopleMover* had to be walled over for Dreamflight, and even the one that remained by the early 1990s (a brief glimpse of a painted Parisian skyline) had a flawed perspective of the diorama's back wall. The room that once contained the vibrant Caribbean Port scene, in fact, became an empty space with just one large screen on its western wall where images of a stunt flyer were projected. Every other surface was covered with black roofing paper with the nails still exposed... a far cry from the artistry of its predecessor. Furthermore, later versions of the ride opted to only use of half the original Mirror Room by pointing the cars south instead of east, leaving the space behind them put to no purpose. This doesn't mean that Dreamflight or Buzz Lightyear's Space Ranger Spin weren't enjoyable - each had its own merits. But the specific ways in which they did not improve upon If You Had Wings reminded those who loved that original ride just how *different* a sensation it provided. Yet even for a huge fan, it's still difficult to fully explain how it managed such a warm effect on the hearts of so many. Perhaps its understated nature and second-class citizenship among the park's larger attractions made it easier to cherish as an underdog. Or maybe it just reminds us of a time in our youth when disappearing into a big globe for five minutes of nonsense in the dark could be innocent, thrilling and life-affirming all at the same time.

The Magic Kingdom has now operated for more years without If You Had Wings than with it. As time passes, I've wondered how long it will be before recollections of the ride pass into the ether of antiquity, like those of old east coast boardwalk attractions whose patrons are long since deceased. It's plausible that an ex-ride built around an ex-airline was not only destined to close, but also to be forgotten in fairly short order.

But its memory persists - and not just because of online efforts to ensure that outcome. In May of 2010 I stood in my driveway talking to some plumbers who were allegedly working on my house. When they learned that I had once worked at WDW, one of them volunteered a list of things she remembered from Orlando-area parks when she a child. This included the Japanese Village at Sea World and the Davy Crockett Explorer Canoes at Walt Disney World. She said she didn't really go to theme parks anymore even though she grew up in them... she hadn't even been to EPCOT Center. Then, without missing a beat, she added, "you know what I really miss? That If You Had Wings ride."

My new favorite plumber got me thinking along new lines: Perhaps the greatest mystery about the ride now is not how long it will be remembered, but whether Claude Coats and Buddy Baker had even the slightest notion as to the wonderful impact their 1972 one-off had on so many people.

As for Grandma Vernice, the most concrete reason she gave for her appreciation was that it was "one of the most beautiful things" she'd ever encountered. I'd venture that the sight of those birds flying by and the Mirror Room, with its lofty vistas and lilting score, made the strongest impression on her. Unfortunately she's no longer with us, so I can't pry for further information. But I like to think that she's enjoying some combination of seagulls and levitation in the hereafter.

Acknowledgments from the author: Thank you to Dave Hooper, Eric Paddon, Jill Rees and Dave Smith for their assistance with my research into If You Had Wings.

Mike Lee *is a former WDW employee, future clairvoyant and part-time contributor to his Widen Your World website. He was the inspiration for the term "no rehire" and is currently not working on his sixteenth unfinished novel, I Think Jane Samuelson Waited Tables at King Stefan's Banquet Hall, But Who's Asking?*

Thunder Mesa & the Western River Expedition: A Neverending Story

Mike Lee

It has been 47 years since Marc Davis first worked up concepts, in 1963, for Walt Disney Productions' unbuilt St. Louis "Riverboat Square" project. In 1968 he revisited those ideas and rolled them into plans for a new attraction at Walt Disney World, which at the time had yet to break ground. His project was initially titled Western River Ride, renamed The Western River Expedition by 1970. It has been 36 years since the WRE concept was shelved by Disney management and about 30 years since the last public mention of the ride as a "coming attraction" for either WDW or Disneyland; those mentions had reached their apex between 1973 and 1976 when plans for the ride were put on display for guests in both the Anaheim and Orlando parks.

In terms of "looking back at looking back," it has been 25 years since Marc Davis's artwork for the WRE started turning up in retrospectives such as "The Disneyland that Never Was," fourteen years since I attempted my first web-based account of the ride's troubled history and ten years since Jim Hill put the ride's development and 'permanent deferment' into grand perspective in a ten-part essay on his website. More recent online mentions of the ride have essentially repeated what was already written long ago or lamented that there isn't much new to add to the tale.

Why, then, do we keep writing about, and looking for new insights, on a nearly 50-year-old ride concept that has been explored to the point of diminishing returns and stands virtually no chance of ever being realized?

For me the answer is plain – The Western River Expedition remains the single-most dynamic unbuilt Disney attraction in the entire history of Disney attractions (EPCOT, the city, doesn't count as an attraction). The WRE's basic conceit alone – a 'Cowboys and Indians' version of Pirates of the Caribbean – is perfectly intriguing. The artwork Davis produced for the ride takes the premise to greater heights with its intoxicatingly rich detail and humor. Furthermore, the sprawling scale model of the attraction that WED Enterprises built in the late 1960s (seen by guests at WDW and reproduced periodically in rare photos) spoke to a combination of animatronics and stunning scenery that would have potentially topped Pirates.

As a kid I spent quite a bit of time staring at a six-foot-wide section of that model in the post-show exhibit area of The Walt Disney Story in Florida's Magic Kingdom. That was my first, and remains my most vivid, exposure to the WRE as something still "in the works." At the age of six, however, I didn't grasp the context of what the ride represented in terms of a major accomplishment in the themed entertainment art form. Back then it was just a cool idea that I assumed would be built, as promised, in due time. When construction began on WDW's Big Thunder Mountain Railroad in 1979, for all intents and purposes spelling out the WRE's fate, the meaning of that eluded me also. If I'd been ten years older then and known what I was missing, my insane enthusiasm for a runaway mine train ride would have been tempered.

The WRE was actually the headlining act for a larger production called Thunder Mesa, first described for the public in 1970's Walt Disney World – Preview Edition as a feature of the Magic Kingdom that would "tower high above dense pine forests, offering a spectacular panoramic view of Frontierland."

How high above Frontierland? Pretty high. If Phase One of Walt Disney World panned out as originally envisioned by its designers, Tom Sawyer Island would fall under twilight shadows a little earlier than the rest of the Magic Kingdom. Due west of the Rivers of America's southern circuit there would be an immense rock wall, looking something like Big Thunder Mountain but much wider and deeper – a looming backdrop for Frontierland, rising up at about the same place where the Briar Patch shop now sits and spreading north to where Big Thunder Mountain Railroad now meets the canal off the west side of the river. Thunder Mesa, the conceptual forerunner of Big Thunder Mountain and proposed home of multiple attractions unique to Disney's Florida Project, would have topped off at roughly 60 feet tall at its highest peaks and spread some 600 feet from north to south.

Among the attractions within its scope was a runaway mine train ride – the one Thunder Mesa concept that did eventually evolve its way into four Disney parks across three continents. Another was a series of hiking trails atop the mesa, past natural arches, waterfalls, desert flora and fauna and a Pueblo Indian village. There was also to be a pack mule ride working its way across the stone bluffs. But the star attraction would be staged *inside* the mountain, which of course was the WRE.

When the master planning of WDW kicked into high gear in late 1967, after Walt Disney's death and the securing of vital legislation from the Florida State Senate that granted Walt Disney Productions autonomous control over its 27,443 acres of property, the company had no intention of building a Pirates of the Caribbean ride for their new venture's theme park. They believed pirate lore was too close to Florida's history to warrant such an attraction at WDW. The prevailing sentiment was that southeastern U.S. audiences would be better entertained by a taste of something less familiar and more removed from their geographical region's past.

Primary responsibility for an alternate attraction fell to Marc Davis, the WED artist and former Disney animator who was at that time largely responsible for DL's Pirates of the Caribbean (opened 1967); concept work on the final versions of DL's and WDW's Haunted Mansions (1969 and 1971, respectively); and designs for WDW's *Country Bear Jamboree* (1971). His comical touch and talent for setting up a scene had also brought some welcome levity to DL's Mine Train through Nature's Wonderland and Jungle Cruise rides in the form of animatronic animal humor. In 1963, shortly after Davis had joined WED, he had worked up concepts for a Lewis & Clark-themed boat ride for a proposed Disney venture in St. Louis called Riverfront Square. The ride idea included animal vignettes rooted in western lore. While that project ultimately fell through, Davis drew from those ideas, one of his favorite television programs (*Gunsmoke*) and films of the period such as 1965's *Cat Ballou* in developing the basis for his new boat ride. It would transport guests past scenes of buffalo, bears, cattle and other animals in natural settings, dance hall girls doing the can-can to the delight of townsmen, bandits engaging the law in shootouts, American Indians rain dancing to immediate results and other frontier situations both humorous and menacing.

Company literature of the era described the new project as a wild west version of Pirates of the Caribbean. That label probably robbed the WRE of its due, as it was intended to be a step up from its predecessor in at least two key respects. First, it was going to be more technologically complex than Pirates, with more animated figures performing a wider range of motions. Second, it was going to be more musical in its execution, with nearly all the scenes united in song. Davis hoped to further explore the limits of three-dimensional animation in the WRE while at the same time creating a very fluid, rousing and funny experience.

Because the ride would have been housed in a show building larger (about 64,000 square feet) than the Haunted Mansion or It's A Small

World, there was a need to mask it well; the space reserved for the attraction - a plot of land on the western edge of Frontierland - would be highly visible from three directions. Davis' solution to the question of prominence was to couch the entire affair in a Monument Valley-style stone edifice which would also support secondary attractions such as the train ride and the meandering footpaths while creating an ideal mise-en-scène for all of Frontierland.

Thunder Mesa's size and scope would have made it, by far, the largest and most dense single component of the Magic Kingdom. This is why Walt Disney Productions decided to hold off on its construction at first, slating it for realization toward the end of WDW "Phase One" i.e., the first five years after opening. It made sense, as it would provide WED and the construction crews an opportunity to get the Kingdom's other attractions up and running before tackling this behemoth. If the park was the success they hoped for, operating revenues would help offset Thunder Mesa's construction costs. Plus it would be something that the company could promote extensively to entice visitors back to WDW after their initial visit.

It seemed like a great plan, and certainly one with which the company intended to follow through. Ground was even cleared in the acreage that the attraction would later occupy. A similar scenario happened for the Asian Resort, where the squared-off hotel site was reserved on the western shore of the Seven Seas Lagoon. Both were WDW Phase One elements deemed imminent, just slightly delayed, along with *Space Mountain*, the Persian Resort and the Venetian Resort.
Back at WED, all the homework and scripting for the WRE was complete. Davis and longtime Disney collaborator Mary Blair had produced a large number of paintings and illustrations that told the ride's story. What follows is a synopsis drawn from that artwork, other written accounts of the ride and interviews with those both involved in and familiar with the project.

Guests approached Thunder Mesa from the south and entered a cave marked "Western River Shipping & Navigation Co." The cave led them into a canyon at twilight (*perpetual* twilight, as its placement would be inside the show building similar to Disneyland's Blue Bayou

Lagoon), and to a riverside dock where they would board a freight levy just like the ride vehicles in Pirates and It's A Small World. The trip began with an introduction to the ride's "star," a recurring audio-animatronic owl named Hoot Gibson, as the boats are hoisted up a waterfall and channeled into a canal for a (momentarily) low-key cruise down a frontier river. Oversized dime novels, their covers depicting western icons such as Annie Oakley, Buffalo Bill Cody and Davy Crockett, gave way to dioramas of bears cavorting on the banks, bison sniffing prairie dogs and a cowboy strumming a guitar and singing the WRE's signature song... along with a chorus of longhorn steer. The ride's musical theme was introduced early and would carry on throughout the remainder of the experience. Desert animals such as owls, even cactus, picked up and carried the tune.

Things got more interesting as the boats passed a group of bandits holding up a stagecoach on a wooden bridge. Both the thieves and their horses wore bandanas across their faces. The lead villain, virtually hidden beneath his dark sombrero, sang to guests as they passed and suggested they would meet again further down the river. Then the boats entered a western town called Dry Gulch. It's Saturday night and the streets are filled with revelry. Dance hall girls are singing and performing can-can feats as cowboys cheer them on. Wranglers on horseback are firing their six-shooters into the air - one has even managed to get his horse onto the roof of a saloon's front porch. Some townspeople look on in shock or disapproval, but it has no effect on the wild behavior. In fact, things only ratchet up from there. Around the bend there is a raging exchange of gunfire between a group of bank robbers and the law. A sheriff on his horse fails to detect underground tunneling trailing below him from the nearby jailhouse. Fearsome ruffians in dark hats shoot Colt 45s from behind troughs and a purloined bank's safe while congenial deputies in white hats answer back from the windows of a bathhouse. Seemingly everyone is caught up in the action, save for a smiling mortician sizing up his prospects for timely business. Guests narrowly avoid injury in the crossfire as they drift through the chaos.

The sound of bullets is soon replaced by that of tribal drumming and chanting. Along the banks is a diorama of the painted desert, in which a gathering of Indians are enacting a full-blown rain dance ceremony.

On a tabletop rock, a storm is already washing down on a circle of braves, over the sides of the plateau and into an adobe homestead. Five maidens sit in a row, swaying in time with the music. A trio of coyotes howls in front of a bonfire while medicine men shake gourds. Lightning from the gathering rainstorm sparks a forest fire and guests cruise through a mass of flames. The once-peaceful river yields to rapids and things start to get rough.

To make things worse, the bandits from the stagecoach scene have caught up with the boat and demand the passengers' valuables at the headwaters of a raging waterfall. Before guests have a second chance to consider their predicament, their craft tips over the falls and plunges them down a passage that leads out of Thunder Mesa and along a channel hugging the Rivers of America, similar to the main drop on Splash Mountain. Then the boat re-enters the mountain and arrives at the Unload dock, where guests disembarked from their vehicle.

It was an ambitious project to say the least, and the company seemed to be sharpening its teeth in order to bite into it completely:

- A 1" to the foot scale model of the ride was built at WED, just as one had been built for Pirates a few years earlier, for purposes of finalizing the spatial relationships of visual elements. Ken O'Brien sculpted an army of figures to populate the miniature show scenes. Those who saw the model in its entirety, such as Bill Cotter, say it was phenomenal to behold, with multiple animated features and beautiful lighting effects. Thunder Mesa had also been sculpted in its entirety as part of a 1/100th model of the entire Magic Kingdom.

- Buddy Baker, the mastermind behind countless Disney film scores and park tracks (including If You Had Wings), reportedly began writing theme music for the attraction in a variety of different styles such as an introductory ballad, a double-time saloon style and an Epic Western style evocative of films like The Big Country and The Magnificent Seven.

- Full-size animated figures were being sculpted. In a 1972 interview with *Orlando-Land* magazine editor Edward L. Prizer, then-Walt Disney Productions Chairman Donn Tatum said the WRE would contain approximately 150 animatronics. That would be an increase of 30 figures over Disneyland's Pirates ride. According to Imagineer Belinda Winn, in the October/November 1996 issue of WDEye (Imagineering's in-house newsmagazine) animated WRE figures actually went into production.

It was in the midst of this work that WDW opened to enthusiastic crowds in October 1971. Enthusiastic, that is, save for a recurring question: "Where's the Pirate ride?" Many WDW visitors fully expected to enjoy the Pirates of the Caribbean attraction from Disneyland, which they had seen on Walt Disney's Wonderful World of Color, the company's Sunday-night television show and heard about from relatives who had traveled to California. When people arrived in the Magic Kingdom to find nary a buccaneer, there were (to put it mildly) a few complaints.

So now there was a problem, and we all know how it was "solved." While Imagineering still felt that building the Pirates-like WRE and promoting it on its own considerable merits was the appropriate route, that was going to be a more costly - and more risky - option than simply repeating Pirates, especially when Pirates was a sure-fire success with great word-of-mouth. That's certainly how Walt Disney Productions' management saw it, specifically then-president Card Walker. He insisted the Pirates be added to the Florida park post haste. And it was, in an abbreviated form built for a rumored half of the WRE's projected $60 million price tag. It opened to the public in December 1973.

The decision to build Pirates was made in early 1972, at which time the future of Thunder Mesa and the WRE was immediately put up in the air. With Pirates on its way to the park, the urgency to build another major attraction on its west side (especially considering that Tom Sawyer Island was also slated to open in 1973) was massively diminished. If the key component of Thunder Mesa hadn't been a boat ride, placed so close to Pirates, there may have still been a compelling argument to proceed. There were still the various peripheral attractions like the train ride and the mules to consider, but in the eyes of management there were enough factors to table the project in its entirety.

What's interesting is that it didn't get axed outright. In this capacity Thunder Mesa and the WRE hold a unique position for the amount of notoriety they maintained well past the point where most unbuilt attractions would have fallen off the radar. Page 10 of the company's 1972 annual report painted (what is in retrospect) a strange picture of the unfolding saga. Pirates of the Caribbean was accurately slated for its 1973 debut; the expansion of Tomorrowland, including a new thrill-ride concept called "The *Space Mountain*" was previewed; and a new attraction was being introduced for Frontierland in 1974... the Big Thunder Railway. According to Jim Hill, Imagineer Tony Baxter's concept for an adaptation of Thunder Mesa's mine train component (one that would spread across the whole of Thunder Mesa's Florida real estate), sat in WED's model room and was known only by WED staff until Card Walker first saw it in Spring of 1974. But that 1972 annual report, which was published in early 1973, demonstrates via a concept painting by Clem Hall that the Big Thunder Railway attraction was fleshed out thoroughly, almost exactly as it would be built (under the name Big Thunder Mountain Railroad) for its 1980 opening. And even though it was billed in that report as a "step toward the completion of Thunder Mesa," anyone familiar with that attraction's scope would rightly wonder how the rest of Thunder Mesa would figure into the arrangement. The train ride was supposed to have sat OVER the WRE; certainly no one was going to slide a boat ride underneath a series of stone bluffs built at ground level.

Baxter, not wanting to alienate Marc Davis by rolling out a concept that would completely kill the WRE, did have a plan for that. He envisioned Big Thunder Mountain sitting side by side with a show building (encased in rockwork) that would have contained the WRE and even created a model showing that arrangement. This seemed like an afterthought, but in many ways it was the most practical approach for giving the train ride maximum free run as a thrill ride while salvaging what would have been a fantastic boat trip. But that hardly mattered, because Davis had already formed an opinion that he would carry with him the rest of his life: that he had been upstaged and a project very close to his heart was the victim. It probably wasn't that simple, but there's no doubt that the eventual green-lighting of Thunder Mountain for Florida was the symbolic snuffing of the WRE's candle.

But what a wick this thing had! Not only had the ride been promoted in WDW pre-opening literature dating back to 1969, but four years later, in spite of all the maneuvering associated with Pirates and Big Thunder, the WRE became the centerpiece of the Walt Disney Story's post-show on Main Street. A section of the WRE model - depicting the scene with the dance hall girls and the cowpoke whose horse jumped atop the saloon's porch - was displayed in its own private hallway. In an adjacent alcove, the electronic version of a feathered Hoot Gibson could be found snoring away on a tree branch. When guests pushed a button the owl came to life and introduced himself as "the star of a brand new Western show being made for Walt Disney World." He then gave a brief run-down on the process behind audio-animatronic technology. At the conclusion of this tutorial he urged guests to come back and visit him "at the Western River Expedition." This was extensive publicity for a ride still being developed - let alone a ride whose prospects for realization had been largely doused *before* this display opened in April 1973.

Unfortunately, this was the last true bright spot in the ride's history. From 1973 onward, Marc Davis dealt with an increasingly frustrating series of disappointments regarding the WRE. One thing he had to contend with was of his own doing... a smattering of American Indian stereotypes throughout the attraction. Davis had worked in pretty much every potentially insulting sight gag for what he surely intended as maximum comic effect - big noses, drunkenness, the war hoop, dancing around wildly in circles, sitting "Indian-style," you name it. That Walt Disney Productions perpetrated these stereotypes (in films like Peter Pan and The Saga of Windwagon Smith) into the 1960s was lamentable. To have carried the tradition forward as part of a 1970s attraction, one which surely would have lasted into the 21st century, would have been egregious. Davis actually had a respect for indigenous cultures in North America and around the globe; he studied them thoroughly when attempting authentic depictions - such as the New Guinea warriors in his works of fine art. But he saw nothing wrong with taking the opposite road for a laugh, and that's where things got thorny. In a 1999 interview, Davis denied that his Indian renderings were a source of real contention. There is, however, some evidence to the contrary. A comparison of two renderings Davis created for the "Doc Cogwheel's Magical Elixir Wagon" vignette, one in 1968 and another in 1974, showed some funny Indians in the earlier art replaced by Caucasians in the later version. This suggests that Davis was willing to make some compromises on that point to advance his project's chances of moving forward.

Another obstacle confronting the WRE was its projected cost; management simply could not see the inherent benefit to spending tens of millions on an attraction that wasn't called *Space Mountain*. By the end of 1973, the expansion of WDW's Tomorrowland was going full-tilt. It not only included a major thrill ride, but also the Starjets, WEDway *PeopleMover* and a revamped *Carousel of Progress* that was returning to the East Coast from a six-year, post-World's Fair run in California. With this project eating up tons of money, with many other attractions that had recently debuted in other parts of the park (Tom Sawyer Island, Plaza Swan Boats, the Walt Disney Story, Pirates itself) and with major work taking place in the resort areas, there was a tremendous push toward achieving higher capacity throughout WDW. And throughout this time, the WRE sat on the sidelines.

Nonetheless, management at least *appeared* to be receptive to finding ways of making it happen. Marc Davis was approached with a proposal to reduce the cost of the WRE by recycling molds cast for Pirates in order to create a large number of the ride's animated figures. As first published in Bruce Gordon and David Mumford's *Disneyland: The Nickel Tour*, Davis wasn't keen on the idea. Inflexible, to be exact. Had he sensed how tenuous his negotiating position was at that time, he might have been more amenable to giving in and then finding ways to get some aesthetic problems with the ride fixed later on. But it must not have seemed feasible to Davis that management would pull the plug on the WRE over something like that. And they didn't. They did nothing... and kept doing nothing with the WRE up through the present day.

In May of 1974, Card Walker announced that WDW Phase One would be complete by year's end, paving the way for the company to concentrate more heavily on the development of EPCOT Center. That didn't bode well for Phase One projects that had yet to see groundbreaking, and it's when plans for the WRE in Florida were essentially - if not formally - over. The model in the Walt Disney Story post-show remained visible until walled up in 1981 for an EPCOT Center preview (the model was "rediscovered" in 1994 with lights still burning). Hoot Gibson got dressed up as a tour guide and spoke of another theme park with Spaceship Earth serving as a backdrop; he never uttered another word about the old west.

Plans for the WRE's inclusion at Disneyland and Tokyo Disneyland never amounted to much either. A display was put up on Disneyland's Main Street touting the WRE's arrival in Frontierland, but that effort was displaced by the *first* version of Big Thunder Mountain Railroad, which broke ground in 1977. Marc Davis left WED in 1978. In the *Orlando Sentinel* there was some brief talk about WDW's next park (following EPCOT Center's debut in 1982) being themed to the old west, but we don't know if the WRE was linked to that. The plans for such a park, if they truly existed, must have evaporated quickly. The name Thunder Mesa did eventually make it to a Disney park, albeit anticlimactically: The Frontierland section of Disneyland Paris, 1992, is home to the town of Thunder Mesa, which overlooks a river that was *not* full of guests in boats venturing into the fabled days of cowboys and Indians, but *was* wrapped around a rocky thrill ride called... Big Thunder Mountain Railroad.

Regardless of whatever role Tony Baxter played in sidelining the WRE during its infancy, for a while it seemed to me that he was likely the only old-timer left at Imagineering who could successfully bring the WRE to life. His intimate knowledge of both the attraction's history and the realities of modern-day theme park politics make him uniquely qualified to shepherd a project of this magnitude from the dusty archives to an actual three-dimensional creation that guests could enjoy firsthand.

The truth is, however, that it would take more than vision and clout to get the WRE built. It would also require the desire. There is a lot of talent at 1401 Flower Street, but it's rolled up inside an organization that seems more likely to continue modifying the classics left to us by WED's earliest roster of artists (such as Davis, Blair, Claude Coats and Rolly Crump) than to actually get another one of that first generation's unused concepts off the ground... especially a major one. Resurrecting something like the WRE would require WDI to look past the obvious physical and financial challenges that the project presents and see their way clear to make it happen. While the genius of Marc Davis is recognized by enough people to never be forgotten, it also may never be enough to overcome the hurdles associated with putting one of his projects ahead of others dreamed up by those artists who are still on the payroll.

That's a sad thought, given that delivering the WRE would provide everyone involved with the chance to take part in an effort that would be heralded as miraculous for the rest of their lives – something that speaks to the very core of their organization in terms of both artistry and history.

But even if the ride still hasn't been built come 2063, chances are someone will still be talking about it how great it would have been.

Acknowledgments from the author: Thank you to Dave Barker Jr., Howard Bowers, Russell Brower, Bill Cotter, Michael Cozart, Alice and Marc Davis, Jim Hill, Mike Hiscano, Bob Kammerer, Jerry Klatt and Ross Plesset for their assistance with my research into Thunder Mesa and the Western River Expedition.

History of the Hoop Dee Doo Musical Revue

Chuck Mirarchi

The various shows and attractions at the Walt Disney World Resort have always been popular. Many guests plan their days not only around parade and show schedules, but also meals and dinner shows.

With over 35,000 performances and more than 10 million guests who have seen the show so far, the *Hoop Dee Doo Musical Revue* is one of the most popular dinner shows at the Walt Disney World Resort.

Located in Pioneer Hall at the Fort Wilderness Campgrounds, the *Hoop Dee Doo Musical Revue* is performed three times a night, seven days a week at 5:00, 7:15, and 9:00 pm. As with other advanced dining reservations (ADR), guests call months in advance for one of the coveted seats and there is almost always a cancellation line at each show.

From those who are loyal followers of the show to those who haven't seen it...but will, we are going to explore the history and creation of this loveable goofball of a wilderness vaudeville dinner show.

Ron Miziker, who was not only the creator of many classic pieces of entertainment for the Walt Disney World Resort, but also was involved in every new show at the Resort, was one the creators and writers of the *Hoop Dee Doo Musical Revue*.

The show, which is considered one of the longest, continuously running musicals in American theatre history (if not the longest), holds a special place for everyone who has seen the performance. When you first try to describe the show to someone they will typically look at you skeptical, but interested. It's not until someone experiences the show for the first time do they understand the undying love and affinity for the show.

For all its longevity, the evolution of the *Hoop Dee Doo Revue* has just as many do si do's as a square dance.

PIONEER HALL

After the park had opened, there was a company-wide directive to find ways to increase revenue streams throughout all the divisions. Card Walker, as well as the other park executives, was pushing to maximize the park's facilities to bring in additional revenue. When Pioneer Hall was going into its final design phase there was a heated discussion about some of the design suggestions for the Hall. After getting their food from the cafeteria, the Hall was meant to serve as a "meeting" or "town hall" where guests would go to play various games, to hear lectures, and watch nature films while eating. Originally the Imagineering department wanted Pioneer Hall to be constructed to complement the cafeteria.

Recreating a sturdy lodge in the Northwest Territory, Pioneer Hall, which opened in April 1974, was assembled with 1,283 hand-fitted logs. Since Florida pine trees were not tall enough, nor was their bark suitable, a six-month search went on to find the right trees. The search ended in Montana where Western White Pines had the exact specifications needed. They were packed up and shipped by rail across the U.S. to the Resort. When Pioneer Hall opened, it housed Crockett's Tavern, a full-service lounge and dinner restaurant featuring wall-to-wall, floor-to-ceiling Davy Crockett memorabilia.

Since Pioneer Hall, built after the park had officially opened, was expensive to build, it needed to generate as much revenue as possible. Card reviewed the plan proposed by the Imagineering department and decided that no one would pay to see nature films and hear lectures. He then asked Bob Jani, Vice President of Entertainment and his team to come up with a pioneer show for the Hall. At the time, Bob had three division directors reporting to him: one in charge of show operations at Disneyland, one in charge of show operations at Walt Disney World, and one in charge of show development responsible for creating, developing, and producing projects at all the Disney Park, as well as special large events and shows Disney was called on to do... that person was Ron. Larry Billman, the show director, reported to Ron along with 35 other individuals. Typically once one of Ron's team's shows opened, management of that show was the responsibility of that Park's operating director.

With this new directive, the Entertainment Division looked at the final designs for Pioneer Hall and realized that what was being proposed would not be conducive for a live stage show. Their two biggest objections were the proposed size of the balcony and the size and placement of pillars. They won one battle and lost the other one.

The Entertainment Division objected to the placement and size of the pillars inside because they said they were too wide and would ruin the sight lines for the guests. The pillars, originally constructed from 70 tons of rare ebony stone from North Carolina, remained as they were, but over the years the width of the pillars were reduced. Imagineering had also wanted to install a wide balcony to accommodate multiple rows of tables. The Entertainment Division objected to this and wanted a single row of tables. Their reasoning was that those not in the first row would be so far back they would see little to none of the show. The Entertainment Division won.

According to D23, in 1973, shortly before the *Hoop Dee Doo* was created, the Star Spangled Washboard Band, a New York-based group of country-western musicians, began performing at Pioneer Hall. During the time the *Hoop Dee Doo Musical Revue* was being planned, written, and readied for Pioneer Hall.

Sonny Anderson probably booked this musical group, along with others. Sonny, somewhat independent of Jani's three producers, was responsible for booking all the musicians, bands, headliners, etc for the parks. When each team needed a specific act for a regular or holiday show, Sonny would work with that division to find an act. For example, when Ron needed a circus-style dog act for a Christmas parade, Sonny found and hired the act. Once hired, Ron's team was responsible for integrating them into the parade.

CASTING THE SHOW

Since the show wasn't planned as a permanent show, but something to fill the space and bring in some additional revenue, Walt Disney World started auditioning college students from the summer intern program – the Disney/CalArts Work Experience. The Disney/CalArts Work Experinece was an 11-week work experience program in entertainment that involved both Disneyland and Walt Disney World. The intern program was beneficial to both the students and the company. The students would gain valuable show experience, received classroom instruction, and get eight units of college credit... (and possibly future employment) and the company was able to have an inexpensive source of labor for busy periods. Traditionally there were 97 participating students each year; coming from over 50 universities.

During this time auditions were being held for the three female and three male character performers. Those roles were: Six Bits Slocum and Dolly Drew (comic relief), Jim Handy and Flora Long (the singers), and Johnny Ringo and Claire de Lune (the dancers).

Three of the six original cast included Marilyn Magness, Tony Christopher, and Gary Goddard. Marilyn has held a number of jobs in the entertainment industry including working on projects for Ron's company, Miziker Productions. Today, Marilyn is back at the Disney Company as Creative Director of Parks and Resorts Entertainment. Both Tony Christopher and Gary Goddard went on to successful entertainment careers together and individually at Disney and on their own.

When the summer was over and the college students headed back to school, the *Hoop Dee Doo*, which proved to be an incredibly popular show, continued on. This time auditions were held and on September 5, 1974, Disney performers continue in the six roles.

THE SHOW

According to Ron, the script for the *Hoop Dee Doo* was a collaborative effort. The writers, as with many Disney shows and productions, tried to incorporate something that was a nod to the Disney legacy. In the *Hoop Dee Doo Musical Revue* it was Davy Crockett. Playing off of the coonskin cap and killing the bear wove Davy in. A large section of the show is the Legend of Davy Crockett – complete with bear puns and jokes.

When asked how much of the original script has changed over the years, Ron said that the script is exactly the same from 1974 except for one thing. When the show first started its run – in the show's finale the troupe would ask the audience to stand up on their chairs with their red and white checkered napkins in their hands and wave them high above their heads. Well, due to safety issues and liabilities that part was discontinued. Other than that – everything else is virtually the same. The cast generally follows the script for each performance. However, some of the cast members who typically have been performing the show for quite some time will ad lib on occasion.

THE MUSIC

The principle songwriter was Tom Adair. Tom's first work with Disney was in the fall of 1954. In 1956 his first big project was to write words for George Bruns' score for Sleeping Beauty. When the

Mickey Mouse Club started production, he wrote a few songs for the first season, collaborating mostly with Jimmie Dodd.

Over the years Tom picked up enough music theory from his many associates to try handling some composing. His work can be heard on The Tennessee Ernie Ford Show, then Hazel and The Ann Sothern Show. While working on the latter he met writer James B. Allardice, with whom he formed his newest partnership. Together they wrote scripts for some of the most popular television sitcoms including My Three Sons, I Dream of Jeanie, Gomer Pyle, The Munsters, Maude, and, F Troop. He also wrote Annette Funicello's first hit record, *How Will I Know My Love?*

Ron Miziker said, "Tom was brilliant. You can tell him the idea, theme, or play some music and he would have the lyrics for the song in no time. He was the quickest songwriter I ever knew."

Most of the songs in the show are parodies of actual songs previously recorded by top artists. One of those songs is the opening song of the show – *Hoop Dee Doo*. The song, written by Milton De Lugg and Frank Loesser, was first recorded by Perry Como in March of 1950 on RCA Victor Records. (Como initially didn't want to record the song. He is rumored to have said, "I hate that song. It makes me sick." It stayed in the Top 10 for almost 5 months.) Years later, when Ron was producing Perry's popular television network Christmas specials he asked Perry about the song and if he had ever seen the *Hoop Dee Doo* show. Perry said to Ron, "Why would you ever select that song?" Then Perry asked... in his typical style... if Ron could get him comp tickets to the show!

Most of the *Hoop Dee Doo* song's original music score was kept, but the words were changed to suit the show. And it is typically the song that you will hear most of the guests humming or singing on the way out of Pioneer Hall.

Another popular song in the show is the *All-State Song*. According to D23, two years earlier, a tune called the *All-State Song*, was written for an unproduced Magic Kingdom live experience in Frontierland. The song was resurrected for the *Hoop Dee Doo* show.

The *All-State Song,* which was a take-off of the American folk song, *She'll Be Coming Around The Mountain*, written in the 1800's, was written with a verse for every state in the U.S. as well as verses for some of the more visited foreign countries including Canada. Each performer was given a set amount of states / countries and they memorized those verses. The way it worked was when all the performers moved into the audience and talked with the guests – they would indentify a guest and mention where they were from to the crowd. If that state were not part of their repertoire then the performer whose state it was would sing the verse. Eventually those performers who had performed the show multiple times started to memorize and sing the other cast members' states as well.

THE FOOD

A 1974 brochure states, "*The Pioneer Hall Show* features frontier entertainment nightly in two exciting dinner shows. Adult, $11, Junior (12-17), $8.25, Child (3-11), $5.50." Today, the price structure is based both on age and seating section.

Today, the *Hoop Dee Doo* runs three shows a day every day. In all these years the menu hasn't changed much. The salad course, along with the cornbread, is pre-set on the table. When the players come bursting through they get the show started and continue until the main courses are ready to be served. At that time the servers come through the dining room – literally slamming small metal kettles of fried chicken, smoked barbecued pork ribs, mashed potatoes, and country-style baked beans not on your table but right down on your plates. For dessert, originally it was apple pie, but now the Pioneer Hall Players not only introduce the dessert – strawberry shortcake – but the servers come parading off the stage with the dessert to the tables.

The *Hoop Dee Doo Musical Revue* is one of those shows that may not be on the top of first-time visitors lists, but it should. Once you experience not only the majestic Pioneer Hall, chow down on all-you-care-to-eat vittles, and are thoroughly entertained by the Pioneer Hall Players, but also understand what went into creating this toe-tapping revue it will be on the top of your list for future visits.

About Chuck Mirarchi

Ever since his first visit in 1972, author, blogger, and Disney aficionado Chuck Mirarchi has been a lifelong Disney fan. He has written for a number of Disney-related outlets and currently is a columnist for WDW News Today.

History of the Main Street Electrical Parade

Chuck Mirarchi

From hotels to restaurants, parks and attractions, parades and special events; everyone has their favorite. Every time they eat at a particular restaurant, stay in the same hotel, ride the same ride or see the same parade – it's like it's for the first time. One of those is the Main Street Electrical Parade.

The Main Street Electrical Parade (MSEP) is a nighttime parade that features floats and live performers covered in thousands of electronically controlled lights and a synchronized soundtrack triggered by radio controls along key areas of the parade route.

The parade is known by two different names: at Disneyland it is known as The Main Street Electrical Parade, which is the officially registered name of the parade, and at Walt Disney World it is simply known as Main Street Electrical Parade. The last time the parade was seen at Walt Disney World was on April 1, 2001 before heading cross-country to Disneyland. The parade has undergone a number of incarnations since its debut and the current Disneyland version is expected to arrive pretty much intact at Walt Disney World.

There are a lot of stories out there on Walt Disney World "history" usually consisting of a mix of facts, myths, and urban legends. The stories surrounding the Main Street Electrical Parade are no different. Some report that Walt Disney himself had conversations about the parade and that there needed to be a nighttime parade. If there was indeed a conversation about evening entertainment at Disneyland, it would have more than likely been between Walt & Tommy Walker, who was the entertainment director at the time. And it would have more than likely have been about Magic Music Days – where school bands & choirs come to perform in the park (at Disneyland, the performances happen on the Carnation Plaza Gardens stage).

Ron Miziker, Founder and Creative Director of Miziker Entertainment Group and The Howdy Show in Mesa, Arizona was intimately involved with the birth of the parade. Ron, then Director of Show Development, was the co-creator and producer of the Main Street Electrical Parade.

According to Ron's bio, he started his career in advertising, produced a daily variety show in Cincinnati, and then joined the Disney Company as Director of Entertainment and Show Development. He was responsible for the planning and production of all shows to open at Walt Disney World. Later he was responsible for shows at all the Disney parks including Disneyland, Epcot Center and Tokyo Disneyland including many original shows, spectacular parades, dazzling revues, atmosphere shows, dinner theater shows, celebrity headliner specials, character and animal shows, fireworks, laser extravaganzas and "almost any other kind of production you can imagine." He also participated in the master planning of some of Disney's largest outdoor entertainment projects. Ron left Disney to produce network television specials and numerous other award-winning projects and then returned to the Disney Studios as Producer of television programs including the Wonderful World of Disney. He was then named Vice President of Original Programs and Productions for the launch of the Disney Channel.

Robert Jani oversaw the events for Walt Disney World's grand opening, one of which was the Electrical Water Pageant. Jani was the head of Disneyland Guest Relations from 1955-1957, then after a 10-year hiatus from the company, returned in 1967 as director of entertainment, and was eventually named VP of Entertainment for Disneyland & Walt Disney World.

The Electrical Water Pageant was created not only for the grand opening events at Walt Disney World but also, initially, it served as a backdrop for the Polynesian Luau when the luau was performed on the beach at the Polynesian (before construction was completed on Luau Cove).

The pageant's popularity prompted Disney to make it into its own stand-alone show after the luau moved into its permanent home.

THE BEGINNING

Ron Miziker, who worked under Jani, was asked by Bob if he would take over the planning of all entertainment and shows for Walt Disney World because Bob was having all kinds of production issues with Disney on Parade. Subsequently, Ron became, temporarily, the first Director of Entertainment for Walt Disney World.

Shortly after Walt Disney World officially opened, Ron returned to California where Card Walker, Company President, had called a meeting with Bob Jani and Ron Miziker. Card told them that he had a big problem: not only did Disneyland not have any nighttime business, but also employee morale was low. Since the opening of

Walt Disney World, the Disneyland employees felt little attention was being paid to their park. Card wanted to correct that and quick so he told Bob and Ron that this event should take place at night to keep guests in the park past the early evening hours.

Dick Nunis, Executive Vice President of Walt Disney World and Disneyland, was against working on and implementing the MSEP project. He felt the opening of Bear Band (*Country Bear Jamboree*, March 4, 1972) was enough and there was no need for another big attraction like a parade. Card disagreed with Dick and continued to make the parade a reality.

"The President of The Walt Disney Company said to me if you really believe in this thing then go for it," said Bob Jani. "I don't think one other person in the Company was behind me in this mission."

Ron made his first stop to the local library to research various show ideas. He found one story of particular interest. At the turn-of-the-century big cities, that were the first to get electricity, would hold parades down their main streets with strings of lighted bulbs. This struck Ron as an interesting idea. He went back to Bob and said, "What if we do a parade with lights?"

The overwhelming popularity of the Electrical Water Pageant at Walt Disney World further inspired them to create a west coast equivalent, but instead of being on water, Ron and Bob put wheels to the idea and created The Main Street Electric Parade for Disneyland.

It was almost a literal translation of the Electrical Water Pageant. The first MSEP for Disneyland was mostly a series of flat screen lit images pulled down Main Street by Cast Members. There were a few dimensional floats: the Casey Jr. Train, Mickey's large drum, and the whirly bugs, because they pre-existed and were just fitted with lights, they added the Blue Fairy float, which led the parade.

WE GOT THE IDEA... NOW WHAT?

One of many problems to come up was how to power these street floats. Powering the Electrical Water Pageant was easy; the generators were on the lake. However, for this parade, it was not that easy. The park maintenance department offered the help of one of their electrical engineers, Gerry Hefferly, to come up with a workable power source.

A number of power sources were considered from an assortment of generators to electrifying the tracks in the street, but they still did not have an adequate way to power the parade. The power source had to accomplish three different tasks at the same time: light the bulbs to create the images, power the unit, and power the sound system. "When we first looked at different power sources we had to consider different alternatives," said Gerry. "I have to admit for about a half-a-second I thought about running long extension cords from Small World all the way down to Main Street, but that idea was rapidly put out of my mind."

They reported to Card about their problems. He told Ron and Bob that they, and their team, had about a week to figure out whether it was possible or not. Three days before their deadline, Gerry was working virtually non-stop to figure out the problem. After a number of calculations on various types of batteries he told Ron and Bob that he believed he had the answer.

The Walt Disney Studio had recently purchased a brand new type of battery called nickel-cadmium batteries – commonly known today as NiCad batteries – for lighting and other various film productions. Gerry discovered, based on his calculations, they were more efficient than existing car batteries and, more importantly, would solve their power issue. He determined if they ran the parade in one direction, they could then recharge the batteries and do a second show in the opposite direction.

The week had past and the team went into another meeting with top management to present their findings. They told Card and Dick that they had found a solution to their power problem. Card was ecstatic, but Dick still was against the entire idea. Plans for the parade continued to move forward.

Now that the power issue was resolved there was the matter of where to get the right light bulbs to create the exact desired effect. The team determined the specifications for the ideal bulb for each of the floats. Bob Jani told Ron that he knew of a company in Chicago, the Silvestri Lights Company, who were specialists in little lights and had the technology of how to deal with little light blubs. At the time, this Italian company was the only company manufacturing the tiny Christmas lights. One of the problems was that the lights only came in clear – color bulbs required hand dipping the lights into a color medium.

Planning for the parade took place January and February of 1972. Construction of the floats had to start quickly if they wanted to get the parade up by the mid-June deadline. Relying on Silvestri's working knowledge of lights, they contracted the company in the beginning of March to handle the construction of the floats. With regular updates the team discovered the construction company was falling far behind and not accomplishing what they needed. Ron decided a trip to Chicago was in order. He headed to there to evaluate the situation. "It was a disaster. Very little had been accomplished," exclaimed Ron. "As hard as they tried, Silvestri didn't have enough time or probably the technology to really make the units come together."

Bob and Ron discussed their options by phone and it was decided that the floats would come back to California to be finished. While Ron organized moving vans to ship the floats back to California, Bob began preparations for their arrival, as well as the work that needed to be accomplished. Large circus tents were erected in the back area of Disneyland, and an array of electricians, carpenters and others were hired to begin work on the parade unit pieces. Flying back from Chicago, Ron remembers contemplating that he was flying over a fleet of fourteen moving vans of stuff and with only a few weeks left before the announced opening of this spectacular new parade; none of it was even close to being finished.

Once in California, crews worked around-the-clock on the floats. They cancelled most of the scheduled rehearsals with the performing cast to allow more hours of work on the units. Of the two rehearsals that did take place, the first was an absolute disaster. Some of the units fell apart including Cinderella's canopy of lights. One of the units crashed into a building on Main Street, and two horses (yes, there were several horses with riders in the first version of the parade), fell under the weight of the lighted banners they were carrying. The electricians and other crewmembers became totally dedicated to the task. They were determined to get this parade done and opened on time! In fact, they were working on the floats right up until the moment it premiered, June 17, 1972. As the floats were readying to move from backstage to Main Street, the lights on the units were lit for the first time! Dozens of electricians were still working on the lights and hopping off just before each unit went through the gates into public view. Ron said, "The sight of that happening was like people jumping ship just prior to it sinking. Fortunately the parade was an instant hit!"

THAT MUSIC

From the very beginning, Bob Jani was interested in music from *Fantasia* or calliope music for the parade. However, Jack Wagner, who oversaw music production for Disneyland entertainment, was given the challenge of finding alternate music samples. Jack thought it should be something electronic. He had forty-eight hours to prove Bob wrong. (Bob eventually got to use his calliope music for America On Parade).

A side note about Jack – in addition to him being responsible for finding the music, he had another distinction. He was nicknamed "The Voice of Disneyland." Jack's voice was not only heard over Disneyland's PA system for parades and special events, he also did a lot of voice work for the attractions themselves, including instructions, emergency precautions, and safety spiels. Jack also did some voice work for the Walt Disney World Resort and – what is probably his most famous and popular work to some Disney World fans – his voice can still be heard on the Walt Disney World Monorail System: "Please stand clear of the doors; *por favor mantenganse alejado de las puertas*."

Jack also had one more responsibility with the Main Street Electrical Parade – he provided the very famous announcement for both the original Disneyland Main Street Electrical Parade and Walt Disney World Main Street Electrical Parade. In a vocoded voice, you hear, "Ladies and gentleman, boys and girls, Disneyland/Walt Disney

World proudly presents our spectacular festival pageant of nighttime magic and imagination, in thousands of sparkling lights, and electro-synthe-magnetic musical sounds, The Main Street Electrical Parade!" After the parade concludes, you hear one final announcement before the closing electric fanfare; "Disneyland's/Walt Disney World's Main Street Electrical Parade!"

Jack found a number of musical samples that he thought would work for the parade, but there was one in particular that he was liked the best. They gathered in Bob Jani's office and Jack played each music sample. Jim Christensen, who was the Musical Director, Ron, and others, agreed that there was one piece that was better than the rest, *Baroque Hoedown*. The music, created electronically, was something very new during this time in the music world. According to Don Dorsey website, the electronic sound and its quick, catchy melody were infectious. The tempo was right for choreography and a one-minute and three-second portion could be looped to play continuously; exactly what parade music needed to do.

In 1967, early synthesizer pioneers Jean-Jacques Perrey from France and Gershon Kingsley from Germany created *Baroque Hoedown*. Disney spoke to the composer's agents who agreed to allow them use the music for the parade. Originally, the parade's soundtrack had the same themes as the current recording, but a different arrangement by Jim Christensen and Paul Beaver. In 1977, Don Dorsey and Jack Wagner updated the parade's music at Jack's studio. It was used until January 2009 in Disney's Electrical Parade.

According to Don Dorsey's website, "A quick search of Los Angeles-based musicians turned up synthesizer programmer Paul Beaver. Paul had a small studio and was considered "the only guy" for synth work in Hollywood. On May 17, 1972, Jack and Jim met with Paul for the first time... As they experimented and explored, with Paul programming the electronic sounds and Jim playing the keyboard, two demo tracks were completed. One was a short patriotic medley and the other was the original *Baroque Hoedown* recording with a synth bass line added.

Through discussions with Bob, they decided to build the entire parade on top of *Baroque Hoedown*, a technique similar to *It's a Small World,* where one melody is overlaid with multiple synchronized arrangements. In this plan, instead of moving the audience through the arrangements, the arrangements would move past the audience. Armed with sketches of the parade floats, Jim began the puzzle-like process of fitting Disney melodies into the harmonic structure and format of *Baroque Hoedown*."

He continues to say, "A deal was quickly negotiated… and less than two weeks later, Jack and Jim were back in Paul Beaver's studio recording the masters for the very first Electrical Parade. They created six different musical scenes, each one using *Baroque Hoedown* as the foundation. (Three of those original tracks, *Baroque*, *Alice*, and *The Angry Dragon*, were retired with the original Electrical Parade after its 1974 season but *Cinderella*, *Dumbo*, and the *Patriotic Finale* are still used in the current parade.)

After the summer of 1974, America On Parade, a two-year Bicentennial celebration, replaced the Main Street Electrical Parade. Paul Beaver, who was working on the music for this parade as well, died suddenly. Jack Wagner contacted the Moog Company, the manufacturer of the synthesizer that Paul had used, to see if they knew any local programmers. They suggested a college student, Don Dorsey. He helped to create the Great American Band Organ sound for the patriotic parade.

After Don's work on America on Parade, Jack hired him as his full-time audio production assistant. When the MSEP returned to Disneyland in 1977, Don suggested that they try something different. According to Don's website, "The original parade began with a manually triggered tape of an oscillator sweep, followed by the fade in of the continuous parade music as the lights were turned off. Don wanted to create an exciting musical opening that would incorporate a fanfare that segued directly into the parade tempo. He also wanted to synchronize the light cue to the music for dramatic effect. Because the parade would need this dramatic beginning as it arrived in each different area of the park, Don invented a way to perform automatic synchronized introductions "on demand." This process, called the "opening window" has been used to start Disney parades ever since."

Another important innovation of the Main Street Electrical Parade is that it uses radio-activated triggers as each float enters a zone. When the float passes over a sensor in the street; the audience would hear float-specific music that is synchronized with the lights. Each zone is between 70–100 feet long, and the zoned system means that every person watching the parade would experience the same show, no matter where on the parade route anyone stood.

Don composed the *Electric Fanfare*, reworked the *Underliner/Blue Fairy* track with a livelier bass line and new melody enhancements. He also rearranged the *Alice in Wonderland* section and added creature sounds, and arranged new tracks for *Pete's Dragon*, *Briny Deep/Underwater* and *Disney Neon Finale*. Bob Jani called the new music "electro-synthe-magnetic" and wrote the announcement for the opening sequence.

The parade opened in June 1972. It was such a success that even park guests were requesting copies of the music. Eventually, a seven-inch souvenir disc featuring a colorful graphic of the parade pressed directly into the vinyl went on sale.

In January 1978, Disney took several Electrical Parade floats to the Orange Bowl for a spectacular half-time show produced by Ron Miziker. For the half-time show, introductions and endings for the Alice in Wonderland and Pete's Dragon units were created, along with a grand finale for the Blue Fairy track. Don composed the "Fanfare of Lights" for the finale and used the "opening window" concept in reverse to achieve the musical endings. Bob Jani liked the result so much that the closing fanfare was added to the parades in the summer of 1978.

Over the years, new floats were added while others were retired. Some of the retired floats include: "it's a small world" float, Briny Deep float, the Disneyland 25th Anniversary float, and Mickey Mouse's 60th Birthday float. The Blue Fairy float, which led the parade, was also retired and replaced by the Tinker Bell float. The Title Drum float, near the beginning of the parade, was constructed using a real bass drum, one of the world's largest in 1972. Before that, the drum was used in Disneyland parades in the 1960s.

THE PARADE ON THE MOVE

Disneyland's The Main Street Electrical Parade had an East Coast version with the same name and layout at Walt Disney World Resort. It ran from 1977 to 1991. It was replaced by a similar parade, SpectroMagic, which ran from 1991-1999 and then reopened in 2001. In 1992, the Walt Disney World MSEP transferred to Parc Disneyland at Disneyland Paris and ran there until 2003.

Fantillusion, a nighttime parade from Tokyo Disneyland, replaced the Tokyo version of the Main Street Electrical Parade. Tokyo's current electrical parade, which made is debut in 2001, DreamLights, brought back the style of the original parade with updated music and floats.

After a 24-year run, in 1996 Disneyland's The Main Street Electrical Parade was retired. Light bulbs certified as having been part of the show were sold to collectors. The replacement show, Light Magic, which opened in 1997, proved to be not popular and was quickly cancelled. However, Disney held off bringing back the Main Street Electrical Parade. Instead, as part of Walt Disney World's Millennium Celebration the parade was refurbished and in May 1999 returned for a limited engagement. It ended its run at the Magic Kingdom on April 1, 2001 and SpectroMagic returned the next day.

The Main Street Electrical Parade floats were sent back to California for the parade's return to Disneyland. However, Disney management decided that California Adventure, which recently opened needed a boost. Therefore, on April 25, 2001; Disney announced that the popular parade would be heading there rather than Disneyland. The parade made its appearance in July 2001.

The name of the show also changed from the Main Street Electrical Parade to Disney's Electrical Parade. Most of the 1996 parade floats returned, except for the Pinocchio Pleasure Island section and the Snow White diamond mine float. In 1997, they were sent to Parc Disneyland (Paris). During the 2005 off-season, the entire parade was refurbished. The lights on all of the floats were replaced and the parade name on the drum float was changed to "Disney's Electrical Parade, Presented by Sylvania."

In December 2008, Disney announced that a Tinker Bell float would be added to the parade. This would be the first time since the temporary Mickey Mouse's 60th Birthday float in 1988, that a new float was added to the parade. In the spring of 2009, Disney announced that the Snow White and Pinocchio units would also be returning. Most of the major floats received new LED pixie dust effects as well.

When the parade returned to Disney's California Adventure in June 2009, it began using the updated, orchestrated *DreamLights* soundtrack from Tokyo, but with some changes made, as certain floats in the California parade are not included in the Tokyo parade.

THE MAIN STREET ELECTRICAL PARADE ESCAPES FROM THE PARKS

The first time that some of the MSEP floats were seen outside of a Disney Park was in 1977 at the New York City premiere of Disney's *Pete's Dragon*, a live-action/animated feature-length musical film. Since the film was to premiere at Radio City Music Hall, Ron Miziker thought that it would be great if they could also promote the addition of a new MSEP float, Elliott, the dragon in the movie, at the premiere. Therefore, he arranged with the City of New York to not only bring the MSEP to New York City and parade the floats down Sixth Avenue, but he also got the City to agree to turn off the streetlights on Sixth Avenue.

It was done once again on June 14, 1997 for the opening of the New Amsterdam Theater and *Hercules* movie. With the addition of some *Hercules*-themed floats, the parade was temporarily renamed "The Hercules Electrical Parade". Again, Disney arranged for all the lights to be turned off for eight blocks on Broadway leading up to the theater. Every business complied with the exception of Warner Brothers, who had a Warner Bros. retail store at the crossroads of 42nd Street and Broadway.

The MSEP was also seen during the halftime show of the 1978 Orange Bowl college football game.

If you have ever seen the Main Street Electrical Parade or will be seeing it for the first time you will now be able to appreciate it even more and understand why this has been a guest favorite for 33 years.

History of the Contemporary & Polynesian Resort Hotels

Chuck Mirarchi

When one uses the words landmark and iconic, they typically refer to objects and places that are instantly recognizable by virtually everyone, anywhere on the planet. These words can easily be applied to things like the Statue of Liberty, the Eiffel Tower, and the Taj Mahal. However, for a theme park and resort complex? Never… well except for one place, Disney Parks.

In addition to Mickey Mouse, who is one of the most recognizable symbols in the world, a number of other Walt Disney World symbols also fall into that including Cinderella's Castle and Epcot's Spaceship Earth. Another "landmark" that falls in that category is the Contemporary Resort Hotel.

The Contemporary Resort Hotel and the Polynesian Village Resort (as it was known in 1971) were the first two hotels to open at Walt Disney World on October 25, 1971. On opening day, the Contemporary Resort Hotel truly lived up to its name, but to really appreciate this resort, one must understand the hotel's history.

Disney's original agreement was that they would retain the land these hotels were built on, but would allow US Steel to build and own the hotels. Disney would then lease and run the hotels. There were concerns over the financing for the Florida project so mergers were BRIEFLY considered. One of those companies discussed, prior to Walt's death, was General Electric. According to Bob Thomas, "Roy faced the formidable task of financing... Bankers and financiers told Roy that such an investment was too great [$100 million] for a company the size of Walt Disney Productions. He was advised to seek a large corporation as a partner. GE was approached..." The GE deal was thought of as a way of handling the large financial undertaking for the entire Florida project.

The negotiations ended shortly after Walt realized the merger would put GE execs in charge and that Walt would become an employee and could be fired at anytime. A merger with Westinghouse was also considered, but ultimately Roy found a way to go it alone. The one thing he and Walt had learned early in their careers was to share ownership with no one.

THE EVOLUTION OF THE CONTEMPORARY RESORT HOTEL

In 1964, Walt Disney put "Project X" (later known as "The Florida Project") into motion. After Walt's death in December 1966, Roy put most of Walt's plans for his futuristic city, EPCOT, on hold. However, he incorporated many of EPCOT's ideas and companies – already on board – into the creation of the new Florida park and resort. The birth of the Contemporary Resort Hotel came from Walt's vision for his "Progress City," as well as the involvement of US Steel.

The Contemporary Resort Hotel's design was a collaboration between The Walt Disney Company, United States Steel Corporation and Los Angeles architect Welton Becket. One of US Steel's subsidiaries, American Bridge, had been experimenting with modular construction. They had been promoting constructing, assembling, and furnishing rooms off-site and then stacking them next to the skeleton of the building and then slot each room into the frame of the building.

There are some well-known "facts" that are very prevalent about the construction of The Contemporary Resort. One is that the guest rooms were made to be easily removed, refurbished, and slotted back in. Another was that the rooms had settled into the structure and became stuck thereby unable to be removed. These are wonderful Disney urban legends. The fact is that the rooms were never intended to be removed in this way. When the building was constructed and the rooms were slid into place, the frame was simply steel. After the rooms were in place, the concrete was framed and poured for the thirteen 150-foot tall A-frames thereby making the rooms unmovable from the onset.

The original park plans called for five hotels to surround the lake and face the park. Each hotel would be specifically themed and would complement the view of the Magic Kingdom. The flagship hotel, based on Walt's vision for the high-rise multi-use structure he planned for the center of EPCOT, would be the most futuristic or contemporary in design. The original structure was to be a "city" with an open-atrium building complete with shops, restaurants and a monorail running straight through the building. Because of this hotel's futuristic element, it was positioned in line sight of Tomorrowland.

US Steel's vision for this hotel turned it from a high-rise to an A-frame structure. Becket Associates came up with the architectural elements for the resort. Marvin Davis, of the Walt Disney Company, served as a liaison for the project. Marvin gave the hotel its present-day iconic feel and not that of a box. He also made it more accessible from the outside. The final design of the hotel would see the main building standing at 184-feet high, 468-feet long, and 220-feet wide.

Disney had to overcome a number of construction obstacles. They quickly realized that they could not just slide the rooms in one after another. If they did slot them all in one side of the hotel first, it would not only compromise the integrity of the structure, but it would also throw the hotel frame off balance. Therefore, they had to set up two cranes on either side of the A-frame and alternately slotted in the rooms.

Another problem was the monorail. The original plans called for the monorail to run straight through the middle of the hotel; however, the vibration from the monorail caused the hotel to shake. The contractors said the monorail feature would be impossible. Walt's planners argued that without the monorail the hotel would resemble, "a place where the Goodyear blimp comes to mate." Roy realized that without the monorail the Contemporary would be no different from any of the Hyatt style atrium hotels. All Roy said was "build it." After reengineering the hotel multiple times, the engineers decided to move the monorail to one side of the hotel and anchor the track to the ground instead of the building.

In David Koenig's book, *Realityland: True-Life Adventures at Walt Disney World*, the working title everyone referred to the hotel as was the Contemporary Hotel. Marty Sklar always had reservations about using that name as it might "stick." In early 1971, they came up with the permanent name, the Tempo Bay Hotel. Roy Disney had also known the hotel as the Contemporary Hotel and when he saw the plans for a Tempo Bay Hotel, he wanted to know what that hotel was. When he was told the Contemporary was only the working title, he said, "I just don't like it. I like Contemporary. I like names that are simple and say what they are. The other name is phony and plastic." Shortly after that, everything changed – again – and the hotel bore its new name – the Contemporary Resort Hotel.

THE CONTEMPORARY RESORT HOTEL OPENS – FINALLY

Another misconception – that has become fact – was that construction on most of the resort was running on or close to on time, and the

Contemporary was falling behind. In fact, construction was a challenge in and out of the entire park. For example, in the fall of 1970, only about one year from scheduled opening, the main contractor hired to oversee construction announced that the timeline was unrealistic and suggested that Disney change the planned opening date. Within days of that announcement, the two Joe's – Joe Fowler & Joe Potter – filed the necessary paperwork to create Buena Vista Construction. In the spring of 1971, after a visit east to check on the state of the construction, Dick Nunis was asked if he honestly believed that the Resort would open on time. His response was, "Only if we put the entire force of the Disney Company behind the effort."

The following week he was asked if he would relocate to Florida to ensure that the park opened on time. He moved to Florida on the reassurance that if he needed ANYTHING from another department, he would get it. Over the next few months, he and his team would earn the nickname of "The Nunis Raiders."

The hotel was plagued with various setbacks and difficulties, some were minor, and some were significant. Workers were sleeping on the job, some were creating phantom employees to cash additional checks, and others were outright stealing. The park opened on time, but it took a few more months to complete the Contemporary Resort Hotel tower and garden wings.

According to Charles Ridgway's biography, *Spinning Disney's World*, the Thursday before opening giant construction cranes were still towering over the Contemporary. Since appearance is everything to Disney, the sight of these cranes would not only be unacceptable, but would also spoil the view for the first guests. Therefore, the cranes were dismantled, laid down on the ground, and covered with grass for the remainder of the weekend. The following Monday, the cranes went back up and stayed there working over the hotel until the day before the Grand Opening. In the end, the hotel was completely finished in the New Year, but enough of the rooms were completed to accommodate the Grand Opening day guests and various activities.

During the whole process, the Disney-US Steel relationship grew so strained that it was a constant bother to Roy Disney. A few weeks before his death, Roy negotiated a deal with the company to not only buy their interest in the hotels, but also assume all remaining construction costs. When The Contemporary Resort hotel finally did open to guests, those lucky enough to stay there, and at The Polynesian Village Resort, were paying the *exorbitant* room rates of $28 to $44 per night.

The hotel's original dining outlets included Grand Canyon Terrace Cafe, Grand Canyon Terrace, Top of the World, Gulf Coast Room, El Pueblo, The Dock Inn, Monorail Club Car, The Sand Bar, and the Mesa Grande Lounge. As for shopping: The Contemporary Man, The Contemporary Woman, Plaza Gifts & Sundries, Kingdom Jewels Ltd., The *Fantasia* Shop, The Spirit World, The Captain's Chair, The American Beauty Shoppe, Bay n' Beach, and The Olympiad spa and gym.

Walt Disney World was officially dedicated on October 1, 1971. A few weeks later, the opening ceremonies were broadcast on October 29 as part of The Wonderful World of Disney's coverage. A number of celebrities were included in the broadcast including Glen Campbell, who arrived at the Contemporary by boat. There is an aerial shot of Monorail Green gliding towards the Contemporary Hotel and sailing right in to the hotel. After the doors open up two Disney Hostesses stepped out with Bob Hope right behind. He does about eight minutes of stand-up on makeshift steps off the Grand Canyon Concourse.

As mentioned before, prior to the construction of the Grand Floridian Resort and Spa, the Contemporary Resort Hotel was designated as the flagship hotel for Walt Disney World. Therefore, the hotel needed to provide any service for a guest. Given the fact that when it opened, both the Contemporary Resort and the Polynesian Village Resort were removed from "civilization" therefore by their very nature, they needed to be self-sufficient. So services like a drug store, liquor store, smoke shop, jewelry shop, florist shop, tennis shop, beach shop, game room, men's and women's hair salons, as well as separate men's, woman's and children's clothing stores were found at the resort. These services, for the most part, became loss leaders. They very rarely, if ever, broke-even let alone turned a profit.

THE CONTEMPORARY RESORT HOTEL – PAST, PRESENT & FUTURE

Back in the 70's, guests entered the Contemporary Resort hotel from the ground floor and off to the left, just past the reception desk, they would have encountered conference & meeting rooms. That quickly became the Fiesta Fun Center, a game room & arcade, movie theatre, and 24-hour snack bar. Years later, the center's name was change to the Food and Fun Center. Today it is home to the Wave Restaurant. On the second floor was the Gulf Coast Room, one of two upscale restaurants that required men to wear a jacket. The other was the former Top of the World.

Going through a large doorway, into the Fiesta Fun Center (now the archway leading into the Wave Restaurant), guests went down a short flight of steps. There was a large snack bar on the right side offering hot dogs, nachos, french fries and sodas. Past the seating area, the game room had a variety of pinball machines, shooting games, video games, and several novelty machines including Morgana, a fortuneteller housed in a blue box. When you put your quarter in and selected your zoological sign, a woman's face would appear on a head mounted inside a viewing window – a la the Haunted Mansion. She gave a few seconds of mystical insight and then would vanish. In the back was a theater that showed Disney movies, and a few ski ball machines. In the room's southwest corner was a light-activated shooting gallery. The Shooting Gallery survived only until the mid-1980s, but the game room (later the Food & Fun Center) received a few updates before closing and converted to The Wave Restaurant. Some of the games were relocated to the fourth floor in an area that was once the original Fantasia shop.

The fourth floor, or Grand Canyon Concourse Level, of the Contemporary Resort Hotel has seen the most dramatic and constant change to the resort. In the beginning, the north end of the Grand Canyon Concourse Level housed a souvenir shop, Plaza Gifts and Sundries, and The Spirit World. Here, guests could buy Disney merchandise, toiletries, flowers and floral arrangements, food and snacks, soft drinks, liquor, and tobacco products. Today it is the Concourse Sundries & Spirits. On the opposite side were the Contemporary Man, the Contemporary Woman, and Kingdom Jewels, Ltd., where guests could purchase men's and woman's clothing and beachwear, as well as costume and fine jewelry. Today the entire location is home to Bayview Gifts. Fantasia Gifts, which stands between these two shopping areas in the middle of the Concourse used to be open lobby space with some seating and funky tree-shaped lighting.

On the south end of the Grand Canyon Concourse, the dining areas have also seen tremendous changes in recent years. Today's Contempo Cafe was originally the home to the Terrace Buffeteria, also known as the Grand Canyon Terrace, then the Concourse Grill, and then the Concourse Steakhouse. The current version of Chef Mickey's also underwent a number of incarnations in years past including the Pueblo Room, Contemporary Cafe, and Coconino Cove (referred to as the Coconino Grove). The space before Coconino Cove was air. Actual air! There was nothing there originally but the outside of the building. They built that section out to make the Coconino Cove cocktail lounge and today it is the dining area for Chef Mickey's, one of the more popular character dining restaurants. From empty space to the Monorail Club Car, the area is now the Outer Rim Lounge.

Moving up to the 15th floor, the Top of the World (also known as the Top of the World Supper Club) was the place to be. It was also the place to see classic Vegas-style performers like Mel Torme, Donald O'Connor, Rosemary Clooney, Barbara Eden, Phyllis McGuire, and many more. There was also dinner and dancing to a full Top of the World orchestra. In the early 1980's, a new show premiered at the Top of the World, Broadway at the Top. Top of the World, along with Mesa Grande Lounge – later called the Top of the World Lounge – offered not only some of the best views of the Magic Kingdom and the fireworks, but also the most scenic brunch around. Although The Top of the World was not very profitable, it was a necessity from not only a prestige point of view, but it also gave guests something to do after dark. The Top of the World closed in 1993 to make way for the current, and spectacular, California Grill Restaurant.

The Walt Disney World Resort continued to grow in popularity throughout the years, and just as each of the theme parks was a major attraction, people flocked to the Contemporary Resort Hotel and the Polynesian Village Resort as if they were… and did become…

attractions in their own right. To this day, all of the Disney Resort hotels have become attractions.

Through the years, more and more groups started holding meetings and conventions at the resort hotels – easily mixing business and pleasure. Seeing the need to be able to continue to host larger groups and shows, in November of 1991 Disney opened a 90,000 square foot convention center, where a parking lot once stood, on the southwest corner of the hotel property. They got an A for effort, but a D for not keeping it in the same style.

THE GRAND CANYON CONCOUSE MURAL

The Contemporary Resort Hotel is known for a number of things. In addition to the A-frame structure, slotted rooms, and monorail, the resort is known for its soaring 90-foot mural.

Walt Disney was fascinated with the Grand Canyon; so it comes as no surprise that many aspects of it pop up throughout the cavernous Contemporary.

Mary Blair, who was an animator, Imagineer, and Disney Legend, designed the mural. She worked on many Disney projects including *The Three Caballeros*, *Song of the South*, and *Cinderella*. Because of her use of color and the child-like way she approached her work, Walt had asked her to work on a new project he was working on for the 1964-65 New York World's Fair – It's A Small World. For the Contemporary Resort, Mary created the world's largest handmade mosaic featuring a modern southwest theme.

The mural, which is classic Mary Blair, took more than a year and a half to design, produce, and install on six, ninety-foot walls. The mural's design incorporated her Southwest Indian children, stylized birds, animals, flowers, and trees. Her drawings were originally used throughout the resort's lobby and as framed prints in the rooms. The giant mural, which also conceals the hotel's elevator shafts, shows Native American Indian children standing along the slopes of the Grand Canyon. The mural that faces the monorail has a goat with five legs, up near the top. Blair did that to honor the culture of the Grand Canyon Indian tribes who felt that artwork could not be "perfect."

Her inspiration for the mural came from a broad spectrum of resources, including prehistoric petroglyphs, Pueblo murals, and Navajo ceremonial art - such as sand paintings. The mural and concourse colors reflect earth and sky tones found at the Grand Canyon, as well as in Indian art.

Each of the more than 18,000 individually hand painted and fire-glazed ceramic tiles were shipped from California to Florida on special air-suspension trucks to prevent them from breaking. The glazes used on the tiles are made from mineral and chemically bases. For example, real gold was used to make the color pink.

ALMOST IMMEDIATE REDECORATING

When the park opened, people flocked to the resort and clamored to stay at one of the only two hotels right at the Magic Kingdom. The 1000+ rooms were full all the time. Since the average resort stay was two to two and a half days, the room turnover was tremendous. Not only was the turnover tremendous, but also the wear-and-tear on the rooms was magnified. As such, room refurbishment began almost immediately. In the fall of 1972, Disney started a continuous rehab of the rooms, eight at a time. By 1975, every room at the Contemporary Resort Hotel had been completely overhauled from top to bottom… only to start again. Each room received new carpeting, drapes, and a new color scheme. Large maps of the Magic Kingdom hung in each room, and to make clean-up easier vinyl wallpaper replaced traditional wallpaper. To reduce "souvenir seekers" from acquiring items not sold at the resort, that is everything that originally had the Walt Disney World logo, (a globe-like circle with Mickey ears in the middle of a large capital D) from dishes to towels to trashcans and virtually anything that was not nailed down – the company replaced them with generic ones.

THE NORTH GARDEN WINGS TAKES FLIGHT

In November 2006, Disney filed plans for a project on the site of the Contemporary Resort's North Garden Wing and erected a construction fence encompassing the wing, part of its parking lot, and Disney's Racquet Club. The North Wing itself was demolished in 2007 and construction on the new building continued throughout the year… with Disney never making an official announcement as to what they were building.

Originally dubbed "Project Crystal" in the Disney boardrooms, on September 2008, Disney unveiled their plans, Bay Lake Tower at Disney's Contemporary Resort. The units are not only part of an offering from the Disney Vacation Club, but some are available for regular guests. Some of the resort's features include full-length windows with views into the Magic Kingdom or onto Bay Lake and some bathrooms, on the Magic Kingdom side, include movable partitions to permit watching the park's fireworks displays from the bathtub.

Bay Lake Tower, which opened on August 4, 2009, offers 295 units including studio, one-, two-, and three-bedroom units with a majority facing either the Magic Kingdom or Bay Lake.

The tower has a pedestrian bridge connecting to the original A-frame tower. The new addition also includes its own set of amenities including a swimming pool with a water slide, tennis and shuffleboard courts, zero-entry pool, and a cookout pavilion.

Atop Bay Lake Tower is a "resurrected" Top of the World Lounge. The lounge, which is only accessible to Disney Vacation Club Members after 5 pm, includes a viewing deck and an indoor seating area with a full bar and appetizers. Guests can view the Magic Kingdom fireworks display from the viewing deck with the firework's music simultaneously piped in through speakers along the deck's wall.

Unlike the convention center, which is perceived as a total disconnect in design to the Contemporary Resort Hotel, Bay Lake Tower is a perfect complement to the resort.

ONE MORE BIT OF CONTEMPORARY TRIVIA

Many presidents have visited both Disneyland and / or Walt Disney World, but none has had more of a connection to the parks than Richard Nixon. Vice-President Nixon and his family were at Disneyland to cut the ribbon dedicating the monorail and he visited Epcot prior to its opening. However, what is considered his most famous – and notorious visit – came on November 17, 1973. During the height of the Watergate crisis, President Nixon spoke in front of 400 Associated Press managing editors in one of the meeting rooms on the second floor at the Contemporary Resort.

During his speech, Nixon said, "People have got to know whether or not their President is a crook. Well, I'm not a crook."

THE POLYNESIAN (VILLAGE) RESORT

Like the Contemporary Resort Hotel, the Polynesian Village Resort was also designed by Welton Beckett, constructed by US Steel Realty Development, used the same pre-constructed modular rooms for the longhouses, and was strategically positioned to be on a specific axis and line sight… this time with Adventureland.

The first thing most people will notice about the Polynesian Resort Hotel is that it underwent a slight name change – when it opened on October 1, 1971 the hotel was known as the Polynesian Village Resort Hotel. In the 1980's, Disney dropped "Village" from the name and now it is simply known as the Polynesian Resort Hotel.

Another change, one that guests never knew about or saw, was the design of the hotel. The original design of the resort called for a large pyramid structure at the entrance that would have included the lobby, shops, meeting space, and guest rooms. Additional guest rooms would have been located in sprawling, low-storied hut-like structures behind the hotel and stretching out towards the beach. In 1970, that design had changed in its entirety and what we know today as the Great Ceremonial House and the various longboat structures took its place.

The Polynesian Village Resort, like its sister hotel The Contemporary Resort, had its own share of renovations, additions, and deletions. In the 70's there were a number of minor decorative changes, but the major renovations included the addition of a formal Luau Cove and a guest room expansion.

The 1980's and 90's saw an increase in Resort changes. In the 80's, additional guest rooms were added, as well as décor changes to the guest rooms and public spaces including the walkway from the Resort to the Ticket and Transportation Center. The 90's saw a 'philosophy' change in the way the hotel ran. The general manager and other cast members, along with the help from some native Hawaiians, changed the way people worked at the hotel. Many say that the hotel now has a more authentic feel. One of the other big changes was the renaming of all but one of the Longhouses.

In the millennium, the Polynesian Resort saw some of the most significant changes in its history. They included not only a new pool, a revamped luau show – now called The Spirit of Aloha, and major renovations to their guest rooms, dining and shopping outlets, but also received a AAA-rated Four Diamond Award.

THE LONGBOAT HOUSES

In addition to the Great Ceremonial House, the 23,000 square foot lobby, modeled after a Tahitian royal assembly lodge, the hotel opened with 8 longhouse buildings housing 492 guest rooms. The original eight-longhouse buildings were Bali Hai, Bora Bora, Hawaii, Fiji, Samoa, Tahiti, Tonga, and Maui. Using traditional construction methods as opposed to the pre-fabricated modular method used in the past, three more longhouses were added: the Oahu in 1978 (this year the Maui longhouse was renamed the Maori), and in 1985 the Moorea and Pago Pago were added. This addition brought the total number of guest rooms to its current 847.

In 1999, to represent the Polynesian islands accurately, ten of the Resort's longhouses were renamed. With the exception of Fiji, the Bali Hai longhouse became Tonga; Bora Bora became Niue; Hawaii became Samoa; Maori changed again to rarotonga; Moorea became Tahiti; Oahu became Tokelau; Pago Pago became Rapa Nui; Samoa became Tuvalu; Tahiti became Aotearoa, and Tonga became Hawaii. Some of the longhouse names did not disappear, but flipped to another building to reflect a more accurate geographic location to their real island counterparts.

Excluding the three-story rock and waterfall rainforest, much of the Great Ceremonial House has undergone dramatic changes including the green & blue tiled floor giving way to an earth-toned slate lobby, as well as the dining and retail outlets.

THE POLYNESIAN RESORT HOTEL – PAST, PRESENT & FUTURE

The Polynesian Resort's past restaurants included the Papeete Bay Verandah and the Coral Isle Coffee Shop, Tambu Lounge, Captain Cook's Hideaway Lounge and the Barefoot Snack Bar. The Papeete Bay Verandah was a French Colonial restaurant that served breakfast, lunch, and dinner with nightly floorshows – the Polynesian Review. It was closed in the latter half of 1994 and reopened in 1995 as Ohana's. The Coral Island Cafe became the Coral Island Coffee Shop and today is the popular Kona Cafe. The other dining outlets have survived in one form or another.

Shopping options at the hotel during the earlier years included The Polynesian Princess, Robinson Crusoe, Esq., Village Drugs & Sundries, Trader Jack's Grog Shop (aka Trader Jack's Grog Hut) and News From Civilization. Later on came Kanaka Kids, Maui Mickey's News from Polynesia, and Outrigger's Cove. None of these retail outlets exists in their original state, but some remnants have survived.

For the first three weeks in October of 1971, between opening day and Grand Opening, Disney World hosted press from around the world. Part of their experience was a luau on the beach of the Polynesian Village. Unfortunately, all six luaus were rained out and they moved indoors. For the Grand Opening television special it did not rain and a spectacular luau was held on the beach. In addition, that night the Electrical Water Pageant sailed across the Seven Seas Lagoon for the first time. To this day, both of these opening events are now Walt Disney World classics.

Shortly after the Resort had opened, and until 1978, guests would have found a Chinese Junk docked at the hotel. Originally known as the Outrider, the ship's name was changed to the Eastern Winds. According to March 20, 1979 edition of *The Virgin Island Daily News*, the sixty-five foot Chinese Junk was built in Hong Kong in 1964 and went through a number of owners including a Texas oil tycoon and Joe Namath. Disney used the vessel as a floating nightclub, lounge, private charters, and a backdrop for promotional materials. Its last known location was St. Thomas where the ship was used for pleasure cruises. Other watercrafts that were once available were a 40-foot Polynesian War Canoe and Bob-A-Round boats.

ALOHA TO THE WAVES

Dick Nunis thought that waves crashing into the shore of the Polynesian Village would give guests a more realistic experience so there was a wave machine installed in the Seven Seas Lagoon off the shore of the Polynesian's beach – on the coastline of Beachcombers Island. The wave machine worked…too well in fact. The crashing waves caused so much beach erosion that is was abandoned. Most of the wave machine was sunk in the Lagoon as a reef; however, a small piece of it can still be seen off the Island – mostly from aerial shots.

THE POLYNESIAN RESORT AND MUSIC HISTORY

Not to be outdone by The Contemporary Resort, The Polynesian Resort holds its own place in infamy. In May Pang's book, *Instamatic Karma: Photographs of John Lennon*, she writes, "At the end of 1974, after three years of court battles and acrimony, the final dissolution of The Beatles was about to happen. The meeting was scheduled for December 19 at New York's Plaza Hotel - ironically, this was the first place the group stayed in America in 1964. George Harrison was in New York on his Dark Horse tour. Paul and Linda McCartney came in, and of course, John and I were already in the city. Only Ringo was missing, but he had signed the documents in England."

"George, Paul, assorted lawyers and family members were at The Plaza and were waiting on John to arrive. George said out loud what everyone was thinking: 'Where's John?'...I was with John and it was up to me to tell Harold he had decided not to attend the meeting. Although John was concerned with shouldering a major tax burden because he lived in the United States... His official reason for not showing was 'the stars aren't right.'"

"John, Julian, and I left New York the following day to spend Christmas in Florida. On December 29, 1974, the voluminous documents were brought down to John in Florida by one of Apple's lawyers."

“Take out your camera, he joked to me...He finally picked up his pen and, in the unlikely backdrop of the Polynesian Village Hotel at Disney World, ended the greatest rock ‘n’ roll band in history by simply scrawling John Lennon at the bottom of the page.”

Each of the original resorts has their own unique history and stories to tell. In the end though they have remained as popular as ever and that is a testament to the vision that was set forth from Walt, Roy and the original team.

Walt Disney World Resorts That Never Were

Lou Mongello

When looking back into Walt Disney World's past, we often think of extinct attractions, shows, or even some of our favorite places to dine. But many people may never know of the incredibly-themed resorts that were once planned for, yet never came to be. Properties that would have changed the literal landscape of Walt Disney World, as well as afforded Guests experiences unlike any other.

Beginning near the Magic Kingdom in 1971, the Polynesian Village and Contemporary Resorts sat on the monorail loop, nestled on the shores of the Seven Seas Lagoon and Bay Lake, respectively. But when Walt Disney World was first being planned, things were set to look a little different. Believe it or not, the Grand Floridian was not part of the original concept for this part of the property. In fact, there weren't going to be just three hotels on these shores, but five!

The planned resorts were the Contemporary (which would be the "flagship resort"), the Polynesian Village, and the unrealized Asian, Persian, and Venetian resorts. While the Contemporary and Polynesian opened as planned in conjunction with the Magic Kingdom in 1971, the other three resorts were to be built over the following five years.

Walt Disney Productions President Donn B. Tatum explained that other hotels would "*be ready to meet the demands of our audience as experience dictates.*" These resorts, which were some of the very first "themed" properties in the world, were the Asian, the Persian, and the Venetian. The concept of theme was actually novel at the time, and as Disney explained, they would be "planned around a single theme that represents a culture or architectural style around the world... In design motif, food specialties, recreation activities, convention facilities and even the type of entertainment to be presented, these major hotels will complement each other and the attractions of the theme park."

The 500-room Asian hotel was set to be the first resort to be built, with construction set to begin in early 1974. The hotel would have consisted of a large center tower building more than 160 feet tall with a high-end restaurant on top, and convention facilities located underneath the main guest areas.

By December of 1971, prep work on the site had already begun, as a large, square piece of land that extended out into the Seven Seas Lagoon was prepared. Unfortunately, plans were scrapped for the resort in 1973, and the area was left barren for almost 15 years until the Grand Floridian opened on that site in 1988.

The second resort, the **Venetian**, was set to be located between the Transportation and Ticket Center and the water bridge between Bay Lake and the Seven Seas Lagoon. Designed as a small harbor with a series of canals, its main building would have housed 500 rooms and resembled St. Mark's Square, complete with a 120-foot campanile. (Sound familiar? Take a look at the Italy pavilion in Epcot). Imagine visiting the hotel's various shops by riding a gondola through the waterways.

While this project was also abandoned in 1973, it was reconsidered briefly in the early 1990s. At that time, Chairman Michael Eisner was considering building a new hotel, but the Venetian idea was discarded in favor of a **Mediterranean** Resort at the same location. Themed after a small Greek island, the resort would have served as Disney's flagship, 5-star property. Styled after Mediterranean beaches, the hotel was to house 760 rooms in 12 buildings, as well as have two full-service restaurants. Rather than have a monorail station, it would have a large marina, with watercraft being used as the primary means of guest transportation.

However, a problem that plagued the Mediterranean would also have befallen the Venetian. During initial tests, wet, swampy soil on land that had been cleared revealed that no structure could be built on that site.

The last of the Magic Kingdom resorts would have been the **Persian**. Located on the shores of bay Lake, its presence would not only have changed the resort landscape, but the monorail route as well., as it would have had the line passing through it, much like the Contemporary.

Instead of the monorail curving from the Contemporary to the station located at the front of the Magic Kingdom, it would have continued north to the Persian Resort, then curved around through the park to a station in Tomorrowland. Following that stop, the monorail would continue to a stop in front of the Magic Kingdom, and then on to the Asian.

The theming of the resort was described best by Disney itself in an early guidebook:

> *"Stepping right out of The Arabian Nights is the Persian resort which will reign like an exotic far-Eastern palace on the Northwest shore of the lake. Jewel-like mosques and columns will rise above landscaped courtyards, while terraced sundecks offer sculptured swimming pools and 'old Persian' dining facilities."*

The resort's main building would have been octagonal in shape, with a 24 foot dome which would have housed the entrance area and meeting facilities. Decorated in whites and blues, the 500 rooms would radiate out from the central lobby.

Sadly, this very unique and opulent property also never left the drawing boards and modeling tables.

In 1982, plans for another resort were revealed, **Cypress Point Lodge**. A smaller hotel, it would have been located on the south shore of Bay Lake near the Fort Wilderness Campground. In addition to the 550 rooms, it would also be home to 50 log cabins – on the beach! Themed after a turn-of-the-century hunting lodge resembling Yellowstone Lodge, nestled in a deep forest, it was set to be one of the most immersive experiences on property.

> *Cypress Point Lodge will offer a romantic notion of a turn-of-the-century hunting lodge secluded in a deep forest. Neither the trees nor the buildings dominate the entire area; but blend together in a natural harmony... One can almost hear the crackling fireplace and feel the large wooden beams offer a haven of security and comfort.*
>
> *Cypress Point Lodge will also include: two restaurants, a pool, extensive beach, and lake dock. Guests will commute in and out of Cypress Point Lodge by watercraft.*
>
> *–Walt Disney World Eyes & Ears, November 4, 1982*

Want to see where it was planned to be located? Look for a cleared chunk of forest along the southwestern shore of Bay Lake across from Contemporary – that would have been the site of Cypress Point.

According to Walt Disney Productions' 1974 annual report, inflation, the gas crisis and other factors took their toll on the U.S. and the Disney Company, forcing plans for the new resorts to be scrapped. However, the Cypress Point idea did not die (as no good idea ever dies at Imagineering), and guests now have many of the Cypress Point themes and features in Disney's Wilderness Lodge.

Then again, the idea of 50 cabins nestled along the shores of Bay Lake sounds like the makings of a wonderful option for a Disney Vacation Club Resort... but that's just me.

Speaking of Wilderness Lodge, there were also plans at one point to resurrect the nearby Fort Wilderness Railroad, which had operated from 1973 until 1977.

It is well known that Walt Disney had a love of trains, and he also believed that on some level, most everyone also was fascinated as well, which is why he featured a railroad prominently in his designs of Disneyland, and eventually Walt Disney World. The Fort Wilderness Railroad was a unique and prominent feature of the campground, and transported guests throughout the resort (a necessity because of its sheer size), and also added to the allure of being transported out of modern-day central Florida, and instead escape into another time and place.

The Fort Wilderness Railroad only existed for a few years due to a variety of operational issues. And although the trains were put in storage for many years, some turned up around Walt Disney World - some as the original ticket booths at Pleasure Island, while another car could be found in the Typhoon Lagoon parking lot.

But during Michael Eisner's "Disney Decade" in the early 1990's, there were plans to rebuild the railroad. But instead of simply taking guests through the confines of the Fort Wilderness Resort & Campground, it would transport them to a new resort in between

Fort Wilderness and Wilderness Lodge, with a station near what is currently the Villas.

Known as "**Buffalo Junction**," (also referred to as "**Fort Wilderness Junction**"), this Moderate resort would have been an incredibly well-themed, western railway town. The 600-room resort was planned as part of the Disney Decade's goal to significantly expand the Walt Disney World resort's offerings to guests.

Imagine more than simply a series of buildings with a western theme. Instead, picture an entire themed area and 19th century town, with horses along the sawdust-strewn streets, and appropriately-themed shopping, dining and entertainment offerings - much like the Cheyenne Resort in Disneyland Paris, which extends the Frontierland story and experience from the Magic Kingdom. In fact, plans included creating a version of the incredibly popular Buffalo Bill Wild West Show from Disneyland Paris as well.

Unfortunately, due to a downturn in the economy in the early 90's, plans for Buffalo Junction (and many other projects developed as part of the "Disney Decade") were put on hold indefinitely.

But not every new resort was going to be centered around the Magic Kingdom area. In fact, going back to May of 1982, Dick Nunis, then executive vice president of Walt Disney World and Disneyland, said in an interview in Eyes & Ears (Walt Disney World's internal Cast Member newsletter), that Walt intended to develop

> *"....an area where all types of corporations, governments, and academia could come together to really try and solve some of the problems that exist in the world today. We started with the recreation area, and then began the community, which is Walt Disney World Village, and now we're building the center... Epcot Center, and we're going to connect it all with the monorail system... In addition, we have some dreams for the Walt Disney World Village. From the Empress Lilly, we're going into a New Orleans street, and you'll walk right into a beautiful New Orleans hotel."*

That's right. In what is now known as Downtown Disney, located near what is Fulton's Crab House (formerly the Empress Lilly), would have been a New Orleans-themed resort. Plans were underway to extend the monorail, and even displayed a scale model showing the Walt Disney World Village expanded to include office buildings, more shopping venues, a monorail station, and even a *PeopleMover* to help transport guests throughout the complex.

The area in front of the Empress Lilly would have been analogous to Disneyland's New Orleans Square. According to the proposed story, the Empress Lilly had just pulled up to the dock in New Orleans to unload passengers and goods. Across the plaza would be a magnificent and ornate resort, with shopping on the lower levels and guest rooms on the upper.

Again, like Buffalo Junction and Cypress Point, because of the economy, and changes within the Disney Company, with Michael Eisner and Frank Wells joining the company in 1982, just two years after Dick Nunis spoke about these projects, they never were fully realized (although the New Orleans theme would eventually find a home at Port Orleans).

While rumors of themed resorts with similar concepts to those that never made it off the drawing board many decades ago being built in Walt Disney World surface from time to time (most notably the idea of a Mediterranean Resort or Disney Vacation Club property realizing the Buffalo Junction dream), it's always fun to wonder what could have been… and speculate as to what may be next.

Lou Mongello *left the practice of law and his IT consulting company to pursue his passion and follow his dream of sharing his love for Walt Disney World with others. He is the author of the Walt Disney World Trivia Books and Audio Guides to WDW. He is also the host of The WDW Radio Show, voted Best Travel Podcast for 2006, 2007, 2008 and 2009. The show, products, blog, videos and discussion forums can be found at http://WDWRadio.com. Lou is also the publisher of Celebrations magazine, a print publication dedicated* *to the magic of Walt Disney World (http://CelebrationsPress.com) and founder of the Dream Team Project, which raises money for the Make-A-Wish Foundation of America. He has appeared on television and radio as a Disney expert, and has been interviewed for, written about and featured in: the Orlando Sentinel, StarWars.com, Robert Scoble, Southern Living magazine, Cookie magazine, Fodor's and many others, and he speaks around the country at fan gatherings, as well as educational and corporate events.*

Goodnight, George:
A Ghost Story

Foxx Nolte

What follows may rate as a bizarre exercise in nostalgia, if you will permit it, and so I most humbly suggest that it be read in a whimsical state of mind. I will attempt to faithfully relate the colorful stories and myths, as they were first told to me, which make up such a vital part of the oral tradition of the Walt Disney World "underground". So much of this tradition is unrecorded and so the reader may, as she chooses, read the following merely as an account of the superstitions and urban legends which are whispered through break rooms and utilidors. Those of us who worked there, however, will probably never be as sure...

> *"The most famous faux fatality was 'George', the imaginary welder who was killed during the construction of Pirates of the Caribbean... [...] The imaginary victim is most likely a Disneyified amalgam of the actual fatalities at Disney World..."* - *David Koenig,* *Realityland*

The first day I ever walked into Pirates of the Caribbean was a bright Florida winter morning in 2005. I don't mean I rode it - I walked into it, through a tunnel, around a large pool of water, opened a door which looks so real and textured from the boats but is really a painted plywood flat, and was looking right at a grotesque mannequin of a fat woman. She has no legs, just a pole extending up into her body, and up close the already garish makeup was like a clown's face. The building was quiet and still, the water glassy and calm, and the figures… they were twitching. Those things move after they're turned off, a sort of spasm occasionally at the wrist or neck. But the eeriest thing was the silence - it isn't until you've seen a Disney park utterly abandoned and quiet and left to the painters and pressure washers and mechanics that you realize that they aren't places for human beings, and that all that warmth you feel in the bright light of day comes from that reassuring music, the crowd, the faces. Under worklights and powered down, those attractions are more like ghost houses, museums staffed by nobody for a crowd that may never return.

Eventually a voice echoed from the PA system: "Good morning, George."

On page 144 of *Realityland*, David Koenig reveals a fact I have long suspected, which is that in his years of research he has failed to find any mention of a fatality regarding the construction of Pirates of the Caribbean, the death of a young man named George. Since Koenig's research is otherwise maddeningly complete regarding all manner of death and dismemberment at Walt Disney World, I have no reason to doubt him. However, that does not remove the fact that for those of us working at Pirates of the Caribbean then and, I'm sure, to the Cast Members working there today, George was a day to day reality.

George has a way of making a believer of you. A day of constant and inexplicable breakdowns, a door that will not open for you and only you, or the strange way you often feel followed while crossing one of the attraction's many crosswalks, eventually you too will meet George. Who he really is and why he is called "George" will probably forever be a mystery. You can, after all, call a ghost whatever you want.

Now Cast Members are a strange and fairly superstitious bunch, perhaps by necessity. When you're working at an aging attraction and walking through corridors which sunlight has not penetrated in some 40-odd years, a rather Gothic mindset becomes something of an occupational hazard. Those twisted backstage corridors are dark and scary places, full of disused props, dark and winding paths, and sounds both distant and near from some unidentifiable source; the hiss of compressed air or the dripping of some water pipe or air conditioning unit. Add these work environments to attractions which by dint of age or another agent may start or stop for reasons rarely explicable, and a paranoid atmosphere is inevitable. It may be outside the realm of supernatural behavior that a ride is unreliable, but what about a ride that only breaks at 4 pm on Sundays? Or that lone footfall you heard when you were alone in the backstage corridor? Keeping rides working sometimes seems less to be a matter of technical mastery and more one of kharma and blind faith.

And so such stories arise. There were the whispers that the whole of the Animal Kingdom theme park was built on sacred burial grounds and that prior to opening Imagineering had Native American shamen on property to placate the angry spirits. I've never heard of wispy figures wandering Animal Kingdom in the dead hours of night, but then again the park is never open late enough for anybody to be sure. But stories of a figure near the load area of Kilimanjaro Safaris, visible only on rainy or misty days, are told, a shape of some sort where rain does not fall, just in the shape of a man, right alongside the jeeps as they careen off into the jungle.

Perhaps in a variation of the phantom hitch-hiker tale, stories of a straggling guest who you can never quite catch up to after park closing - always walking away from you - have been circulating for years, especially on Main Street – a woman with a bag, or sometimes just a grayish shape. In late night jaunts through Tomorrowland, gathering abandoned strollers after the park had closed to push back onto Main Street for collection, I know I saw some figures that should not have been there. I'm fairly sure I saw that woman with the bag walking off into the shadows at least twice. Or maybe not, maybe it just shadows, after all - Tomorrowland is a dim place at night. Less explicable were frantic, clanging steps up and down metal staircases I heard backstage on several occasions – but never a corporeal body on the staircase to cause such a sound. When this happens a few times you get to wondering.

I've heard of inexplicable shadowy forms appearing in empty Star Tours Star Speeders, forever jumping light speed to Endor, visible only on security cameras. Perhaps nearly every attraction of any substantial age must have a few ghosts, whether by inheritance or invention. There will always be new hires to scare and oral traditions to carry on, after all.

And so George, the typical story goes, was a young man who, while welding or perhaps bolting in a high area of the superstructure of the building which would one day become Pirates of the Caribbean, met with a horrible accident and fell to his death. From day one of the operation of the attraction - December 15, 1973 - inexplicable events plagued the attraction. Breakdowns were constant and unmotivated. Female Cast Members were mysteriously patted on their rear or had their bra straps snapped. Stories of George grew. In the early years, it is said that an old woman would often enter the ride and ask for a boat to herself. On the in-ride security cameras, she could be seen weeping and talking to nobody. There were stories that she was talking to her son - George.

A second component of the story comes into play surrounding the Down Ramp, or waterfall, and it is partially confirmed by Koenig - although his version differs significantly from the version traditionally told. At the very bottom of the Down Ramp, the boats take a sharp left turn to proceed into the show building behind the Walt Disney World Railroad tracks. This turn is the single point in the ride where the sides of the metal troth that guide the boats through the attraction poke above the water... although it is a hazard for any hand trailing in the water, the boats are safely steered through the "Down Ramp

Runoff" area and into the famous scene of the pirate ship attacking the fort known as Bombardment Bay. Legend tells us that for a few months these raised metal guides were not present, which resulted in one particularly light boat hitting the bottom of the drop, hydroplaning out of the troth, and killing a woman sitting in the front row. Whether by George or by fate, this woman (sometimes there are two of them) entered into myth and became perhaps the most feared inhabitant of Pirates of the Caribbean.

George casts a long shadow over the Cast imagination. The town scenes which constitute the bulk of the Florida version of the show are contained in a single, huge room which has a large, central pillar supporting its' roof. The top of this pillar is decorated to appear to be a multi-windowed tower, and can be seen to the right of Carlos' house in the Well scene. If you are lucky, you may even see a lonely little light burning in it. This pillar is supposedly the very one which George fell from, and his initials, carved on the bottom of the pillar, cannot be painted over - they will bleed through the paint. The tower is called "George's Tower" - a play on the term for the ride's central control booth overlooking the Load area, called "Tower" - and it has a special trick to it. If one sees a light burning in George's tower from the Well scene, it means that George is "home". If you get to the fire scene and look back up to George's Tower (the two scenes are only a few feet away from each other, on the other side of the village facades), and if that light is still burning in George's Tower - it often is not – then, you are inevitably told by your trainer, something *bad* may happen.

I've been to the bottom of that pillar, and can verify that it does indeed feature a set of initials, a G followed by perhaps a C. It also features dozens of other bits of graffiti, and I cannot vouch for their ability to bleed through paint without the aid of a less ghostly agent. I have, however, seen the light in George's Tower go through its' disappearing and reappearing act many times and I cannot account for its' cause. As the tower is some many dozen feet up, I was not about to climb the vertical ladder and see if there's really a light installed up in that tower or not. I suspect that there is none; not even at Disney are lighting fixtures so unreliable that the tower is dark more often than not.

Continuing from the base of George's Tower, and proceeding further into the show building, one comes across an inauspicious set of steps which lead up to a door. On the "show scene" side of the door is the famous dog, keys dangling from mouth. This door is George's Door, and it must be closed at all times. If George's Door is left open, the ride should not be powered up in the morning. This is fine for show quality reasons in the morning, and building maintenance and Imagineering know well enough to shut it behind them. However, sometimes, the door begins the day shut and will, in the middle of the day, mysteriously creak open.... and if George's Door is open, it is said, a serious breakdown is sure to follow. As you can imagine, if the light is on in George's Tower and George's Door is open, it is considered to be an especially bad portent.

George is, for whatever reason, especially active in that part of the building, perhaps because it is indeed the most far-flung and least traversed portion of the ride. He seems to especially lurk around "Storage", which is a spur line that runs underneath the Burning City show scene where boats may be moved on or off the main ride path in order to be sent to or released from the maintenance bay. The spur line begins at the end of the chase scene near "Old Bill". Storage Out is near the Jail scene, and if you're one of many who sometime feel a little uneasy after going under the pirate with the hairy leg and before coming upon the Jail; you may have had an encounter with George. He especially seems to be near that particular bend in the track, close to his door.

Behind the faux stone show walls near the hairy leg pirate and just a few feet down, is the cement foundation of the building. In this narrow backstage passage, to facilitate dry passage along the edge of the spur line, a number of plastic grates are laid across the floor, which is often flooded with a bit of water. Many have crossed these grates (during an evacuation or during after-hours events where Cast are stationed in the ride to watch guests) and heard a second pair of feet walking behind them a few grates back, or even felt cold breath on their neck. On the opposite end of the spur line, a shadowy man is sometimes seen sitting in a prop chair near Old Bill, or crossing the bridge which divides the Chase scene from the Fire scene - an impossibility since such an action would set off several alarms.

I don't feel the need to comment too much on the customary habit of saying good morning and goodnight to George, as this is famous and needs little further explanation at this point.

What a textbook account of all these customs, traditions and/or superstitions fails to convey is the day-to-day nature of the 'reality' of George. The morning and evening greetings were in fact nearly mandated by management, and any deviation will result in the day's woes being explicitly blamed on the closing Cast Member in Tower of a previous night. Switches, doors, water sensors and other basic mechanics sometimes inexplicably malfunction, causing the ride computer to enter "cycle out" mode - the Load Area gates lock and the computer enters a countdown until it will shut down the ride. This will initiate the regulated but still mad dash to fix the ride with as little disruption to the operation as possible - and resulting in the single most feared task by any new Cast Member, the need for the Unload Cast Member to enter the ride building and re-open, or "key", the Down Ramp.

A brief bit of explanation here: for safety reasons, the Down Ramp is designed so that the bottom of the Ramp must be opened before the top; just like a playground slide, the bottom must be clear before the boat at the top can come down. This is facilitated with a key turned in a lock and, in order to reach the Down Ramp, one must proceed on a labyrinth path through the guts of the building and emerge in what is known as the "Transition Tunnel". What follows is an endless-feeling wait in a very dark tunnel, and it is often here that your thoughts turn to that woman in the front row of that very light boat.

I cannot here exaggerate when I say that those times I have spent at the bottom of the Down Ramp, waiting to be called on the park phone by Tower, count as among the most miserable moments of my life. The mild illumination is not helpful, the water continues to rush past you, and you fully expect for a boat to turn the corner into sight at any moment, perhaps with two bloody figures seated in the front row. Even the walk to get to the Down Ramp is traumatic, dimly lit and wet, with the chest-high wading pants (used during ride evacuations) slung every few feet over handrails providing a jolt, so easy are they to mistake for a just-noticed figure or dead, limb legs jutting from the shadows. At the bottom of the ramp, the atmosphere is oppressive - you fully expect to be jumped. Worst of all was the ear splitting volume of the ghostly narration which once echoed through this scene prior to the 2006 refurbishment:

> *No fear have ye of evil curses says you! Properly warned ye be, says I!* ***DEAD MEN TELL NO TALES!*** *Now proceed at yer own risk! These be the last friendly words ye hear! You may not survive to pass this way again...* ***DEAD MEN TELL NO TALES!***

I've spoken to several Cast Members about their "George Stories" over the years, but the most chilling stories always involve the ghost of a very mad woman still haunting the ride. She's even been spotted on security cameras, standing upright in the current at the bottom of the Down Ramp, hair over her face. To give an indication of the impossibility of this, consider that the current in the ride needs to be strong enough to move a boat which is several hundred pounds as well as some two dozen people seated in it.

One Cast Member related a story about an unusual place for an encounter with this angry ghost. Load 1, the side of the queue with the skeletons playing chess, once had a single emergency exit – a door set into a wall just out of sight in the Load Area, actually part of the little diorama of a ship out at sea known as Moonlight Bay. Although I never used it, in my tenure at the ride I knew of it, because in order to use the door you would have to actually step out onto the plywood board which created the illusion of an ocean in the diorama. For obvious reasons, we called it the "Jesus Door", because you would have to walk on water to get there! Miracle achieved and door opened, you'd then have a very big step down to the concrete foundation backstage. It was rarely used for these reasons.

After being summoned away from the Load Area, this Cast Member made his exit using the Jesus Door and ended up in the narrow backstage corridor between two faux rockwork walls. At that moment a malevolent female voice whispered right at his shoulder: "You're not [f']ing supposed to be here!"

The Lady or Ladies generally confine themselves to the Down Ramp runoff portion of the ride, and although the tunnel has been significantly relieved in atmosphere by the removal of those voices and the insertion of the upbeat Hans Zimmer soundtrack, I still shudder as I pass by the hidden exit point, and I know that ghosts still linger. George, however, may be observed anywhere, at any time. I have been told of odd white points of light which occasionally float out of boats and into the rafters of the ride, observable only on security cameras. Shadows sometimes crawl along walls where you know they are not supposed to be. One spectacular and probably fictional manifestation I was once told about involves a cloud of mist engulfing a boat before it plunged down the Down Ramp.

Guests sometimes report seeing "someone" looking down on them from the Bombardment Bay fortress, but even more uncanny things have happened, especially if the guest makes idle chat about George in the Load Area in the early morning or late night. One guest questioned me at length about changes to the dialogue in the attraction until finally I realized that they were telling me that the voice which ordinarily says "Dead Men Tell No Tales" was in fact saying something about the dead "not having a face" and furthermore had felt that many of the ride figures were visibly malfunctioning and appeared to be looking at them! Although we will never be fully sure of the truth of this story, it does make a delightfully spooky addition to George's tale. And if it matters at all, this guest seemed to be honestly confused rather than deceitful and left looking unsure. I, for one, had trouble standing down at Unload for the rest of the night. The Unload position, in fact, is quite unpopular with Cast Members, especially at night. It may be because it's lonely and boring, or it may have something to do with the fact that it's mere feet away from the Down Ramp in one direction and George's Door in another.

Although the 2006 refurbishment changed the nomenclature, the queue or waiting area at Pirates has two sides; what was then known as Load 1 and Load 2. Load 1 winds past the famous skeletons playing chess, while Load 2 headed through a once uncommonly seen portion of the queue, with a dining hall and cannon pit. Load 2, however, had been modified to include a wheelchair ramp out of the building, and late at night we would have to lead guests in wheelchairs down to this side of the load area, turn on the load console, load just that group into a boat, turn off the load console, and push the chair back out the exit ramp all because Load 2 was considered the "secondary" side of the holding area and thus would close earlier.

On many trips exiting Load 2 with an empty wheelchair I knew George was loitering in this usually quiet part of the building. I even saw him once. He was all black, like a shadow standing off the wall.

I don't often get nostalgic for my days at Disney but pre-Jack Sparrow Pirates of the Caribbean is a wonderful memory for me, a time when the lines were often short, steel drum music echoed through the plaza, and a green parrot by the entrance would have to be muted five minutes before the start of the fireworks. And George was there, perhaps just in our minds, but present none the less. But then again, perhaps he was really there, you know. I'm sure inexplicable breakdowns persist to this day, and those plastic grates laid down all over the foundation of the show building which let you walk dryly even though the floor is usually slightly flooded, I'm sure that to this day you can hear another set of feet clanging across them, just a few feet behind you at that one special spot. His name may have been any number of things, but we called him George, and in a way he is the protector of Pirates of the Caribbean. More than a nuisance when his door isn't closed or he isn't greeted by name, we knew George wouldn't really do anything to hurt us.

That was, at least, the hope...

Foxx Nolte *has been studying, writing about, and thinking about Walt Disney World since a first trip in 1990 - with a recent emphasis on the first ten years of the property. The fruits of this labor may be found online at Passport to Dreams Old & New (http://passport2dreams.blogspot.com), a personal essay vault, and also at 2719 Hyperion (www.2719hyperion.com), a collaboration with George Taylor and Jeff Pepper. Longtime Haunted Mansion aficionados may also remember another, early project, the now-departed fan effort GrimGhosts.com*

Another Magic Corner of the World

Foxx Nolte

To look at Downtown Disney today, you'd never know what was there before. Indeed, the massive tripartite complex, housing something like seventy shops and eateries, is one of the traffic and economic centers of Walt Disney World. But the historical reality of the Village which preceded it is a complex tale, and one well worth retelling. In it, we can find everything about Walt Disney World, in a way – her relationship with the city of Orlando, the original aspirations, those dreams realized in an uncommon way, the later rampant commercialization – everything that went into the big crazy cultural pot of Walt Disney World is reflected here.

"A collection of more than two dozen waterfront shops, each dedicated to the fine art of browsing." – Walt Disney World Village Directory, 1980

In the tale of how the economic behemoth of Downtown Disney evolved from an adult little half day diversion called The Walt Disney World Village, we can see much that is central to the overall Walt Disney World story.

A bit of an overview, then, is probably desired before we descend too maddeningly into the hows and whys, so that the unwary Walt Disney World time traveler will not find herself too turned around in the serpentine twinings of history. The most valuable thing to impart is what The Walt Disney World Village was, and what made it different from her current incarnations.

This is how Disney themselves described their brand new creation in the spring of 1975:

"YOU HAVEN'T SEEN ALL OF
WALT DISNEY WORLD
UNTIL YOU'VE SEEN THE VILLAGE

The Shopping Village. Walt Disney World's newest addition. So different. So unique. So exciting. Only the Disney people could've done it. Just ten minutes away in the Host Community, Lake Buena Vista.

At the Village, you'll watch Old World craftsmen at work with pottery. Crystal cutting. Toledo gold engraving. You'll discover European and Oriental antiques. Candle crafts. Custom-blended tobaccos. Designer originals. And posh pets. You'll savor the flavors of imported beers in frosted mugs. International cheeses. Oysters on the half-shell. Fresh-ground coffees. And tasty homemade candies. You'll explore 29 cedar-shingled shops and four distinctive restaurants clustered on the banks of a beautiful blue lagoon. After you've seen the Magic Kingdom. See the

Village. Today. Or on your way home tonight. Open every day 10 till 10."

The Village, in the form that it opened in - in 1975 - was modeled on a quaint shopping village of vague stylistic origin. Captain Jack's Oyster Bar, with its strong diagonal wood siding, hexagonal seating area, and position out on piers on the lagoon "floating" over the placid surface of the water bespoke strong New England colorations, while other shops had a slight Swiss atmosphere to them, housed in Alpine-style chalets and little bungalows. The Village landscape was dotted with lush trees, six-sided planters, descending staircases, reflection ponds, flowers in little boxes, and a number of Renaissance-style statues arranged along the waters' edge, giving the whole area a slight European flavor. *"Flowers and trees have replaced the concrete and chrome of most shopping centers. And weathered brick, warm wood, and cedar shingles are the rule,"* wrote Disney in an issue of *Lake Buena Vista Village News* from 1976, and they were right in highlighting the radical departure the Village represented from the burgeoning clutch of mega-malls across America. Rather than the steel enclosed concrete box, the Village was intended to recall the market, the European High Street, or the historical commerce center of old. It may have been impossible to imagine without the 1970's love of earth tones, but in her earliest days the Village had a dreamy timelessness that many revived downtowns in cities across the United States would be envious of today.

Shaded verandas stretched between buildings and goods spilt out beyond the confines of the shops. There was the Gourmet Pantry, with her dim interior dotted with neat little piles of cans and bottles, gleaming brass light fixtures accenting sunset hued walls, and the walk in freezer with onsite butcher. Then, Toys Fantastique, an emporium of import toys and Disneyland Records, with the wall-length wood-carved dioramas from Pinocchio. Or The Pottery Chalet, where potters worked on the wheel all day and the pots were finished in an onsite kiln, this shop the largest of the buildings with an unmistakable massive open air entry under the arch of the chalet roof. Inside was more than just pottery: kitchenwares, interior finishing and even The Candle Chalet, where ongoing demonstrations on wax sculpting produced remarkably opulent results.

There was Pipe Dream, which housed Walt Disney World's first walk-in humidor and sold blended tobacco and pipes. Heidelberger's Deli, offering imported beers in frosted mugs and sandwiches often described as "palm stretching" on a shaded outside patio. And The Village Lounge, which had the distinction of housing any number of jazz personalities over the years attached to an upscale dining room with an open hearth. As Disney themselves said, the Village was truly "Another Side of the World".

The Community of Lake Buena Vista

A planned community had been a part of the Walt Disney World project from the very start, and much pen and ink and pixels and megabytes has been spilled on Walt Disney's EPCOT city – Disney's El Dorado. It's very debatable whether anybody inside the Walt Disney Company following the death of Walt Disney actually planned or wanted to build EPCOT once its' primary use had elapsed – as a bargaining chip with the Florida Legislature. Following a media blitz involving press announcements, panels, and a screening of the famous Walt Disney EPCOT film in Winter Park's Park West theater, the Disney-drafted package of three bills was quickly moved through the Florida House and Senate in an astonishing three days (Richard Fogelsong, "Married to the Mouse", pg. 72). Although then carried along on a wave of popular support and goodwill, these laws would have long term and serious consequence for Florida, having not only given Disney carte blanche to build whatever they wanted without having to go through the usual local and state formalities, but frozen the agreement in time at the moment where Central Florida was most in need of, and most likely to bend to, Disney's demands.

Disney spoke of a future city with a population of 20,000, all living and working at Walt Disney World, residing in model homes with the latest innovations in home appliances, furniture and textiles - all prototypes installed and tested at EPCOT by the real backers of the experiment, American Industry. Since all residents would be fulfilling a yearlong lease, there would be no property owners in EPCOT – and thus no citizens with those voting rights Disney was having so much trouble finding a way around. Yet there was also discussion of a second community in which some degree of land ownership could be expected. The story of how EPCOT the city became EPCOT the theme park has been well tread, but we find that the story of the Walt Disney World Village begins here too, back in 1967 and in the Florida Legislature. The Village was not built to be another attraction to extend the day of the average Walt Disney World visitor, although that is how Disney promoted it internally. It was created to be a downtown for an actual city, a planned community - much like those springing up all over the United States - and which still appear today.

The moment where the first seed was planted which would eventually spring into being as not only the Village but all of Walt Disney World is when the Florida legislature approved the formation of two municipalities within the Disney property: Bay Lake and Reedy Creek. These would later become known as the "City of Bay Lake" and the "City of Lake Buena Vista", self-governed by the "Reedy Creek Improvement District". And indeed the very first part of Walt Disney World to open to the public was *in* Lake Buena Vista, not far from where the Village would one day be: the Walt Disney World Preview Center.

Located on what was known for many years afterwards as Preview Blvd, a winding, tree lined road led to the Preview Center: a squat, rectangular building which still stands on the shores of what was then known as Black Lake. Employing a limited number of hostesses, for two years the Walt Disney World Preview Center offered interested travelers a peek at the vacation kingdom Disney was building just to the northwest, including artwork, models, and a film. At the end of the tour one could buy her first Walt Disney World souvenirs, including a thin paperback souvenir booklet labeled as the "Preview Edition"; these books are today amongst the rarest of all early Walt Disney World items.

It was not long before Black Lake was rechristened Lake Buena Vista, the name an imaginative melding of Disney's skill at romantic evocation and the name of their own film distribution company. And as part of General Joe Potter's master plan for Walt Disney World, the lake was integrated into the property's elaborate canal system to allow for natural drainage throughout the swampy property. As the Preview Center closed in September 1971, many of the hostesses were given new jobs in the brand new Vacation Kingdom, even as Disney was busily selling land all around it to outside hoteliers. Disney wasn't yet done with Lake Buena Vista.

Master Planning for Walt Disney World, a fascinating early document detailing Disney's thinking about what their property would be like circa 1969, has fascinating details about Disney's projected "Residential Community", which they appear to have planned to have ready for opening in 1971.

"25,000 Visitors Annual Daily Average – Development Plan Year 1" we find on page 35, with a note below a map: "Residential Community – 625 residents, 1000 employees, 1000 motel units and 250 residential units".

> *"The residential community will, in effect, 'branch off' from the commercial development at the intersection of State Road 535 and Interstate Highway 4. The community will grow along the east and northeast portions of the Walt Disney World property, and, the company believes, will form an underlying economic base for the whole area. The concept in development is a small, balanced community that can be the focus for early expansion in the entire south-of-Orlando region. Ultimately, it will have a carefully conceived network of community and recreation facilities. [...] The residential Community will have an integrated theme... a chain of lakes and open spaces that will make recreation and Florida's natural resources of sunshine, fresh air, mild climate, and scenic beauty a part of everyday life."*

On page 38 of their document, Disney projects the scope of their project all the way forward to Year 20, with 100,000 visitors a daily average. Under "Residential Community" on their map they project "16,500 residents, 4,000 employees, 3,000 motel units, and 4,500 residential units".

Disney wasn't able to get everything ready for opening day, but by early 1972, things were starting to come together in Lake Buena Vista. The first of several hotels in the Motor Inn Plaza had opened –

a Howard Johnson's, a Dutch Inn, TraveLodge, and Royal Plaza had sprung up along Preview Blvd and were drawing steady local and tourist business, for their restaurants and night clubs as much as their central location. And in 1972, Disney put up the first of a series of experimental little grey bungalows along a widened stretch of canal out in their Florida wilderness. Their idea was to rent townhouses to the corporate arm of Disney's operating partners such as RCA or Gulf. Before Disney had even begun construction, they had more than 70 interested companies (David Koenig, *Realityland*, pg. 124).

> *"More than 100 townhomes, incorporating four distinct design styles, already are completed and are available to corporations for two- or three-year-term leases or outright purchase in full. Ideal for executive family vacations, customer entertaining, or sales-incentive-reward holidays, the townhomes come furnished or unfurnished", Disney breathlessly describes in a 1974 publication, "A limited number of one- and two-bedroom villas, fully furnished and complete with linens and kitchenware, are available to families visiting the Vacation Kingdom for short-term rentals." (Walt Disney World Vacationland, Spring 1974)*

All of this was laying the foundation for the most ambitious aspect of the project, the planning and construction of the Village itself. A man made inlet south of the Townhouses was carved out of the canal and dubbed the "Village Lagoon", around which sprung up 29 shops and 5 restaurants in ten weathered chalets and bungalows embracing the lagoon. An early promotional piece described the Village as

> *"...The Shopping Village, the newest addition to the Walt Disney World Host Community of Lake Buena Vista. Joining an already established Disney community of townhouses, hotels, and country clubs, the Village, like its neighbors, has been landscaped to blend in with the natural wooded and lake-studded environment around it."*

In the original arrangement, the Lake Buena Vista Shopping Village featured some eccentric establishments. In addition to shops like "Miss Merrily's Madness" for the young miss, there was an Apothecary which also served as a post office, an antiques shop – Von Otto's Antiques, named for Disney's antiques buyer Otto Rabby – and another establishment called "Posh Pets Etc". The center of the little town was a tall six-sided structure called the Captain's Tower which hosted local and visiting authors and artists, celebrities, or whatever else could be housed in the practical if not climate controlled little pavilion. In fact, everything about the Village was hexagons, from the stepped reflecting pond, the flower filled planters, and even the paving tiles, as if to offset the Vacation Kingdom's insistence on circles – especially those three circles in that special pattern.

The earliest beneficiaries of the Village were certainly those guests staying in the motor inns on Preview Blvd and at the Lake Buena Vista Villas, which by 1975 constituted both Townhomes and Treehouses. The Lake Buena Vista Club, a clubhouse facility servicing the Lake Buena Vista Golf Course, had opened in 1974 with a pro shop and high end eatery. Described by Disney as "a country club where you are already a member", the Lake Buena Vista Club was amongst Walt Disney World's most ambitious early restaurants, featuring sommeliers and strolling musicians. Disney scribes penned this beautiful paragraph to describe it in a 1975 issue of *Vacationland* Magazine:

> *"The Lake Buena Vista Club supplies excellent Gallic fare. Built like a chalet with exposed beams, copper sculptures, wall rugs, plush furniture, and smelling of cedar, it overlooks the beautiful tall pines and lush greenery of the Lake Buena Vista Club fairways. The menu offers gourmet meals of fish, fowl, veal, lamb, and beef served in an atmosphere of cozy, yet sophisticated, comfort."*

1976 brought further embellishment to the Village. Originally situated in a near circular alcove off the main water cannel leading towards the Townhouse Villas and the Lake Buena Vista Club, Disney dug out the western shore of the lagoon and began laying the submerged concrete foundations for a massive restaurant expansion of the Village. Opened May 1, 1977, and christened by Walt Disney's wife Lillian, the Empress Lilly was a massive reconstruction of a nineteenth century steamboat. From a Fall 1977 issue of *Disney News*:

> *"Twinkling lights, dancing on a placid nighttime waterfront are reflections of a new era in dining and entertainment at the Walt Disney World Village at Lake Buena Vista. The Empress Lilly has arrived! [...] An authentic reproduction of earlier stern-wheelers, the Empress Lilly is decorated in the grand style of those 19th century steam crafts. Satins and velvets are lovely accents to the dark mahogany and bentwood furniture and beams, brass lamps, crystal chandeliers and silk damask wall covering."*

Although most often described as a "Riverboat restaurant", the Empress Lilly was in reality an ambitious complex of almost a dozen separate "establishments", from family oriented to the highest of high end. On the bottom level, at the bow of the boat, was the "Baton Rouge Lounge", most famous for housing the "Riverboat Rascals", a lively quintet performing Dixieland jazz in what could be described as "dinner theater" style. In later years a massive (for its time: four feet across!) television would be wheeled out on the raised stage backed by a stained glass window for game nights, and the Baton Rouge Lounge holds the distinction of likely being the only "peanut shells on the floor" bar Disney ever created.

A world away in atmosphere but in reality right next door, the Starboard Lounge was distinctive for only being available to guests via silent Flote Boat launch from the Village or Lake Buena Vista Club - with a private dock just outside. It constituted a long, cozy room stuffed with furniture alongside the water-level windows looking across the Village Lagoon at the twinkling shopping village. And at the back of the boat, The Steerman's Quarters, clustered around a large central staircase, offered steak and ale with a view of the Lilly's churning paddlewheel through huge windows.

Upstairs, above the Steerman's Quarters could be found the Promenade Lounge, a sort of waiting area for the Lilly's main culinary attraction, the Empress Room. The Promenade Lounge, according to a slim 1982 menu, offered shrimp, clams and oysters by the dozen or half dozen, as well as a variety of blended drinks such as the Delta Queen (midori liqueur, light rum, cream of coconut) and the First Mate (rum, pineapple juice, lime juice, and grenadine).

The Empress Room, one of Walt Disney World's most ambitious pre-Eisner eateries, was the truly most unique and high end restaurant at Walt Disney World. Described by *Disney News*:

> *"The Empress Room, also on the second deck, will feature the finest in gourmet fare and exclusive French service. The intimate, evening dining room seating 68 is designed with a private entrance. Satins, glittering Maria Theresa chandeliers, and etched glass will accent the sophisticated Louis XV setting. Selections from a daily list of hot and cold appetizers, soups, entrees, and desserts will be complimented by the finest wines from an exclusive cellar. The adjoining Empress Lounge will provide an elegant atmosphere for Empress Room guests to sip their after-dinner cups of Coffee Flambe or other specialty drinks mixed at their table and enjoy the magnificent view of the shimmering moonlit waters."*

At the front of the second deck (yes, there's more!) was the Fisherman's Deck, a 126-seat two-tied restaurant offering seasonal catches from local sources in a family-oriented setting. The top level of the boat, comprising The Captain's Table and the Texas Deck Lounge, was mostly reserved for private functions (as it still is today). The Texas Deck Lounge, in particular, with massive tub seats, private bar and scrollwork, was easily the largest entertaining space on the boat, and the Captain's Table – the thing itself - was actually an antique table, seating 20, which Disney brought over from Club 33 at Disneyland, making it likely that Walt Disney had selected the table himself before his death.

The Empress Lilly herself provided a remarkable visual centerpiece to the entire Village, a visual icon of Walt Disney World as distinct as Cinderella Castle or Spaceship Earth. Massive, her gilded sign proclaiming "The Empress Lilly – Port of Lake Buena Vista", churning red paddle wheel, and twin smokestacks, she appeared part of the Village but also on its outskirts, always perpetually ready to churn out of port into the swampy wilderness beyond. *"The Empress Lilly, designed by WED East (the master-planning, research and development arm of the Disney organization), is an authentic reproduction of the earlier steam crafts such as the Robert E. Lee and Natchez, which negotiated the waters of the Mississippi. Thorough attention to detail, such as four-foot railings circling each deck with gingerbread detailing, two 84-foot smoke stacks, special made-to-order China, and a 1896-inscribed, nickel and brass bell that can be heard for 20 miles around, add to the realistic atmosphere of the riverboat."*

1977 saw changes "on land" to the Village as well. The Village Pavilion, a cozy gazebo-like structure with two hexagonal wings, appeared between the Pottery Chalet and the Lilly, along the way to the massive boat beside a winding, wooded path dotted with gorgeous craftwork lanterns hanging from rough-hewn wooden posts. The central structure of the Pavilion housed the Verandah Restaurant, casual at lunch and more upscale at dinner, as well as Borden's Ice Cream Shoppe to the left and the Sara Lee Bakery to the right, which opened at 9 am and, along with the Verandah Restaurant, functioned as the Village's early morning breakfast option. A number of shops in the main body of the Village moved or changed as well, such as Von Otto's Antiques being replaced by the Great Southern Craft Company and Toys Fantastique moving across the street. The Chummery, the original name of the lounge adjoining the Village Restaurant, gave up its Disney-sponsored entertainment of clean cut kids singing John Denver songs and became The Village Lounge, home to its signature lineup of traveling jazz acts.

The Village Post Office moved down the street to the old Preview Center, becoming part of a complex which offered check-in services to Disney's growing fleet of Villas and offices for the Walt Disney Travel Company. The former resident of the Preview Center - Buena Vista Interiors, an interior design firm owned by Disney meant to offer their services to companies buying unfurnished villas and headed by WED veteran Emile Kuri – moved to the Village into a space to the immediate right of the Pottery Chalet and became the Home Furnishings Gallery. This allowed Village Spirits to move into the vacated Post Office space and add their prestigious Vintage Cellar. And with all these changes, the whole complex got a new name – The Walt Disney World Village.

Company Town

It was in this sedate arrangement that the Village remained from 1977 to around 1989, and it is this that most people who visited the Village will remember it. Changes, however, were underway. 1977 is the year that WED Enterprises first linked up the separate EPCOT theme center and World Showcase attractions to create EPCOT Center theme park as we know it today, and the next five years the company would be heavily involved in funding, planning, and building the multi-billion-dollar behemoth. Following a fallow period of financial decline in the wake of EPCOT Center, the old guard at Disney would be out and Michael Eisner and Frank Wells would be ascendant. Following a concentrated effort to turn around the Disney movie production pipeline, Eisner would begin a period of rapid expansion throughout Walt Disney World that would mean the end of much of the type of atmosphere which had defined the resort for her first 15 years.

Now, as part of Eisner's entry into Disney in 1984, he was required to appease the majority shareholder in the company, Texas oil baron Sid Bass. To prevent a hostile takeover attempt Bass increased his share in the company to 25%, under the condition that Eisner would begin aggressive expansion of the Florida property. Bass saw huge potential in hotel building in Lake Buena Vista and Eisner would begin his expansion plans just a few years later in an agreement which would become his legacy in Walt Disney World.

The opening of Pleasure Island and Typhoon Lagoon nearby were the first signs that massive changes were afoot, but by this time much of the adult charm of the shopping village was being eradicated anyway. Lite Bite had become Goofy's Grill, Heidelberger's Deli transformed into the far less continental Great American Sandwich Shoppe, and the Village Restaurant became Chef Mickey's. The Village Lounge, no longer home to famous jazz musicians, was showing Mickey Mouse cartoons daily from 5 pm to 9 pm. The large Port of Entry import decor shop had long since transformed into Mickey's Character Shop, well remembered for its' central sculpture of Disney characters in a flying machine at the apex of a mountain of plush. The days of an adult diversion were over. And of course with the opening of Pleasure Island, the Village got her third name change, becoming the Disney Village Marketplace.

Some of the original charm held on for a few more years, but in 1994 a massive renovation effort pretty much brought an end to what could be referred to as The Walt Disney World Village. Planters were removed to make way for wider, theme park-like walkways. Water play fountains began to appear. The original reflection pond by the Captain's Tower became a train ride for children. All of the original shaded breezeways were torn out. Goods no longer spilled from open shops. Those original potters, ring engravers and glass etchers became relegated to a small alleyway between a surf shop and a beach wear store before fading away entirely. All of the original efforts to create something "different" and "unique" were stripped away by the corporate mentality of post-Eisner standardization and by, it must be said, changing fashion.

So what happened to those ambitious plans of community building–that promise of a city that Disney promoted in 1967 as part of its legislative campaign? It was, likely, sadly, lost in the shuffle. In 1975, a fascinating document simply called "Lake Buena Vista PeopleMover" was published, which detailed plans to connect the motor inn hotels and Village via an automated, coin-operated *PeopleMover* system, all the way through the Village's expansion area (filling the spaces currently occupied by Pleasure Island and West Side) over to what Disney was describing as a "Multi-Modal Station", a transit hub which would link *PeopleMovers*, monorails, and local busses. The actual document indicates how serious Disney was back in 1967 when they pledged to help alleviate urban congestion and help the entire area achieve productive growth:

> *"The downtown Lake Buena Vista multi-modal transportation terminal includes intra-urban, inter-urban, and inter-state facilities which will provide the critical 'location' and 'link' to the achievement of a viable regional public transportation system. According to the east Central Florida Regional Planning Council recent study estimates, by 1990, the public transit system will provide daily trips for 34,610 Orlando area transit passengers, with 24,570 of these trips going to/from Walt Disney World. For these visitors, the multi-modal terminal at downtown Lake*

Buena Vista will be the 'showcasing' stop while on their way to Walt Disney World." (pg. 15)

Assumedly, all this was put on hold as work proceeded full speed ahead on EPCOT, and was again put off following the completion of EPCOT Center - although Disney did purchase some extra monorail track from Morrison-Knudsen, manufacturer of the EPCOT leg of the monorail loop, for the Lake Buena Vista monorail system. Disney did advertise a model of the completed Lake Buena Vista downtown through the late 70s, showing a monorail, *PeopleMover*, and a fully developed office building plaza across the street, only one of the planned thirteen buildings ever being completed (it is today known as the SunTrust building). According to Disney's plan, the Lake Buena Vista Villas were phase one of an elaborate four-community vacation community, comprising recreation themed communities – golf, tennis, boating and horses – and a transient population of 30,000!

A transient population of 30,000? A *PeopleMover* through a downtown area of shopping and dining? Commercial highrises? Monorails? Modern homes situated in grassy, pastoral suburbs? Haven't we heard of all this before? Arguably, it's nearly every component of Walt Disney's Progress City – only spread out across a huge area instead of the compact circle Walt Disney was envisioning in 1966. Disney was building a community – a real community – or at least, maybe, trying to.

Sadly none of this came to be following the arrival of the Eisner team in 1984, and this is, unfortunately, where our story ends. In the years since 1994 – during the so-called Disney Decade - even more of the original Village structures have been torn down, making it somewhat hard to correctly identify those which are original to 1975, even more so now that their signature natural woods have been painted over in cartoonish colors. In 1996 the Empress Lilly was leased to an outside restaurant firm who have stripped away all the careful interior finish, redecorated it in the manner of a Red Lobster, painted it grey and rechristened the vessel Fulton's Crabhouse. Even the red paddle wheel has been removed. But some things continue. The Festival of the Masters, inaugurated by Disney in 1975 with the opening of the Village, has been held every year. Another early promotion, the Easter

Flower Festival, later moved to EPCOT and expanded to become the International Flower & Garden Festival. Even the EPCOT Food & Wine Festival has roots at the Village, in a wine tasting weekend once centered around the Vintage Cellar.

Of course the most obvious legacy of the Walt Disney World Village is in the growth of the "Downtown Disney" concept across the globe. Although the mega-multiplex-anchored retail wonderland Disney has today installed worldwide has only a tangential relationship to the Village, they do share the same the same heritage of diverse shopping, dining, and entertainment –all under the auspices of Disney. But next time you're in the midst of the sensory pleasures of Downtown Disney, take time to walk the Village, or what's left of her, and reflect. Reflect that once upon a time this was meant not to be a Disney Downtown but a real downtown of a real population center, where ecologically friendly construction and natural colors were the rule. Where the emblem was a white bird flying across a blue circle and the lagoon was bright and blue and the ambiance quiet. Another magic corner of the world.

EPCOT 1939

Jeffrey Pepper

The World of Tomorrow

Over the course of its 25 years, Epcot has often been described as a permanent world's fair. It's an interesting, and very accurate reference that is likely lost however, on the vast majority of guests, especially those under the age of fifty, who walk in the shadow of Spaceship Earth every day.

Built as showcases primarily for industries and governments, these fairs and expos have by and large become anachronisms in these early years of the 21st century. People attended these often massive expositions to view the wonders of technological progress and celebrate the accomplishments of the industrial complex. They also sought to bring themselves closer to other peoples and cultures from around the world, by visiting pavilions hosted by numerous nations. The countless media outlets available today have largely rendered world's fairs obsolete. People need only go as far as their televisions or their computers to be exposed to the latest hallmarks of progress, or to explore distant lands.

Epcot was clearly designed and built around these very same concepts of progress and international cooperation. But its similarities to one fair in particular are striking. While most associate the Disney Company and Walt in particular, with the 1964-65 New York World's Fair, it is in fact its 1939 predecessor that Epcot most closely resembles, especially the EPCOT Center that existed from 1982 through the early 1990s.

Both 1939 and 1964 World's Fairs occupied the same location in the Queens borough of New York City. It sprawled over 1,216 acres of former marshland adjacent to Flushing Bay. That's four times the size of Epcot. An illustration from a 1939 pre-opening guidebook provides an idea of just how large it was:

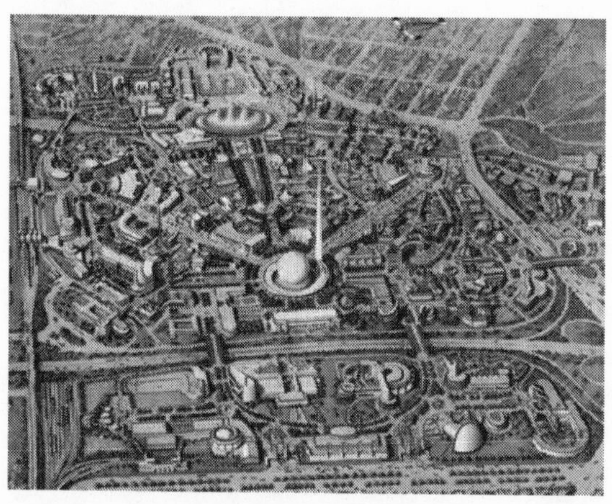

A close examination of this aerial view reveals how Imagineers likely took inspiration from the fair's extensive layout, when mapping out EPCOT Center. Known as the Theme Center, the Trylon and the Perisphere, like Spaceship Earth for Epcot, serve as the Fair's focal centerpiece. Immediately surrounding these dramatic icons are seven different zones and focal exhibits, each with a distinct theme: Communication, Transportation, Community, Food, Health, Production, and Science.

Beyond these areas, at the rear portion of the grounds, was the Government Zone. Radiating out from the Lagoon of Nations were over twenty large pavilions featuring the likes of Italy, France, Japan, Great Britain, Brazil and the U.S.S.R. The Hall of Nations surrounded both the lagoon and the Court of Peace, and offered slightly smaller scale pavilions representing an additional forty countries. The nearby Court of States featured pavilions from 22 different states. Centered directly behind the Lagoon of Nations and the Court of Peace was the United States Federal Building, anchoring the area in much the same manner as the American Adventure in World Showcase.

It's interesting to compare the overall layout of the Fair to this concept art of EPCOT Center, featured on a pre-opening postcard:

And the similarities extend well beyond layout and design. Take for instance the theme of the Fair, as expressed in its official slogan: "Building the World of Tomorrow with the Tools of Today."

And then compare this excerpt from Card Walker's dedication of EPCOT Center–

> *"Here, human achievements are celebrated through imagination, wonders of enterprise and concepts of a future that promises new and exciting benefits for all. May EPCOT Center entertain, inform and inspire, and above all, may it instill a new sense of belief and pride in man's ability to shape a world that offers hope to people everywhere."*

–to the following statements from the aforementioned Official Guidebook of the New York World's Fair 1939:

> *To the millions of visitors the Fair says: "Here are the materials, ideas, and forces at work in our world. Here are the best tools that are available to you; they are the tools with which you and your fellow men can build the World of Tomorrow. You are the builders; we have done our best to persuade you that these tools will result in a better World of Tomorrow; yours is the choice."*

The same forward thinking idealism that EPCOT Center embodied was very much alive and well in 1939. Sadly, it would soon be dampened by Germany's invasion of Poland and the onset of World War II.

Icons Past and Present

Like Spaceship Earth at Epcot, the Trylon-Perisphere Theme Center was the visual centerpiece of the 1939 New York World's Fair. And in the same manner that Disney uses Spaceship Earth, Cinderella Castle and the Tree of Life as marketing icons for their respective parks, the Fair's promoters spared no opportunity to brand everything they possibly could with representations of these two very dynamic structures.

Disney established Spaceship Earth as the symbol of EPCOT Center well prior to its October 1982 opening. Nearly every piece of pre-opening publicity material featured the distinct likeness of the giant geosphere.

The New York World's Fair 1939 Corporation was no different with the Trylon and the Perisphere. The terms "trylon" and "perisphere" were specially created to describe these structures. Two years prior to the Fair's opening, the dual icons were featured prominently on this "coming soon" poster:

It didn't stop there by any means. There were few types of consumer products in 1939 that escaped Fair licensing. Furniture, cameras, typewriters, watches, radios, china, and countless other items all carried some type of image or graphic of the Trylon-Perisphere.

The Trylon-Perisphere Theme Center was dramatic and imposing to say the least. The Trylon stood some 700 feet high while the Perisphere measured 200 feet in diameter. In comparison, Spaceship Earth's diameter tops out at 165 feet.

Like Spaceship Earth, the Perisphere also housed an attraction. While the Fair did have a zone that was identified with Spaceship Earth's communication theme, the Perisphere's resident presentation, Democracity, embraced the fair's broader theme of "The World of Tomorrow."

Visitors entered on what was then the longest escalator in the world. At its top, they were deposited onto either one of two revolving balconies that hung suspended over the sphere's vast interior. Below was a highly detailed model of a city of the future. The Fair's guidebook provides this description:

> *"As the interior is revealed, you see in the hollow beneath the sky, "Democracity"—symbol of a perfectly integrated, futuristic metropolis pulsing with life and rhythm and music. The daylight panorama stretches off to the horizon on all sides. Here is a city of a million people with a working population of 250,000, whose homes are located beyond the city-proper, in five satellite towns. Like great arteries, broad highways traverse expansive areas of vivid green countryside, connecting outlying industrial towns with the city's heart."*

In theme and message, though not in presentation, Democracity is most similar to Horizons of all EPCOT Center's first wave of Future World attractions. But more striking is the miniature city's uncanny resemblance to models and artwork of Walt Disney's original vision of his Experimental Prototype Community of Tomorrow, right down to the single imposing skyscraper that tower's over each concept's city center. I have never come across any information that documents a visit by Walt to the Fair, but I have to feel it's likely he attended at some point during its two seasons of operation. One must wonder if he viewed a performance of Democracity, and if he carried away any impressions that later influenced his plans for EPCOT.

Chrysler's World of Motion

In 1939, the most readily accepted hallmark of progress was the automobile. Therefore, it's not surprising that the Transportation Zone was the most popular destination at the 1939 New York World's Fair. Many of the longest lines at the Fair were to exhibits and attractions belonging to General Motors, Chrysler Motors and the Ford Motor Company. And many of these crowd pleasers would distinctly foreshadow EPCOT Center attractions created some forty-plus years later.

The Chrysler Motors Building was at the forefront of the Transportation Zone and was home to the area's Focal Exhibit. It embraced the very same theme as EPCOT's World of Motion--the history of transportation. It however approached the subject with a much more serious tone, and a distinctly different presentation. Let's flip to page 199 of our Official Fair Guidebook for a description:

> *"Within the rotunda of the building, the FOCAL EXHIBIT—-a part of the Chrysler Motors presentation— tells its graphic story of Transportation by means of moving pictures projected upon a great map of the world, and by the "Rocketport," a display that seizes upon your imagination and projects it into the future. The show consists of three parts—The Early Period, The Middle Period, and The Mechanical Period."*

Like World of Motion's cast of animatronics, these *periods* chronicled the history of transportation from foot and animal power all the way through to the arrival of automobiles and airplanes. The show culminates in the following dramatic finale:

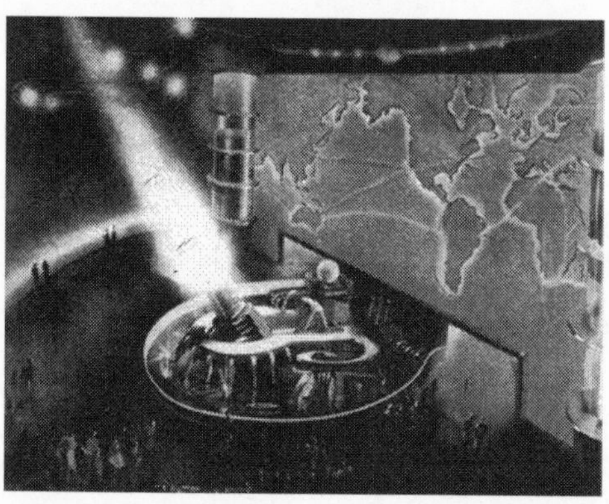

> *"As the airplane finishes its flight across the screen, lines shoot out and harness the earth with other planets. Twinkling signal lights, the hum of gigantic motors and the warning sound of sirens indicate that the Rocketship is loading passengers for London. You see futuristic liners unloading at nearby docks; sleek trains glide to a stop, auto¬mobiles whisk voyagers to the spot, high-speed elevators rise and descend as the Rocketship is serviced for the coming journey. The moment for departure arrives. A great steel crane moves, a magnet picks up the Rocketship*

and deposits it into the breach of the rocketgun. A moment of awesome silence. A flash, a muffled explosion, and the ship vanishes into the night."

Another popular attraction at the Chrysler Motors Building was in fact the first Technicolor 3D film ever made. After donning special Polaroid glasses, audiences were entertained by singing and dancing auto parts that magically assembled into a fully built automobile. EPCOT Center connection? Picture Journey into Imagination's Magic Eye Theater dropped into World of Motion's Transcenter.

Other points of interest in the pavilion included the standard showroom of new model Chrysler-made vehicles, and an exhibit featuring a talking car that answered questions, gave interviews and demonstrated its many then high-tech features.

The Road of Tomorrow

While the Focal Exhibit at the Chrysler pavilion, like Epcot's World of Motion, told the story of the history of transportation, Ford's main attraction, the Road of Tomorrow, drew parallels to the World of Motion's successor–Test Track.

A stainless steel sculpture of the god Mercury towered high above the entrance to the Ford building, representing one of the four Ford brands that also included Lincoln and Zephyr. But the more striking feature of the building's exterior was the half-mile spiral ramp on which visitors rode in Ford-model vehicles as a part of the Road of Tomorrow attraction. The ramp surrounded the Garden Court, a beautifully landscaped courtyard where fairgoers could partake in a picnic lunch, listen to a musical performance, or just relax and people watch.

Let's take a look at our guidebook for a quick description of the exhibits inside:

> *The "Exposition" has four main divisions: the Entrance Hall, the Industrial Hall, the Garden Court, and "The Road of Tomorrow." Each of the first three demonstrate in graphic style some significant phase of the company's work, showing how mass production of automobiles at moderate cost has contributed to a new way of life. The Entrance Hall is dominated by a series of striking exhibits. The first car Henry Ford built will be seen with current models of Lincoln-Zephyr, Mercury and Ford V-8 cars. "Everytown" is a large three phase map activated on a series of synchronized prisms, depicting the changes the automobile has wrought in our country. A huge activated mural by Henry Billings shows how the basic sciences are utilized by industry. Outstanding in the adjoining Industrial Hall is the "Ford Cycle of Production." A revolving turntable 100 feet in diameter, it contains 87 exhibits showing the progression of raw materials from*

earth to finished cars. Industrial Hall also offers various exhibits demonstrating Ford manufacturing methods.

While not sharing the same theme, these exhibits were very similar in design to the Fountain of Information display and the Age of Information animated mural that were a part of Communicore West's FutureCom area at EPCOT Center.

The popular highlight of the exposition was The Road of Tomorrow, demonstrated by the long queue lines that overlooked the Garden Court. Here's how our trusty guidebook described the attraction:

From a broad mezzanine you embark on your wondrous trip over "The Road of Tomorrow." The winding course takes you through a tunnel lined with murals depicting ultra-modern highway construction, circles the top of Industrial Hall and through still another tunnel high in the nave of Entrance Hall. Descending at last to the second floor level, you circle Garden Court and return to the mezzanine and the end of a thrilling and delightful adventure.

Granted, this "thrilling adventure" did not rival the 65 mph speed of Test Track, but it was certainly entertaining in its day. In fact, Test Track would have been far cooler had the speed ramp circled a public area much the way "Road" surrounded the Garden Court. Instead, it exposes guests to some fairly unattractive backstage scenery.

Highways and Horizons

It was the talk of the 1939 New York World's Fair. It had the longest lines of any attraction. It was state-of the-art in design and execution. It was the centerpiece of the General Motors Building. It was Futurama.

In 1939, Futurama was to fairgoers what Horizons was to Future World guests in the mid-1980s. Just as Horizons' travelers were transported into the 21st century, their 1939 counterparts were taken on a scenic journey twenty years ahead to America in the year 1960. Appropriately, the name General Motors gave to its seven acre exhibit was "Highways and Horizons."

Once again, our handy official guidebook provides a much better description than I ever could:

> *"In 600 moving chairs, each equipped with a sound device which serves as a private guide on the Aladdin-like trip, visitors tour a vast miniature cross-section of America as it may conceivably appear twenty years or more from now."*

The ride mechanics foreshadowed Epcot attractions like Spaceship Earth and Horizons, especially in regard to the vehicles' onboard audio.

"Covering an area of 35.738 square feet, the "futurama" is the largest and most realistic scale-model ever constructed. As visitors in the moving chairs tour this "futurama" they experience the sensation of traveling hundreds of miles and viewing the scenes from a low-flying airplane. As they travel on several levels of the building in their magic chairs, they view a continuous animated panorama of towns and cities, rivers and lakes, country and farm areas, industrial plants in operation, country clubs, forests, valleys and snowcapped mountains. The "futurama" contains approximately 500,000 individually designed houses; more than a million trees of eighteen species; and 50,000 scale-model automobiles, of which 10,000 are in actual operation over super-highways, speed lanes and multi-decked bridges."

The ride culminated in a shining, tower-filled future metropolis. Through a series of transitions, the magic chairs and their occupants were drawn closer and closer into the cityscape, until they finally hovered above a bustling intersection. The ride ends but the amazement did not. Upon exiting their magic chairs, visitors walked onto a full scale reproduction of the street intersection they had just encountered in model form. It was a total "wow" moment.

The guidebook describes how the imaginary city streets of the future formed the overall architecture of General Motors Building:

> *"Spacious open-air terraces with several hundred chairs for visitors' comfort encircle two-thirds of the structure. Actually, "Highways and Horizons" is not one building, but consists of four towering structures (four to six stories in height). Located on the four corners of an imaginary and spectacular, full-scale street intersection of 1960, the four buildings are joined into an overall exhibit structure by broad, elevated pedestrian sidewalks, which extend for a full city block in two directions. This open-air spectacle forms the center section of the Exhibit and at night is brilliantly illuminated by a battery of floodlights"*

The buildings at the four corners of intersection actually contained additional exhibits and attractions. These included a 650-seat theater that housed the Casino of Science, the World Horizons exhibit that focused on GM's overseas operations through a series of animated displays, and a full scale "x-ray" car constructed of "plexiglass," an amazing new transparent plastic.

Yes, in design, theme and even name, the General Motors Building and Futurama, found themselves reborn at EPCOT Center on October 1, 1983.

Interestingly, GM produced a short film in 1939 to promote Futurama. Its title: "To New Horizons."

The Food Zone

People were certainly "living with the land" in 1939, and the Food Zone was a popular destination for Fairgoers at New York World's Fair of that same year. The Focal Exhibit of the Food Zone was called "Miracle of Modern Food." While not in any way similar to any of the future EPCOT Center Land pavilion attractions, it spirit and message ultimately reflected the same themes of "Listen to the Land" and "Symbiosis," The Land's 1980s era attractions.

Let's check our Official Guidebook for a quick description:

> *Though it deals with humble, commonplace things like "bread and butter," the Food Show is high and amazing entertainment. Comprehensive and dramatic, the Exhibit illustrates the progress made in the cultivation, preparation, , processing and distribution of food since 1789. The techniques of Coney Island, the atmosphere of Forty-second Street, comic cartoons, and "slapstick" are among the amusing devices employed to stage the "Miracle of Modern Food" for millions of Fair visitors.*

In describing the show's climax, the guidebook conveys a message that would be echoed by its Future World counterpart in 1982:

> *A startling anticlimax to the show is the exhibit "the challenge to the future," which is housed in a huge chamber under the ovoid itself. Here the walls and ceilings impress you with their grave message of food questions yet unsolved. Springing from the shadows, newspaper headlines and photomontages graphically depict a score of acute food problems darkening man's future. As the show ends, you turn away reflecting on another unfinished job for the "World of Tomorrow." Yet every unfinished task is a challenge—an opportunity for an additional achievement in man's progress.*

The Food Zone did host Walt Disney's most direct connection to the Fair. Let's take a look at the Guidebook's entry for the National Biscuit Company's (more familiar to people today as Nabisco) exhibit:

> *A specially produced Walt Disney motion picture, entitled Mickey's Surprise Party is the outstanding feature of the Exhibit. Fair visitors are invited to see this amusing film in an air-conditioned theatre. The Disney picture is in technicolor and features many of the well-known "Mickey Mouse" characters.*

Robots of Future Past

What would any vision of the future be without robots? EPCOT Center featured a couple during its first decade, and likewise, a mechanical man was one of the more popular attractions at the 1939 New York World's Fair.

At EPCOT, SMRT-1 entertained guests as part of a number of activity islands at EPCOT Computer Central in Communicore East. Small, round, purple and cute would be the best way to describe the little robot, who interacted with visitors by playing simple guessing games via phone hookups.

Just outside Communicore East, another little robot could be found on occasion. Gyro stood just less than 5 feet tall and weighed 150 pounds. Operated by remote control, he would perform twenty minutes shows throughout the day.

While SMRT-1 and Gyro were pretty state-of-the-art for the 1980s, the concept of an interactive robot was nothing new. An example was present and exceptionally popular at Flushing Meadow's World of Tomorrow back in 1939. Elektro was a robot's robot, not at all cute and endearing like his EPCOT counterparts, he held to the more traditional image of robots, as perpetuated by the science fiction pulp magazines of the day–big, slow and lumbering.

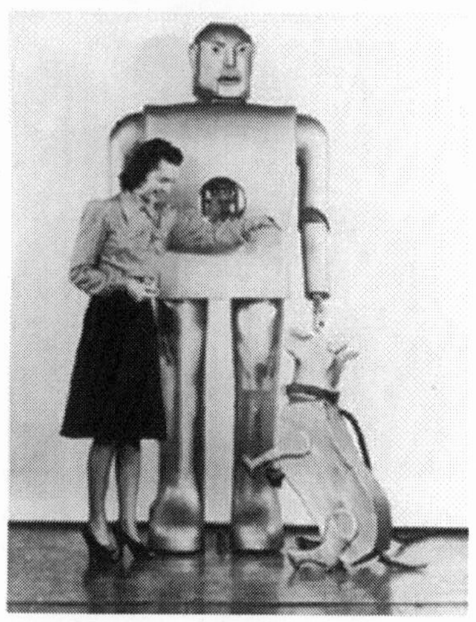

Elektro was a resident of the Westinghouse pavilion in the Fair's Production and Distribution Zone. He was manufactured by Westinghouse in a plant in Mansfield, Ohio. He stood seven feet tall and weighed 300 pounds. As part of his twenty minute presentation, he would walk, move his hands and arms, smoke cigarettes and speak by means of a 78 rpm record player. During the Fair's 1940 season, he was joined by Sparko, a robot dog who could speak, sit and beg.

Elektro made quite impression on fairgoers and entered into the popular culture of the era. Following World War II, Westinghouse used him to promote appliances, and he was a static display at Palisades Park in Oceanside, California for a number of years in the late 1950s and early 1960s. He appeared in the 1960 film *Sex Kittens Go to College*.

Veteran comic book writer Roy Thomas made Elektro a supporting character when he reintroduced the Justice Society of America to DC

Comics readers in the early 1980s. Thomas created a spin-off team know as the All Star Squadron that headquartered in the Fair's Trylon and Perisphere buildings. Their robot butler Gernsback was clearly based on the Elektro robots.

A Slightly Smaller Universe of Energy

The universe of energy was a much smaller entity in 1939. While automobile manufacturers were represented in three major pavilions and dominated the 1939 New York World's Fair transportation zone, oil companies were consolidated to the Petroleum Industry Exhibition and relegated to one building in the Production and Distribution Zone.

Sponsored by eighteen different companies, the Petroleum Exhibit was a generally modest endeavor compared to many of the Fair's other attractions. The official Guide Book of the New York World's Fair reflected the exhibit's lack of flair with the following fairly brief and uninspired description:

> *Plainly land marked by a towering oil derrick in actual operation, the Building (Voorhees, Walker, Foley & Smith, architects; Gilbert Rohde, designer) fronts on the Avenue of Pioneers. Shaped like an equilateral triangle, the structure rests on four huge oil tanks, its metal walls rising in flaring tiers. Four large murals by William T. Schwarz*

> *decorate the inner walls of the Great Hall of Industry, each depicting respectively one phase in the story of Petroleum — Production, Transportation, Research and Refining. Here on a mammoth stage, a motion picture in technicolor, its actors three-dimensional puppets, portrays the importance of petroleum in man's daily life. The Petroleum Garden on the roof is featured by an animated map on which miniature oil derricks depict the growth of oil production since 1860. A model of an oil refinery demonstrates the most up-to-date refining methods. Sponsored by fourteen major oil companies, the Exhibit shows how the industry has made possible and contributed to the advance of civilization during the past 80 years.*

The subject of energy was pretty much as dry then as it was at EPCOT Center in 1982, and a certain amount of window dressing was required for both to create interesting and entertaining presentations. At EPCOT, animatronic dinosaurs, sprawling theater cars and snappy songs generally countered the Universe of Energy pavilion's mostly low key films and Exxon sponsored public relations. Lacking the sophistication and flare of late 20th century technology, the Petroleum Exhibit had to settle for a motion picture called *Pete Roleum and his Cousins*. And what an incredibly weird bunch of characters they were.

Animated oil droplets tell the story of petroleum production in a disjointed and often extremely strange series of vignettes, ending with a chorus line musical number that is both bizarre and more or less incomprehensible. This is partly due to the fact that a person at the exhibit interacted with the film's narrator, and those scripted lines are absent from the film.

What makes *Pete Roleum* somewhat notable is that the stop-motion puppetry was created by silent filmmaker Charles Bowers. Bowers, largely unknown today, was a pioneer in stop-motion special effects photography during the mid to late 1920s. He was famous at the time for two reel features that incorporated his innovative special effects with the typical slapstick antics that hallmarked the comedies of the day. He faded from the movie business in 1930, only to resurface nearly a decade later, assisting director Joseph Losey in the making of *Pete Roleum*. Bowers also provided the film's narration.

The Original IllumiNations

Walt Disney World's pyrotechnic displays have been long recognized as state-of-the-art spectaculars. Epcot's Illuminations, in its series of incarnations, has in particular been lauded for its truly amazing combination of fire, water, music and pyrotechnic elements, with many observers especially praising its stunning originality in both concept and design.

However . . .

> *"This Lagoon of Nations display centers in a giant fountain which rises from an oval lake two blocks wide by four blocks long. Water, geysering in beautiful patterns from 1,400 nozzles, is painted in constantly changing rainbow hues by batteries of powerful electric lights from below. At climaxes in a performance, towering gas flames roar through the columns of scintillating water, from more than a hundred jets. Showers of fireworks burst overhead. Stirring music thunders an accompaniment to the display from the heart of the fountain."*
>
> From the article "Fountains of Flame" by Kenneth M. Swezey; *Popular Science*, August, 1939

As we noted numerous times already, the overall design of EPCOT Center was distinctly analogous to that of 1939 exposition. Similar to World Showcase, the Fair's Government Zone, which was comprised of pavilions representing both states and nations, was located in similar fashion behind the technology and commercial zones and featured a body of water at its center. It was there that the Fair's designers decided to create ". . . a scene to thrill thousands," as noted in the Popular Science article. The article explained that "The whole complex mechanism is 'played,' as if it were some mighty organ, by three operators at electric consoles located in a near-by tower." Regular programs, based on such themes as "The Spirit of George Washington," "Creation," "Isle of Dreams," "Fire Dance," are presented to tens of thousands of spectators each evening." Some of those themes do not sound very far removed from that of the current Illuminations presentation, Reflections of Earth.

In his book, *1939: The Lost World of the Fair*, author David Gelernter observed:

> *The critics raved. Fountain displays like the ones at the Lagoon of Nations and San Francisco's 1939 fair "deserve to be called examples of a new art," wrote Talbot Hamlin. "The best of them are as emotionally compelling as they are visually exciting." The show at the Lagoon gave the New York fair "its most unique and perhaps its most artistically memorable element." "Dramatic and indescribable beauty" wrote Gardner Harding.*

And so the Fair closed out its daily operations every night, over a half a century prior to guests at EPCOT Center being entertained in similar fashion around the World Showcase lagoon.

***Jeffrey Pepper** is a journalist and historian who writes extensively about 20th century popular culture and most especially Walt Disney and the the history of the Walt Disney Company. He is the publisher and author of the popular Disney web site 2719Hyperion.com. He and his family live just outside of Winston-Salem, North Carolina.*

The Carousel of Progress:
What Would Walt Think?

Michael Scopa

"The age we're living in is the most extraordinary the world has ever seen. The human species is still reaching for the stars. Today we are the shapers of the world of tomorrow. Often we can't explain what we see, but the era we are living in today is a dream coming true."

—*Walt Disney*

Within that quote Walt Disney was very much including himself. During his lifetime he truly evolved into someone who shaped the future and redefined what family vacations were all about. This man, a true visionary, was very much focused on bringing smiles to the faces of those who watched his movies, enjoyed his television productions, and of course, visited his theme parks.

But even a visionary like Walt Disney could have never imagined that a spark of an idea that first appeared in his mind would somehow touch the lives of a family decades later. In fact, for one person's life in particular, it would lead to important closure.

This story begins in the late 1950's when Walt Disney was looking to expand Disneyland, specifically Main Street, USA. Walt looked to add some flare to Main Street, USA, but not just any flare. His objective was to add a global flare to this, his Disneyland foyer. Walt toyed with the idea of expanding Main Street, USA with what he envisioned as an International Street or global thoroughfare that would include restaurants, shops, and attractions, bringing a taste of Europe or Asia to partner with the Americana feel already established within Main Street, USA.

In addition to this International Street idea, Walt was also, as always, focused on showcasing the latest technology to his guests in the form of some sort of attraction or show. He came up with something called Edison Square.

Edison Square would be Walt's vehicle to illustrate the latest trends in technology. The chosen name was in honor of course of Thomas Alva Edison, who is often touted as the 20th Century's greatest inventor. As you would expect with any Walt Disney brainchild, the plans were very detailed. The host of this area would be a character named "Wilbur K. Watt" and the attraction would cover electronic technology from the late 1800s to the present and even the future.

Unfortunately, even though Walt knew in his mind what he wanted and was confident that, if given the chance, he could bring his ideas to life, he also knew that in order to accomplish this goal, along the way, he would need to hurdle some rather tall obstacles.

Being a visionary brings with it frustration at times and Walt Disney, a man ahead of his time, often found himself running up against two primary roadblocks in his path, capital and technology; both very much linked together in this journey.

Capital was needed not just to get ideas off the ground but to nurture them, as well, for some ideas, even those best planned, go through some metamorphosis, which translates to unexpected more expense. More importantly, many times Walt's ideas were limited by the technology available at the time and in too many instances the lack of technology would delay the development of these ideas.

Thus it was the lack of both capital and technology that unfortunately led to Walt's decision to put on hold his plans to expand Disneyland's Main Street, USA.

His ideas were put on the shelf until opportunity knocked.

Opportunity came in the form of General Electric, one of several companies involved in the plans for the 1964 New York World's Fair in Flushing Meadows, New York. GE approached Walt Disney and proposed a partnership. The company was interested in creating a special pavilion for the upcoming fair with a plan to build something that would entertain, educate, and generate a lot of interest in what GE was all about…electricity.

Since he was seen as the premier storyteller of his time, who else but Walt and his Imagineers would be the perfect match for GE to partner with and tell their story? So here you have a visionary needing capital to bring an idea to life and a company who had capital but needed a visionary and storyteller to tell their story.

This was exactly what Walt was looking for: an opportunity to work with a large corporation who would enable him to develop the technology he was lacking to bring Edison Square to life.

GE would provide the funding and Walt would provide the creativity, energy, and experience to get the job done.

Walt presented to the General Electric executives a concept in which animated figures he called "audio-animatrons" would help tell the story of electricity. These figures would engage with the audience, just as a great actor does, to provide a means by which the story would be told to all who attended this attraction. The concept was well received and development soon began.

The GE pavilion was called Progressland and it became the number one attraction at the 1964 World's Fair.

The telling of the story of electricity from the 1890s to the present involved a number of theaters connected by dividing walls. These theaters combined to form a large circular structure and each theater would look out into an audience of several hundred guests. The audience portion of the attraction would rotate every several minutes, bringing the audience to a new scene (theater).

Each scene represented another milestone era in the history of electricity and the auto-animatrons, which Walt had described in his presentation to the GE executives, described how electricity affected the quality of their life.

Experienced Walt Disney World visitors recognize this as Walt Disney World's Magic Kingdom's *Carousel of Progress*, which is still going strong after making its debut in Flushing Meadows, NY almost a half century ago.

Walt was very excited with the reception his *Carousel of Progress* had received and he decided that this attraction would have a permanent home in Disneyland's Tomorrowland. The New York World's Fair closed its doors in 1965 and Walt immediately put plans together to move the *Carousel of Progress* to California. Unfortunately time was running out for Walt and he passed away in December 1966 some seven months before Disneyland's Tomorrowland and *Carousel of Progress* became part of the Disneyland landscape.

The attraction enjoyed a run of about six years before its doors permanently closed in 1973. Those doors reopened two years later in Orlando, Florida. The *Carousel of Progress*' new home was in Walt

Disney World's Magic Kingdom theme park where it continues to enjoy the popularity it first felt in 1964.

We could end the story here.

Walt's original concept for Edison Square was finally realized with General Electric's help, at the 1964 World's Fair. We could walk away at this point…but there is another chapter to the tale of the *Carousel of Progress* that must be told.

This chapter touches upon what was mentioned early on as how Walt mentioned how we should all recognize that we are the shapers of the world tomorrow. Well here is how Walt Disney and those who he has inspired, primarily his cast members, helped shape a special day for a special guest.

If not for "The Main Street Diaries" an employee newsletter for Disney Management, this story would probably have never been told…at least I don't know if I would have heard of it.

Right around the turn of the century or so, one particular issue of this newsletter was sent out to Walt Disney World cast members asking them to select a "Magical Memory" for the 100 Years of Magic Celebration. The celebration was to commemorate the 100th anniversary of the birth of Walt Disney.

One cast member, Elizabeth Meyer, picked a magical moment that occurred on January 4th, 2002 because it was, as she says, "…of the opportunity I had to spend a very special day with a very special family."

This all began on December 28th, 2001. On that day, Elizabeth Meyer was working at the Disney Reservation Center and had received an e-mail from Joanne Stolberg-Alger. In the letter Alger talked about her father who was a former executive at General Electric.

Apparently, back in the early 1960s when GE and The Walt Disney Company were in the initial stages of putting together their World's Fair venture, Alger's father was approached by the Disney Imagineers and asked if he would serve as the model for the animatronics host for the eventual *Carousel of Progress*.

He agreed but asked that it be kept a secret. He did not want very many people knowing he was “starring” in the exhibit. After all, wouldn’t it be quite an experience to bring his family to the New York World’s Fair and surprise them?

His plan was to bring his family to the pavilion on opening day and enjoy seeing their reaction when they saw him, or I should say his animatronics self, on stage.

Unfortunately, an illness came on quickly and not only robbed him of this opportunity but also his life as he became deathly ill and passed away at the early age of 40.

He had never told anyone in his family of his secret. It was buried along with him and sadly, the family never made it to the New York World’s Fair.

However, it was his brother’s interest in the New York World’s Fair that would lead to the unveiling of this secret. One visit to Progressland was all it took to reveal the secret.

Some 36 years later Joanne Stolberg-Alger visited Walt Disney World with her children and found her father sitting center stage at the *Carousel of Progress*. Unfortunately her 77-year-old mother, Doris Stolberg, had not made the trip but Joanne knew she had to return to Florida with her mother. She knew that there was some unfinished business that would require her mother to visit The Magic Kingdom and in particular the *Carousel of Progress*.

In her e-mail to the Disney Reservation Center, Joanne mentioned that she was planning on visiting The Magic Kingdom on January 4th and would be accompanied by her mother Doris and her daughter Shannon. She asked if she could purchase a ticket just to see the *Carousel of Progress*.

Reading this e-mail Elizabeth Meyer, who had formerly worked in the Magic Kingdom Event Group and sensed that this was a special occasion for the Stolberg-Alger family, contacted the Event Group to ask if there was anything special they could do for these guests.

After some phone calls Elizabeth was told to inform Joanne to meet her at the Guest Relations Window at the front of the park on January 4th.

On that day Elizabeth and several cast members from the Event Group were there to welcome Joanne, Doris, and Shannon.

Marvin Smith, Operating Manager of Magic Kingdom Guest Relations, had arranged to have special One-Day park hopper tickets waiting at the Guest Relations Window.

Joanne and her family were escorted to Tommorrowland and outside the *Carousel of Progress* where they found a Disney photographer waiting for them.

Judy Paulsen, a Tomorrowland Guest Services Manager, who had arranged for the family to have their own private showing of the *Carousel of Progress* show, also greeted them.

Before everyone went into the *Carousel of Progress* photos were taken of everyone in front of the attraction.

They were then escorted into the pavilion and everyone sat down to watch the show.

As the show started and the audience section began to rotate counter-clockwise to the first scene, Doris caught a glimpse of the show's "host", the animatronics figure modeled after her husband, sitting on center stage.

She immediately placed her hand to her mouth.

As her eyes remained glued to the animatronics figure, Doris started to smile and began to beam and said, "He looks exactly as I remember him!" and her eyes began to well up with tears…followed by everyone else in that audience.

It was truly a very magical moment for all who witnessed this special event.

After the show the photographer took some photos of "Dad" on stage and also a few with the family in front of the stage.

At the end of the show, Doris took out an old photo of her husband to show everyone what he had looked like and everyone was amazed at the resemblance. The Imagineers had truly caught his likeness.

As the group exited the theater, Doris took Elizabeth Meyer's hand and said "Thank you! You have no idea what this means to me."

Doris was very much moved by the hospitality and had waited 37 years to finally experience the *Carousel of Progress* and, more importantly, to see her husband's image be part of an attraction that has brought so much enjoyment to guests for so many years.

The family was warmly told to enjoy the park and was asked to be in front of City Hall at 2 P.M. to receive the photographs of their visit. What Joanne, Doris, and Shannon did not know was that with the help of Dean Gaschler of Magic Kingdom Guest Relations, they were going to ride an electric car as Grand Marshals of the Share a Dream Come True Parade that afternoon.

Dean presented them with Mickey Mouse Ear Hats and challenged them to "wave at each of our guests equally, not only the cute fellas!"

Though Doris was 78 years old that day, the second the car reached the parade route, her eyes lit up and she was a child again.

At the end of the day, Doris was beyond words, but Joanne spoke for everyone when she said it was a day that they would never forget.

This is just one of perhaps hundreds, maybe even thousands of stories of special moments made possible through the actions of Disney cast members.

When we think of this story and how that day evolved we realize it may not have taken place had it not been for the actions of people like Elizabeth Meyer, Marvin Smith, Judy Paulsen, and Dean Gaschler. As Jay Rasulo, current Senior Executive Vice President and Chief Financial Officer of The Walt Disney Company once said of the cast members, "They are the Dreammakers."

However, it was the original DreamMaker, Walt Disney, who served as the catalytic force for how cast members today approach their work and their treatment of their guests.

When you have a formula down pat for treating your guests in a very special manner, along with that drive to bring that unique attraction to fruition, it's a formula for success.

When you add that rare component such as the beginnings of the *Carousel of Progress*, that formula breaks through a higher threshold of service.

We must always remember that in order for the guests to as we say, "Get it!" the cast members had to "Get it!" first…and from whom? Of course we know who that is.

It's that same person who so wisely noted that we are the "shapers of tomorrow."

Yes, when I think of the story of the *Carousel of Progress* and the Stolberg-Alger family the only question left unanswered is, "What would Walt Think?"

***Michael Scopa** is a senior feature writer and blogger for AllEars.net, co-host on the WDWTODAY Podcast, and a contributing author to The Unofficial Guide to Walt Disney World and The Luxury Guide* *to Walt Disney World. He has also served as a peer reviewer for Passporter's Open Mouse for Walt Disney World and the Disney Cruise Line and technical editor for Plan Your Walt Disney World Vacation in No Time.*

In 2005 Mike was chosen by the Walt Disney Company as one of the 50 "Happiest Passholders on Earth" and in 2007 was chosen by the Walt Disney Company to represent the Walt Disney World Annual Passholders at the Year of a Million Dreams announcement in New York City.

An avid runner, Mike has run in over a dozen Walt Disney World sponsored races.

An Island Filled with Tropic Beauty, Colorful Birds,
and the Mystery of Ben Gunn's Buried Treasure!

George Taylor

Discovery Island, situated on Bay Lake, has endured many names and identities over the years. More so than its name changes, the history of this dormant attraction is quite fascinating. The Island was one of the spots that caught Walt's eyes when they were looking for property near Orlando. He flew over Central Florida in the company jet and this island caused him to set aside the surrounding property as the first to be developed.

Visiting the Island over the years would have provided a multitude of different experiences depending upon the timing of your vacation. Was it a deserted pirate island full of treasure and mystery? Was it an island refuge for hundreds of fowl and various animals? Or was it an integral and much needed part of a Walt Disney World vacation?

Island History

From its earliest incarnation, it was known as Raz Island for the family that lived and farmed there from 1900 to 1937. Delmar Nicholson, Florida's first disc jockey, purchased the area in the late 1930's and named it Idle Bay Isle. He lived on the island with his wife and a pet sand crane. When he fell ill, Nick sold the island to some local businessmen who used it as a hunting retreat. It was named Riles Island until Disney purchased the 28,000 acres that included the island in 1965.

The island was named Blackbeard's Island when Walt Disney World opened in 1971. It appeared on guide maps but development of the island didn't start until 1974. At that time, 55,000 cubic yards of soil and over 500 tons of boulders and trees were used to build up the island's acreage to 11 and a half acres. Disney created three elevated lagoons, winding foot paths, streams and hills. It was renamed Treasure Island and opened on April 7, 1974 with hopes to attract and extend vacation stays. It was closed from January to March 1976 for a renovation that included a snack bar and an aviary.

Treasure Island

> *Sail the Seven Seas of Walt Disney World to an island filled with tropic beauty, colorful birds, and the mystery of Ben Gunn's buried treasure!*

Visiting Treasure Island in 1974 and 1975 would have landed you in a tropical paradise that was beginning its theming towards the famous Robert Louis Stevenson story (and the 1950 Disney film). Cast members were dressed in Pirate garb and oil lamps lit the trails. In a promotional brochure from the time, Disney promises multiple themed areas related directly to the book. *Billy Bones' Dilemma*, the *Blockhouse*, *Spy Glass Hill* and *Ben Gunn's Cave* never made it off of the drawing board. *The Remains of the Walrus* would have been converted into the *Wreck of the Hispaniola*. For the most part, it was referred to as the Hispanolia, even though it was the remains of Captain Flint's ship. The wrecked ship was discovered off of the coast of Florida and moved to the Island.

Arriving at Treasure Island from the Polynesian Resort Village or the Contemporary Resort via launch, you would disembark at the Jolly Roger Wharf. Additionally, guests could take the "Walt Disney World Cruise" which was a half-day tour of Bay Lake and Seven Seas Lagoon on a sidewheeler that featured a recorded narration and refreshments. From there, Disney planned a half-day retreat for guests that ended with a fireside singalong and marshmallow roast. Along the route, you discovered 19 stops, vistas and animal encounter areas: Cap'n Flint's Perch, Buccaneer's Cove, North Inlet, Lookout Point, Black Dog Bridge, Doubloon Lagoon, Mutineer Falls, Dead Man's Island, Skeleton Lair, Buccaneer's Roost, Black Dog Swamp, Cape of the Woods, Remains of "the Walrus", Scavenger Beach, Flamingo Lagoon, Rum Point, Toucan Cage and the Mizzen Mast. Each are provided a distinct bird, mammal or specific fauna.

The brochure that Disney released with the map of Treasure Island also previewed coming attractions related to the Pirate theme. Sam McKim, who is also known for early illustrations of Main Street and Frontierland at Disneyland, provided illustrations of the Pirate additions that were promised but never delivered. Let's take a closer look at the proposed attractions:

- *Billy Bone's Dilemma...Captain Flint's first mate falls prey to the perils of the open sea.*
- *The Blockhouse...Site of the battle for the treasure map. "Though fully armed...we were still out-numbered by Long John Silver's buccaneers!"*
- *Spy Glass Hill...A fantastic group of rocks in the heart of the island. In this primeval playground, you'll discover the secrets of this treasure isle!*
- *Ben Gunn's Cave...As mysterious as the strange hermit himself. Its exact location is unknown even today...but we know it's someplace on the island!*

- *Wreck of the Hispaniola...This seagoing vessel led by Captain Smollet, once anchored here in search of buried treasure...only to be overtaken by her mutinous crew, headed by the self-appointed captain. Long John Silver! She was later ran ashore by the brave young Jim Hawkins...never to sail again!*

Unfortunately, the Pirate theme seemed to attract visitors looking for more of a swashbuckling adventure instead of the more sedate walking tour that existed. Disney did not offer a restaurant on the island, so guests were invited to bring picnic supplies from the Disney Village and Fort Wilderness. Swimming was not allowed, but beach exploration was encouraged.

Discovery Island

When it re-opened in April 1976, it was finally named Discovery Island and included one of the world's largest aviaries. The Island was accredited by the American Zoo and Aquarium Association in 1978 and functioned as a breeding facility for rare birds The date of accreditation is noted in some publications as 1979, as well. Discovery Island became renowned for its bird, plant and tortoise populations.

Sail the Seven Seas of Walt Disney World to an island filled with tropical flowers, colorful birds and an untold wealth of discoveries!

In 1978, the island retained many of the pirate-related names from its first two years of operation. Originally, the snack bar was known as the Olde Anchor Inn. Later, it would be called the Thirsty Perch. A few of the stops were renamed or altered during the addition of the Aviary and a second set of restrooms (Mates and Maidens), but most of the route remained the same. The Aviary was one of the worlds largest and measured over an acre. With the re-christening of the Island, Disney added more animals to the sites. Some of the animals featured: peacocks, macaws, rheas, tortoises, flamingos, pelicans, hornbills, eagles, alligators, rabbits, miniature deer, toucans, Patagonian cavies, hornbills, scarlet ibis, cockatoos, cranes, swans and two caged primates.

With the AZA accreditation, the cast members found themselves spending more time taking care of the animals and working on breeding protocols as opposed to guest interactions. By the 1990's the Island boasted over 90 species of animals and 250 species of plants. In 1987, the last of the dusky seaside sparrows died at Discovery Island. There was an attempt to repopulate the species, but it failed.

Sometimes in the mid-1980s, vultures started to appear around the island sanctuary. The disruptive birds caused damage to the island and many of its inhabitants. Cast members tried many alternative devices to dissuade the vultures from staying. Eventually, five Disney employees were brought up on charges of animal cruelty and killing. The employees were reassigned, fines were paid and Disney began a very public campaign throughout the divisions that centered on environmentality. Environmentality is... *a fundamental ethic that blends business growth with the conservation of natural resources. Attention to the environment drives new business initiatives demonstrating how environmental stewardship goes hand-in-hand with bottom line cost savings.*

The island tour stops were completely devoid of any Pirate influences by the early 1980s: Parrot's Perch, Discovery Island Bird show, North Inlet, Monkey Colony, Trumpeter Springs, North Falls, Swan's Neck, Bamboo Hollow, Vulture's Haunt, Toucan Corner, Crane's Roost, Avian Way, Boardwalk, Rookery Pond, Pelican Bay, Flamingo Lagoon, Tortoise Beach, Alligator Pond and Eagle's Watch. It was noted in many of the promotional material that a few of the island's inhabitants would not survive in their native areas due to injuries. The two southern bald eagles were on loan from the U.S. Department of the Interior.

By the 1990s, there were a few additions and changes to the Discovery Island lineup. There was an Education Pavilion; Feathered Friends display; Primate Point (Lemurs); African Aviary; the Discovery Island Headquarters, Animal Hospital and Nursery; Wildlife Walkway; Fishing Cat; South American Aviary; and Shipwreck Beach. By the time that the Animal Kingdom Park opened in 1998, it was obvious that there was not much to bring people to Discovery Island.

The island was officially closed on April 8, 1999, after 25 years of entertaining and educating guests. Many of the conservation and breeding efforts were moved to Disney's Animal Kingdom Park. For a few years after closing, Disney considered the idea of re-creating the island based on the theme of the popular CD-ROM based game entitled Myst. Due to costs, construction issues and technology, the idea never left the drawing board. Other ideas have surfaced that focus on creating a multi-hour attraction that would serve a limited number of guests and charge a larger admission fee. Disney was looking at a boutique experience similar to Sea World's Discovery Cove.

What Happened?

In the first decade of Walt Disney World's public history, Disney was providing a vastly different vacation resort than the one we see today. With the opening of Treasure Island in 1974, the amenities of the Vacation Kingdom were spread far and thin compared to today. The Magic Kingdom, three on-site hotels, Fort Wilderness Campgrounds and various outdoor recreational activities were all that were available to guests. Swimming, boating, horseback riding and tennis were considered ways to round out a week-long stay at Walt Disney World. Most promotional material from the time advised two days at the Magic Kingdom (when operating hours were frequently 9-6) and a day camping at Fort Wilderness. What else were you supposed to do while on vacation? Disney often promoted neighboring attractions and restaurants in Orlando and surrounding counties. For Disney enthusiasts, this seems like a completely foreign concept. When Disney created the Reedy Creek Improvement District and lobbied the Florida governments, one of the major points was that Walt Disney World was going to be a good neighbor; they would spend time promoting local attractions, hotels and eateries.

Many historians cite the lack of transportation to the Island and the dearth of precious vacation time that led to the slow demise of this unique zoological attraction. In the mid-1990s, with three amusement parks, three water parks, a large shopping/entertainment district and 99 holes of golf, vacationers found their time spent away from theme parks a dwindling resource. Early morning entry into the parks for resort guests and hours extending past midnight for parks and entertainment severely restricted where and when guests spent their time and money.

Another area of thought deals with the proposed Phase II development of Seven Seas Lagoon, EPCOT Center and the Walt Disney World Village. The plan for Phase II hotels that would circle Seven Seas Lagoon would have been added to the monorail loop shortly after Treasure Island opened. Imagine the number of vacationers added with the addition of the Persian, Venetian and Asian Hotels that would have launches to the Island.

Walt's original idea for EPCOT Center evolved (or devolved, as the case may be) into a theme park, as opposed to a city with citizens that had jobs, families and social commitments. Would a transitory population of roughly 20,000 citizens have added enough day and weekend visitors to keep the Island open? Would there have been drastic changes to keep up with the surge in population?

One expansion idea for the Walt Disney World Village Resorts was to add a series of life-style based communities that would offer time share resorts. Companies and individuals would be able to purchase a week or two-week period based on whether they were golf, tennis or equestrian fans. The three communities would have added a large number of vacationers seeking more varied entertainment options.

Needless to say, in April 1999, the Island closed its doors. Shortly after that, land at the Animal Kingdom Park was named Discovery Island. Discovery Island was one of the last vestiges of 1970s Walt Disney World; a time when vacations were more carefree and less duty-bound to seek out every last bit of theme park fun.

George Taylor, *a public librarian by trade, runs Imaginerding.com. He is obsessed with Disney-related books and has collected of over 350 different titles. A Disney enthusiast with an interest in the theme parks and animation, he writes frequently about the little details that we often miss.*

Honoring the Cast: Insider Tributes & Homages

Kevin Yee

"You can design, create, and build the most wonderful place in the world… but it takes people to make the dream a reality"

—*Walt Disney*

Continuing a tradition begun at Disneyland, all of the Walt Disney World parks pay tribute to the designers, dreamers, and builders who contributed to the construction and evolution of the parks and attractions. Some of the homages are explicit and obvious, while others are subtle and completely unlabeled. The presence of these tributes creates a rich layer of subtext to the park experience. If you know where to look, you'll discover an entire hidden world of tributes that had been there all this time, right before your eyes.

Some of the homages are not only in plain sight, they are actually labeled. There are surprisingly few of these. On the ferries across the Seven Seas Lagoon, the Disney executives who helped build Walt Disney World are honored by having the boats named after them (they were originally named just MK1 and MK2). Richard Irvine was one of the top executives in the company when WDW was built, while Joe Potter was a retired Navy admiral who led the construction of the Magic Kingdom. Be sure to look for a portrait and biography of each executive on the first floor of each boat, about in the middle of the ship.

Among the few obvious tributes is one dedicated to Disney executive Frank Wells found in the first room of the FASTPASS queue for Expedition Everest. The photo shows Frank resting during an attempt to climb the real Mt. Everest. He was such an avid climber that his window on Main Street reflected the goal of climbing the tallest mountain on all seven continents.

You can find the signatures of several names scrawled into the concrete in one courtyard at the Magic of Disney Animation exhibit at Disney's Hollywood Studios. The names include Marc Davis, Ken Anderson, Ward Kimball, Frank Thomas, and Ollie Johnston. A visitor might easily guess the truth: these are some of the major animators in Disney's history, though there is no sign making it explicit who these folks are.

Nor is there a sign at the Central Plaza of the Magic Kingdom, where an obvious tribute to Walt Disney can be found in the form of the bronze statue. Pictured with his partner Mickey, Walt extends his arm toward Main Street as if waving hello to visitors as they arrive. Look closer. See that tie tack with the letters STR? This was a real pin Walt used to wear. The letters stood for Smoke Tree Ranch, which was used for occasional location filming away from the studio, as well as more recreational weekend getaways.

At the other end of Main Street, a similar bronze tribute to Walt's brother Roy O. Disney sits on a bench with Minnie Mouse. Because Walt had died before the Magic Kingdom opened, Roy took over and made sure Walt's vision was enacted. In a way, the Magic Kingdom is Roy's park as much as it is Walt's park.

The other unlabeled, somewhat obvious, tribute to Walt can be found in the Big City set at Disney's Hollywood Studios. See that subway entrance? The staircase may be a dead-end, but the joke is up top, where the subway lines are labeled as W and D, Walt's initials.

The tributes to Cast Members that many visitors already know about can be seen on the second floor windows of Main Street U.S.A. Here you'll find a couple dozen specially-decorated windows, many attributing unusual jobs to individuals whose names are not familiar to the casual visitor. These were the designers, builders, and longtime executives at Walt Disney World. Here is a list of their windows, displayed in order presented at the park (note: some names appear more than once):

> ***West Main Street, from the fire station up toward the castle—***
> *Roger Broggie, Owen Pope, Buddy Baker, Bob Jackman, George Bruns, Ron Logan, Lonnie Lindley, Ed Bullard, Robert Jani, Charles Corson, Emile Kuri, Charlie Ridgway, Joyce Carlson, Bob Booth, Roger Broggie Jr., John Frankie, Neil Gallagher, Jack Gladish, Rudy Pena, Dave Schweninger, Dick Van Every, Jim Verity, Morrie Houser, Lou Jennings, John Joyce, Don Edgren, John Wise, Ken Klug, Stan Maslak, John Zovich, David Snyder, Michael Bagnall, Bill Walsh, Cecil Robinson, Jack Lindquist, Dave Gengenbach, Bob Gurr, George McGinnis, Bill Watkins, Earl Vilmer, Card Walker, Ted Crowell, Arnold Lindberg, Claude Coats, Marc Davis, John DeCuir, Bill Justice, Jim*

Armstrong, John Curry, Howard Roland, Stan Garves, Tony Baxter, Dave Burkhart, Ed Johnson, Gary Younger, Ralph Kent

East Main Street, from the Plaza Restaurant back toward Town Square—

Larry Slocum, Howard Brummitt, Marvin Davis, Vic Green, John Hench, Fred Hope, Richard Irvine, Bill Martin, Chuck Myall, Bill Sullivan, Bob Matheison, Christopher Miller, Jennifer Miller, Joanna Miller, Patrick Miller, Ron and Diane Miller, Ronald Miller Jr., Tamara Miller, Walter Miller, Don Iwerks, Ub Iwerks, Bill Washo, Bud Washo, Dick Nunis, Ron Miller, Orlando Ferrante, Abigail Disney, Roy Patrick Disney, Patty Disney, Roy E. Disney, Susan Disney, Timothy Disney, Morgan Evans, Tony Virginia, Donn Tatum, Frank Wells, Carl Bongirno, Jim McManus, Warren Robertson, Larry Tryon, Neal McClure, Dick Morrow, Spence Olin, Jim Ross, Phil Smith, Bonar Dyer, Hank Dains, Chuck Fowler, Frank Millington, Marshall Smelser, Bill Sullivan, Bob Matheison, Bob Allen, Pete Crimmings, Dick Evans, Bill Joelscher, Jack Olsen, Pete Clark, Jack Sayers, Norm Fagrell, Bud Dare, Mary Blair, Collin Campbell, Blaine Gibson, Dorothea Redmond, Herb Ryman, Nolan Browning, Roy Davis (aka Roy O. Disney), Bob Price (aka Bob Foster), Elias Disney, Ken Chapman, Paul Hartley, Sam McKim, Elmer Plummer, Ernie Prinzhorn, Vince Jefferds, Lou Tonarely, Wilbur Watt, Bradford Lund, Michelle Lund, Victoria Lund, William and Sharon Lund, Malcolm Cobb, Jack Ferges, Fred Joerger, Mitz Natsume, Bob Sewell, Lee Cockerell, Bruce Laval, Tom Eastman, James Passilla, Pat Vaughn, Tom Nabbe, Yale Gracey, Bud Martin, Ken O'Brien, Wathel Rogers, Bill Bosche, Jack Boyd, Bob Bigeaut, Dick Pfahler, McLaren Steward, Robert Moore, Norm Noceti, Ed Chisholm, Gordon Williams, X Atencio, Al Bertino, Marty Sklar, Doug Cayne, Joe Kramer, George Windrum, Ron Bowman, Glenn Durflinger, Don Holmquist, Dick Kline, George Nelson, Roy O. Disney, Joe Potter, Bill Irwin, Larry Reiser, Pete Markham, Dan Dingman, Francis

Stanek, Bob Phelps, Ken Creekmore, Orpha Harryman, John Keehne, Alyja Paskevicius, Tom Pierce

It's possible to view Main Street as the first reel of a symbolic movie—after all, movies were the primary product of the Walt Disney Company before theme parks—and the names on the windows thus become the credits as the "movie" begins. Just like in movies, where the director's name comes last, one of the last prominent windows on Main Street (facing the castle) heralds Walt Disney. It was, after all, his vision.

While the Main Street windows mention the honorees by name, their exact contribution is not spelled out. Still, the fanciful jobs mentioned often provide hints to the roles played while working for Disney. Bob Gurr, who designed most of the park's attraction vehicles for decades, once said that if something at the park had wheels, he probably designed it. Fittingly, his window is for a bicycle company called Meteor Cycle. Another example can be found in the window for Yale Gracey and three other special-effects artists, which displays a movie projector to imply the visual trickery they were able to create.

Most of the tributes throughout the parks are less clearly explained, even when the Cast Member's name is directly invoked. Take the artificial leaf blade at the Mad Tea Party, which has this inscription: "Be good at something; it makes you valuable.... Have something to bring to the table, because that will make you more welcome. – Randy Pausch." Randy was a former Imagineer that became a professor, and earned fame for giving an inspirational "Last Lecture" before dying of a terminal illness. None of that context is provided on the sign, however—just his name.

The *Carousel of Progress* sports two such tributes. Look for a sign visible through the window of the 1920s scene labeled "Herb Ryman – Attorney at Law." Herb was not an attorney, but he was instrumental in the early history of Disneyland, when he painted the conceptual artwork that helped Walt sell the idea of the park to financial backers. The other tribute is more subtle. Watch for a sticky note on the bulletin board in the final scene, which reads "Marty called. Wants changes." The Marty in question here is Marty Sklar, the longtime head of Walt

Disney Imagineering (and definitely a guy in a position to request changes!)

Hop over to *Space Mountain* and keep your eyes open as your rocket sled gets to the very top of the lift hill. If you glance at the spaceship to your side, you'll see H-NCH stenciled on it, in reference to Imagineer John Hench. John had helped develop the vision of *Space Mountain* from inception to final product.

Next to Peter Pan's Flight is an innocuous brown barrel labeled "Fire Chief W. Ray Colburn, Lost Boys Fire Brigade." It turns out that Colburn was the longtime chief of the real fire department in Walt Disney World, the semi-governmental agency called the Reedy Creek Improvement District. A duplicate barrel with an equivalent homage can be found near the exit to Big Thunder Mountain Railroad.

Slow down to appreciate the tombstones at the entrance to the Haunted Mansion, for these are all folks who worked on the ride: Xavier Atencio wrote the script and the song lyrics, Marc Davis contributed the vision, Yale Gracey conjured up most of the illusions, Wathel Rogers actually built the effects, Claude Coates designed the track layout, Cliff Huet designed the interior, Gordon Williams created many of the Audio-Animatronics, Leota Toombs performed the séance madam, Bob Sewell and Dave Burkhart were model makers, and Chuck Myall, Fred Joerger, and Bill Mart were art directors on the attraction.

Marc Davis has a second tribute up the road, in the form of a crate labeled Davis Tobacco not far from the *Country Bear Jamboree*. Marc was the main creative vision behind this bear show, which was originally designed for the Mineral Springs ski resort in California. Disney eventually decided not to develop the ski resort.

Marc's third tribute can be found inside the Pirates of the Caribbean, a ride which owes its vision to Marc more than anyone else. At the town treasury in the final scene, look high up on the exterior wall to find a shield design. This is the Davis coat of arms, a nod to Marc's contributions to this attraction. There are other significant coats of arms in the Magic Kingdom, principally those hanging in the restaurant inside Cinderella Castle, which are there to honor the family crests for prominent Imagineers. None of them, however, are clearly labeled.

Landscape designer and chief horticulturalist Morgan Evans is honored with his name on the FASTPASS machines at the Jungle Cruise. If you look around at the nearby planters out in the walkway, you'll find Morgan's name emblazoned across the crates holding them as well.

In the Jungle Cruise queue, watch for a barrel addressed to Dr. Winston Hibler at outpost 71755. Winston was the narrator on all the True-Life Adventure films of the 1950s, which gave rise to the Adventureland concept at Disneyland. Even the outpost number is significant, as it references Disneyland's opening on July 17, 1955.

Nearby is a crate advertising "Goff's Brand" of crocodile resistant pants, which is based at 1911 Main Street, Fort Collins, Colorado. Goff refers to Harper Goff, the Disney designer who crafted Main Street and helped significantly with the Jungle Cruise. The mention of Main Street is only half of the tribute. Harper had been raised in Fort Collins, Colorado, and he used that small town—even more so than Walt's youth in Marceline, Missouri—as his inspiration for the design and layout of Main Street at Disneyland. And 1911? That was the year of Harper's birth.

If you strain your ears at the end of the Seas with Nemo and Friends, you can hear mention of "Commander Fulton." This is in reference to Fulton Burley, a performer from Disneyland's Golden Horseshoe Revue but better known as the voice of Michael in the Tiki Room. Fulton has more visible tributes at Port Orleans Riverside (Fulton's General Store) and Downtown Disney (Fulton's Crab House).

A rather large, if quite hidden, list of Cast Member names can be briefly glimpsed at the Great Movie Ride. During the Alien sequence, one of the monitors to the left side of the vehicle (and almost at ground level) displays the names of many Imagineers who worked on the ride, listed with fake job titles. Most of the jobs sound plausible or futuristic to fit with the Alien theme. Eric Jacobson, for instance, is the "system alteration supervisor." But they did manage to sneak in some inside jokes. If you can spot Doug Griffith (about halfway down the list) quickly enough, you'll be rewarded with his amusing job title: "still programming the witch."

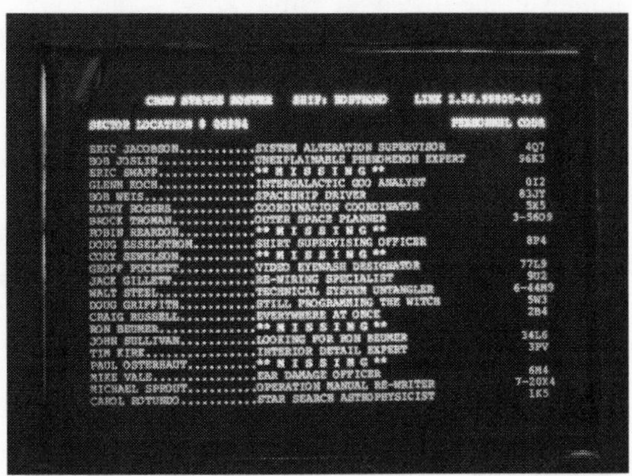

Part of the meet-and-greet location for Monsters Inc., located near the exit to Backlot Tour, includes a nod to the director of Monsters Inc., Pete Docter. A bulletin board on one wall includes handwritten notes signed "Pete D." on Walt Disney Entertainment letterhead reminding employees of recent policies.

Another PIXAR luminary, animator Joe Ranft, was given an homage in the FASTPASS queue for Toy Story Mania. Look for his name on the spine of a blue book. Joe, who died in 2005 in a car accident, is the supposed author of the book "Magic Made Easy," a further tribute to Joe's hobby as a magician.

Nor is Joe the only PIXAR Cast Member honored at Toy Story Mania. The chief creative officer, John Lasseter, is listed as the author on a green book seen at the very end of the ride, just before we disembark. The book listed is "Tin Toy," which was John's first computer animated short in 1988 and the overall inspiration for the Toy Story concept.

Sometimes the Cast Members' names are used without any context whatsoever. A prime example can be seen at the Echo Lake Apartments, where the mailboxes use the names of people involved in the building of the park, then named Disney-MGM Studios.

Perhaps even more famously, on several occasions Imagineers plant just their initials in the rides they build. This is common practice on virtually every ride made since the 1990s—if you see anything that looks like it could be initials, often accompanied by what could be a birth date (or a birth year in the 1960s or 1970s), the odds are good you've just discovered the Imagineer behind that ride. Prominent examples include the electrical boxes in the queue of Rock 'n Roller Coaster, or the pipes along the queue walls in Star Tours (the other numbers are office phone extensions). The Imagineers really went crazy in the Sci-Fi Dine-In Theater, where the license plates of the parked cars offered plenty of opportunity to include initials of everyone working on the restaurant.

While the initials are less obvious than using full names, things really get tricky when the tributes don't use any identification at all. These homages require insider knowledge to even get the joke, and it's likely that a great many of them are simply never noticed by the average visitor.

Some of the photos under the Main Street train station show off the backyard at Walt Disney's Holmby Hills estate, with his backyard locomotive, Lily Belle (named after his wife Lillian). But far more obscure references await just around the corner, where the train schedule on one wall mentions Grizzly Falls. This is a reference to the private backyard railroad of Ward Kimball, the animator and Imagineer who first got Walt excited about railroading. Unlike Walt's miniature backyard railroad, Ward's was full sized.

Some Imagineers are lucky enough to have their photograph—unlabeled—used in the parks. For example, during the "Two Brothers" song at the American Adventure, Imagineers posed for a Civil War era family portrait. A second example might be seen at Casey's Corner, where one photo behind the bleachers is more modern than the other vintage pictures. Everyone sports mustaches in this picture—even the female Imagineers!

The Cast Members are equally fond of painting representations of themselves into the parks. The Imagineers responsible for the expansion of the Emporium on Main Street painted themselves (plus a few extra Imagineers) into one large mural near the ceiling. There are no particular hints or giveaway that the mural depicts Imagineers; this is one of those you simply have to know.

There are actually several such paintings with unheralded portrayals of Imagineers. The image of a family at Thanksgiving, seen in the second floor lobby of the American Adventure, uses several Imagineers as models. The painter, Imagineer Sam McKim, painted his own son Brian as the child with the dog.

Look for prominent Imagineers Marty Sklar, John Hench, and Randy Bright in the American Adventure attraction itself, in the painting celebrating this victory in the American Revolution. As the camera pans out, watch the right side of the screen to see Marty (the flutist), John (one hand in the air), and Randy (two hands in the air).

John Hench reappears again at Cinderella Castle, in the tile mural where Cinderella is being fitted to her slipper. The duke is none other than John Hench, and the footman's face bears an intentional likeness to Imagineer Herb Ryman. Both John and Herb had helped in designing this castle.

Even Imagineer Joe Rohde, the chief designer of Disney's Animal Kingdom, gets into the act. Have you ever noticed all the weathered posters for Captain Bob's balloon rides plastered all over Harambe in Africa? The illustration of Captain Bob is a caricature of Joe. Equally obscure is the sign on the field sample crate at the Kid's Discovery station in Dinoland U.S.A., which reads RD-1. If you allow for the 1 to be read as an "I," as often happens in text messages, the sign can be read aloud as "roadie," which is the correct pronunciation of Joe's last name.

In one case, the Imagineer is represented not by a picture, but by his silhouette. The designer of American Adventure, Rick Rothschild, took his whole team to the Magic Kingdom to have silhouettes made as a celebration for finishing work on their attraction. Some of the silhouettes now hang in the foyer for the attraction. Rick simply added a ponytail to his silhouette to make himself appear more colonial.

A few extremely lucky but anonymous Imagineers have had their faces immortalized as Audio-Animatronics, most notably in Pirates of the Caribbean and the Haunted Mansion. The granddaddy of all such honors goes to Imagineer Al Bertino, whose face, body type, personality, and even first name were allowed to form the core of the Big Al character in the *Country Bear Jamboree*.

But Al is not the only Imagineer to be portrayed directly in a ride he or she helped create. Imagineer Joyce Carlson can be seen as a doll in "it's a small world," hanging from a rope underneath the Eiffel tower. Even this placement is itself a second-order tribute, since the Joyce doll is repeating a tradition begun at Disneyland, where the first "small world" designer Mary Blair was honored with her own doll standing halfway up that Eifel tower.

While here at "it's a small world," look upward at the intricate façade of arches, spires, and turrets that sets the tone for the attraction in the loading area. See those spinning golden toppers that cap many of the spires? Those are exact reproductions of Imagineer Leota Toombs's earrings simply scaled up. Leota (the same Imagineer who performed the Haunted Mansion's séance madam) was given to wearing flashy earrings, and her elaborate jewelry was seen as the perfect accompaniment to the fanciful architecture.

We end with perhaps the most obscure tribute, but an important one to Disney history. Indeed, it may mark the very beginning of the Disney company. When Walt was looking for an office space in Hollywood to hold his newly-formed Disney Brothers animation company, he came across a second-story sign announcing "For Rent" above a business called the Holly Vermont Realty, and he had found a home for his fledgling studio. This same scenario—the realty below and the rental sign up top—is recreated in the Echo Lake corner of Disney's Hollywood Studios, behind the Hollywood Blvd buildings.

In many ways, this sign is the quintessential insider tribute. Those who know nothing about it simply see location-appropriate theming and move on, appreciative of the many-layered details that make Disney parks unique and beloved the world over. But those who know where to look (and what to look for) see a deeper, richer message. The subtle associations carried by history infuse the present. On the surface, it's just an office space. But at the same time, it's also a reminder of the company's humble beginnings, and a reflection on how far it has progressed since then.

But most of all, these tributes add a cultural and historical dimension to the theming right in front of us. Disney parks are beloved because they look and feel real. They capture the essence of escapism by piling up details upon details, so many that it becomes difficult to see these artificial constructs as anything but real. That some of these details have their own internal history—such as tributes to the Cast Members—merely adds another layer onto an already layered experience, and renders it all the more rich and rewarding.

Kevin Yee *worked at Disneyland for 15 years, and has made Orlando his home since 2004. He has contributed extensively to Disney park websites, blogs, and essays, and he is the author of several books about Disney theme parks, including Walt Disney World Hidden History: Remnants of Former Attractions and Other Tributes.*

Theme Park Archaeology

Kevin Yee

Walt Disney once said that "Disneyland will never be complete," and sure enough, the theme parks have continued to evolve over the years. But because the parks have finite space available, when it becomes time to build something new that usually means having to destroy something old. However, every so often, a piece of the old survives to coexist alongside the new, and if you know where to look, you can spot these references to hidden history. At other times, deliberate tributes to the previous attractions are folded into the new ones, giving an intentional nod to history beyond just physical remains.

Like a certain fedora-wearing archeologist, we step now into the parks to hunt for those places where "X marks the spot." Locating these remnants can be as rewarding and fun as spotting Hidden Mickeys, because we become part of the inside joke. Furthermore, these tributes integrate thematically with the Disney park experience, in that so much of Disney's magic formula relies anyway on various types of nostalgia (such as for earlier eras in history, or for our own childhood), and the tributes and remnants provide their own kind of nostalgia for earlier days in the theme parks.

We begin at the Magic Kingdom. You don't have to travel far into Main Street U.S.A. before you encounter the Main Street Cinema, which today is a store. But glance up at the ceiling. See that hexagonal box hanging down from the ceiling, with small rectangle cutouts facing in multiple directions? Back when this facility was a working cinema of side-by-side old-time movies, this box in the ceiling was the housing for the projectors, and it's still here, silently evoking the original purpose of this space.

Just a few doors down you'll find a wooden Indian along the curb. What's he doing here in front of Crystal Arts? It turns out that part of Crystal Arts used to be the Market House, a kind of general store, and such themed items as a typewriter or scales atop displays cases in Crystal Arts are remnants of the Market House. The Indian is a decent thematic match for the Market House, but his original presence on Main Street was in front of a tobacco store, which was located across the street.

At the end of Main Street we find our first attraction remnant. Do you remember the Swan Boats? These stately floating tour boats traveled slowly in waterways around the Central Plaza and even ventured briefly into Adventureland to complete its circuit. There were swan figureheads on each boat, with the conceit being that just like Disneyland before it, the Magic Kingdom would also have "swans" in the moat around the castle. The waterways are still there, and an unlabeled metal shade structure marks the location of the former loading dock for this attraction. Just up the sidewalk from here toward the castle, you can spot swan topiaries as a further nod.

The very first attraction we come to in Tomorrowland has a rich and storied history. Stitch's Great Escape was previously Alien Encounter, where a company called X-S Tech invented transporters that accidentally brought a dangerous alien to us. Much of the infrastructure remains in today's attraction, and watch for a machine actually labeled with X-S Tech's name as you leave the preshow room (with teleportation demo) and head toward the theater. Before Alien Encounter, this facility and its dual theaters had been Mission to Mars (and Flight to the Moon before that).

Monsters Inc. Laugh Floor uses the monster-created "door" technology from the movie to transport us away to Monstropolis for the comedy act itself, but the first queue room is still ostensibly Tomorrowland. In that room, look around for satellite dishes—remnants of the previous inhabitant in this location, the Timekeeper attraction.

Just next door, at Buzz Lightyear's Space Ranger Spin, we can spot several sets that were converted from the previous show here called Dreamflight (also variously called Take Flight, and If You Had Wings over the years). The red, rotating spiral lights in a foggy room near the end once meant to imply we were entering the giant turbine of a modern jet. Or look for rounded bumps on the half-walls near the beginning or end of each room—these were originally cloud designs. The truly obsessed can spot a set of three chickens near the floor in the "volcano" room. These exact cartoon cutouts were previously part of the farm scene in Dreamflight, but they now rub elbows with aliens of all types.

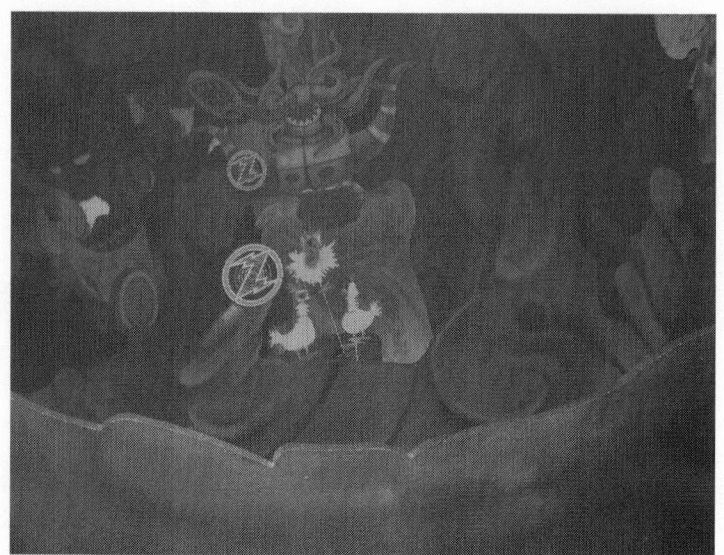

As we step across the way to the Tomorrowland Transit Authority, we need to stay extra vigilant, for there are two tributes on the Tomorrowland Transit Authority *PeopleMover*. First up is the model of Progressland, which is part of the original model built to visualize the futuristic city Walt Disney wanted to build before his death. The acronym for EPCOT—Experimental Prototype Community of Tomorrow—points to his original vision. Epcot wasn't meant to be a theme park, but a living, breathing city, and this was the floor plan for the layout. Later in the TTA, listen as we travel through *Space Mountain* for a terminal-style announcement paging Mr. Tom Morrow, who is to contact Mr. Johnson "to confirm your flight to the moon." This is a multi-layer reference to the Flight to the Moon attraction (later re-themed as Mission to Mars) that preceded Alien Encounter. In these space travel attractions, the robotic host was variously named Tom Morrow (get the pun?) and Mr. Johnson.

The *Carousel of Progress* was originally sponsored by General Electric, and while that company is no longer mentioned by name out loud, their products (and the GE logo) are still highly visible on many of the appliances in the show.

Another company, RCA, was the original sponsor of *Space Mountain*. So it was no surprise that their famous company mascot, a dog named Nipper who had his head cocked sideways (while watching an RCA phonograph), showed up as a robot in the post-show of the attraction. Even though RCA is no longer the sponsor, the Nipper animatronic continues to appear in today's post-show—look for a robotic-looking, metallic dog amid the scenes of alien landscapes.

The booth used to advertise the Disney Vacation Club near the Tomorrowland Speedway is one of the last original ticket booths at the Magic Kingdom. Before EPCOT Center opened, all rides at the Magic Kingdom required individual attraction tickets, and central booths like this one sold tickets for admission.

A pathway of bricks at the start line to the Tomorrowland Speedway serves as a silent reminder of the past sponsor. Previously known as the Tomorrowland Indy Speedway, the race course borrowed a tradition from the Indy 500 of a "yard of bricks." It was meant as a tribute to the Indy 500's original track course, which was made up of bricks rather than smooth pavement.

You can find three references in the Many Adventures of Winnie the Pooh to its predecessor, Mr. Toad's Wild Ride. All three occur in the second room of the ride, in Owl's house, and all three are contained within portraits and paintings on the walls and floor. Look for Mr. Toad handing a deed over to Winnie the Pooh—a rather direct way of "passing the baton." Or you can find the Toad character Moley in another image with Pooh, as well as Owl wearing the outfit and mustache of a third Toad character named Winky. For a bit of tongue in cheek fun, check out the "pet cemetery" at the exit to the Haunted Mansion, where tucked into the far corner is a statue of Mr. Toad.

Right next door to the Haunted Mansion is an unlabeled structure up on a hill. Longtime visitors will remember this as the Swiss chalet that housed the Skyway to Tomorrowland, offering a bird's-eye view of the park below.

Back at the Mansion itself, we'll want to note the ravens throughout the ride. When the attraction was being developed for Disneyland, the original thought was that this raven (a universal symbol of death) would function as the host and narrator, so there is always a raven visible whenever our Ghost Host speaks in our ears.

While we're here, watch for furniture and fixtures that seem to be alive, or at least sport bodily appendages as if part of a larger organism. These are holdovers from one competing concept for the Mansion as a "Museum of the Weird," with semi-living furniture. One classic example can be seen at the end of the ride, when torches are being held by disembodied arms and hands that jut out from the stone wall.

Just outside the Mansion is a loading dock along the water with no apparent purpose. This is the former home of the Mike Fink keelboats, free-floating small watercraft that plied the Rivers of America. An example of a keelboat can be seen at Wilson's Cave Inn (itself a reference to a historical spot for piracy), a themed spot visible from the Liberty Belle riverboat.

While you can't order food on Tom Sawyer Island today, in days past you could eat at a cantina in Fort Langhorn—its name is derived from Samuel Clemens's (Mark Twain's) middle name. Today, the cantina windows are boarded up, though minor themed items like jugs and food crates still advertise the cantina's location. On the other side of the island, an expansive area with chairs and tables still sports a serving window and a sign for Aunt Polly's, though this quick-service eatery has been closed since 2006.

At Big Thunder Mountain Railroad, a major design element is a tribute of sorts: the dinosaur skeleton at the finale is a tribute to a similar dino skeleton once found at Mine Train thru Nature's Wonderland, the predecessor to Big Thunder in Disneyland. When Big Thunder was opened at the Magic Kingdom, this thematic element was duplicated even though there was never a Mine Train attraction in Orlando. This is one of many locations where the changes at Disneyland dictate the designs at Walt Disney World!

Docks visible at the exit to Big Thunder were once used to house canoes. These free-floating vehicles were guest-powered, though you couldn't just explore freely. The guides and canoe steerers made sure that we completed the circuit without too many unwanted adventures.

An innocuous-looking stagecoach wheel in Frontierland pays tribute to the former inhabitant at the Golden Oak Outpost. Before the current structure was built, a broken stagecoach served as the cart from which to sell French fries, with a sign nearby proclaiming how long this stagecoach has been in this exact location.

Up the road is *The Enchanted Tiki Room*, where the preshow pays homage to the Mighty Ducks of Anaheim, which at one time was owned by the Walt Disney Company. The Ducks are mentioned by the bickering birds in the preshow. The team's name can be traced to a small Disney movie from the early 1990s, when then-CEO Michael Eisner was interested in sports of all types. The truly obsessed may also want to track down the Mighty Ducks mask in the store near the Studio Catering Company at Disney's Hollywood Studios, too.

Time to switch parks—perhaps we should take the monorail? Not long after you step into Epcot, you'll come across Guest Relations, where there is a bank of unused windows off to one side. These are the former Worldkey video kiosks, where you could use a futuristic videophone to make same-day dining reservations with a helpful Guest Relations Cast Member. With today's Internet and phone capabilities, the kiosks sit empty and unused.

Around the corner at Ellen's Energy Adventure, visitors with keen senses can detect the homage to the Universe of Energy attraction that preceded it, courtesy of a voiceover near the end that proclaims "Energy: you make the world go around" in deference to a song of the same name at the previous ride.

At Mission: Space, look for the logo for the previous inhabitant, Horizons, at the center of the giant spinning wheel in the queue and again at the cash register in the shop after the ride. If you're lucky, you can witness an albatross landing on the video screens in the "control room" located at the queue. This is a holdover from Mission to Mars (as is a mention of Mr. Johnson on the Gantry Cam heard on the very last safety video just prior to boarding, if visitors are delayed on their entry).

Test Track replaced World of Motion, a ride similarly sponsored by General Motors but focused more directly on the evolution of the automobile as a transportation device. As a tribute, one antique car from World of Motion was retained at the start of the queue for Test Track.

Across Future World at the Seas with Nemo and Friends, there's a hint of the former occupant here, when the Living Seas was host to a "Seabase Alpha." The lifeguard tower in the queue is labeled 5A, an approximation of the initials for Seabase Alpha. You'll also hear mention of "sea cab" knowledge on the ride, as well as see domes in the ceiling reflecting water as if we were fathoms underwater in a giant seabase.

One of the major attractions, Turtle Talk with Crush, began life across the other side of the pavilion. Today, the oversized video screen dominating one wall displays mere oceanic images, but it was once used as the primary window into Crush's world.

A plaque outside the Land pavilion makes mention of symbiosis, both the operating principle of the pavilion (dedicated to balance and avoiding overuse) and the film of the same name in the upstairs theater.

The original logo for the Land pavilion, now largely downplayed, still appears on the FASTPASS machines for the Living with the

Land boat ride. The use of such logos for each pavilion has greatly lessened over the years, though you can still spot the original logo for all of Epcot behind the Fountain of Nations and again on the security gates outside of the main ticket booths.

At the Imagination pavilion, a previous incarnation of this attraction featured a character called the Dreamfinder, so it's no surprise to find mention of "Dean Finder" on one door in the ride through the Imagination Institute. Sharp-eyed visitors will also spot tributes at the finale of the ride, courtesy of sheet music for "One Little Spark" (the former theme song) and a silhouette for the Dream Vehicle balloon atop the sheet music. The actual Dream Vehicle prop, meanwhile, can be glimpsed near the ceiling in Mouse Gear.

In World Showcase, be sure to visit the meadow in Norway where you can spy the remnants of a Viking ship playground, now used as pieces of the Kim Possible interactive cell phone game.

If it's ride remnants you're after, be sure to look at the mega-buildings looming over both the Japan and Germany pavilions—these were meant for the "Meet the World" and "Rhine River Cruise" attractions that have never been built, and they largely sit empty these days. In Germany, a mural depicting the Rhine River castles covers an archway that would have been the entrance to the ride.

Among the more esoteric remnants can be seen in the area populated by African designs. You'll probably guess that this was meant to be an entire pavilion dedicated to Africa, and you'd be right. But would you have known enough Swahili to translate "Mdundo Kibanda," the sign above the hand-carved trinkets? It means "good beats," which makes sense only if you know that this stand was once home to drum sets for sale.

Switching gears over to Disney's Hollywood Studios, we train our attention on a window at the far end of Hollywood Blvd. It mentions Sights & Sounds, a clear reference to a store of the same name from 1989. In that store, visitors could create their own music videos and purchase a tape of it to take home.

Just outside this shop is the bronzed statue of The Filmmaker, which is also home to the park's dedication plaque. Look carefully, and you'll find one of the only references left to this park's original name, Disney-MGM Studios (the name changed in 2008).

When the park first opened, one of its premiere attractions was to watch Disney animators at work on actual production. The large glass walls seen in the Magic of Disney Animation attraction, right after the exit to the pre-show, are now frosted over but once allowed visitors to gaze below to watch the animators at work at their desks.

The park was also a working facility for film and radio production. While some of the soundstages have been converted with nary a trace remaining, there's still a hint of Radio Disney's broadcasting location, courtesy of a stenciled sign on one glass door around the side of Sounds Dangerous.

At Backlot Express, search atop the storage cabinets until you find the vaguely triangular clay-colored vehicle; this is the mold used to create the harvesting vehicle once seen at Horizons in Epcot. In the same room, look around for a go-cart type car on the ground. As you can learn by reading the nearby signs, this is the actual Benny the Cab vehicle used in filming *Who Framed Roger Rabbit*.

While the Residential Street was long ago removed to make room for the car stunt show stadium, the restrooms at the Studio Catering Company retain at least an indirect connection to Residential Street. In the men's restroom only, photos on the tile walls show film production that occurred on the former street.

Just around the corner, the Backlot Tour promises a look behind movie magic, and indeed many movie props can be seen just prior to boarding the trams, when passing through a prop warehouse. But some of the props here come from former Walt Disney World attractions, like the balloonist, flying man, and masks that were all once part of World of Motion at Epcot. Once on the Backlot Tour itself, don't miss the consummate bit of hidden history in the form of Walt Disney's airplane, the very vehicle that was used to scout out the Walt Disney World property from the air.

Even the newest theme park, Disney's Animal Kingdom, has undergone significant change in its brief history. Perhaps the most noticeable would be the vacant waterways and the loading docks seen at Asia and Discovery Island. This was the onetime home of the Discovery River Boat Tour, a taxi service around the park that only operated for a couple of years.

Along the banks of that same river can be seen a clump of rocks arranged in the shape of a dragon—try looking for them from the bridge to Camp Minnie Mickey. These rocks herald the eventual home of Beastlie Kingdomme, an idea originally meant to be the park's first expansion (Camp Minnie Mickey was supposed to be temporary). The planned inclusion of imaginary animals in the park's lineup is further reflected in the park logos visible on benches, where a dragon outline can be seen adjacent to the other, existing animals.

Changes to the storyline at Kilimanjaro Safari have left virtual traces in the queue. The original co-host of our safari was Dr. Catherine Jobson, who spoke with our tour guide from the plane. While Dr. Jobson no longer appears in the attraction spiel, she can still be glimpsed on the video in the queue.

Even more subtle changes at the Pangani Forest Exploration Trail require knowledge that this attraction was once called Gorilla Falls. That original name is mentioned in Swahili at the start of the trail, and a crate at the gorilla observation post mentions the Gorilla Falls Conservation School.

Nor is this the only name change. The Dinosaur attraction was once called Countdown to Extinction, and references to this name continue to abound in the land. Parts of the walls and vehicles in the ride are still marked with CTX, and a map of the land opposite Dino Dig mentions Countdown to Extinction by name. Over in Restaurantosaurus, a faux newspaper article next to the ordering stations not only shows the blueprint for the time rover, it mentions T-shirts emblazoned with "I survived extinction!", which made more sense when the ride was still called Countdown to Extinction.

We've saved the tastiest remnant for last. The former sponsor of Dinoland U.S.A. was McDonald's—can you locate the subtle tribute on Dinosaur to the fast-food corporation? Here's a hint: look up. Ceiling pipes near the loading zone staircase are adorned with chemical formulas for ketchup, mustard, and mayonnaise. The pipes are even colored red, yellow, and white!

The McDonald's "leftovers" are not labeled, like most of tributes found in the parks. As a result, it pays to keep your eyes peeled, especially when a new attraction displaces an older one. Who knows? Perhaps you can be the first to spot the newest homage at Walt Disney World!

Authors' Notes

Jason Diffendal
The Walt Disney World Monorail System

American Society of Mechanical Engineers. http://www.asme.org.

Anderson, Paul F. Persistence of Vision.

Auction Bytes. http://www.auctionbytes.com.

Big Florida Country. http://www.bigfloridacountry.com.

"Bob Gurr's Designer Times." http://www.laughingplace.com.

Fjellman, Stephen M. Vinyl Leaves: Walt Disney World and America.

Keys to the Magic Forum. http://www.keystothemagic.com.

Kurtti, Jeff. Since the World Began: Walt Disney World, The First 25 Years.

McGinnis, George. "Disneyland: The First Thirty-Five Years." On Track. http://www.mouseplanet.com.

Monorail Teal. http://www.monorailteal.com.

MonorailExpress. http://www.monorailexpress.com.

Pirate 4x4 Forums. http://www.pirate4x4.com.

The Monorail Society. http://www.monorails.org.

The Original EPCOT. http://www.the-original-epcot.com.

The Orlando Sentinel. http://www.orlandosentinel.com.

TrainSpottingWorld. http://train.spottingworld.com.

Thomas, Bob. Walt Disney: An American Original.

"Walt Disney World." Modern Marvels. The History Channel.

WDWMagic Forums. http://forums.wdwmagic.com.

Jason Diffendal
Spaceship Earth

Alucobond USA. http://www.alucobondusa.com.

Frank Heger Website. http://www.frank-heger.com.

Jeff Lange Theme Park Videos. http://www.jefflangedvd.com.

Laughing Place. http://www.laughingplace.com.

Lefkon, Wendy, Ed. Walt Disney World Resort: A Magical Year-By-Year Journey.

Lost Epcot. http://www.lostepcot.com.

Martin Smith Disney Park Fan Videos. http://martinsvids.net.

Mouse Planet. http://www.mouseplanet.com.

Ray Bradbury Website. http://www.raybradbury.com.

Siemens. http://www.siemens.com.

Original EPCOT. http://www.the-original-epcot.com.

Walt Dated World. http://www.waltdatedworld.com.

Walt Disney World. Souvenir book. 1986.

Walt Disney World News. http://www.wdwnews.com.

Walt Disney's EPCOT Center. Beard, Richard R.

WDW News Today. http://www.wdwnewstoday.com.

WDWMagic Forums. http://forums.wdwmagic.com.

Widen Your World. http://www.widenyourworld.net.

Wright, Alex and the Imagineers. The Imagineering Field Guide to Epcot at Walt Disney World. Second Ed.

Yesterland. http://www.yesterland.com.

Didier Ghez

Joe and Carl: Two Men Who Built the World

1. All biographical information and quotes about and by Carl Bongirno come from two interviews conducted with Bongirno by the author on August 18 and 25, 2008.
2. Zehnder, Leonard E. "More Than Three Years of Planning and Preparation Required Before Construction of Walt Disney World." Florida's Disney World: Promises and Problems. The Peninsular Publishing Company, 1975.
3. Wessel, Harry. "The Admiral of 'Can Do.'" The Orlando Sentinel. February 08, 1993.
4. Wessel, Harry. "Joe Fowler, the Builder of 2 Disney Parks, Dies." The Orlando Sentinel. December 04, 1993.
5. McAleenan, John. "Building The New World, Why Disney World Isn't In St. Louis, And Other Tales From The Creation." The Orlando Sentinel. April 10, 1988.
6. Joe Fowler to Jay Horan on March 12, 1984.
7. Head of Disneyland lessee relations.
8. Joe Potter to Jay Horan on March 7, 1984.
9. McAleenan, John. "Building The New World, Why Disney World Isn't In St. Louis, And Other Tales From The Creation." The Orlando Sentinel. April 10, 1988.
10. Wessel, Harry. "The Admiral of 'Can Do.'" The Orlando Sentinel. February 08, 1993.
11. Wessel, Harry. "The Admiral of 'Can Do.'" The Orlando Sentinel. February 08, 1993.
12. Wessel, Harry. "The Admiral of 'Can Do.'" The Orlando Sentinel. February 08, 1993.
13. George L. Bagnall, President of George Bagnall and Associates.
14. The "city," in keeping with Walt's original philosophy for the Epcot project, included many innovations. It was the first time in Florida that underground cables were used for the phone system. Other items that existed in no other city in Florida, like

the AVACs trash collection system at the Magic Kingdom, were considered remarkable at the time. Disney had not just built a small city but one that showcased the newest technologies available. This area was accountable to its own Reedy Creek Improvement District, not the two Central Florida counties of Orange and Osceola on which the property was built, which allowed even more innovations when the time came to preparing the land.

15. Joe Fowler to Jay Horan on March 12, 1984.
16. Where Potter spent some time during his career in the military.
17. Joe Potter to Jay Horan on March 7, 1984.
18. Joe Fowler to Bob Thomas in 1973.
19. Reynolds, Robert R. Roller Coasters, Flumes and Flying Saucers. Northern Lights Publishing, 1999. 154.
20. Koenig, David. Realityland: True-Life Adventures of Walt Disney World. Bonaventure Press, 2007. 72.
21. McAleenan, John. "Building The New World, Why Disney World Isn't In St. Louis, And Other Tales From The Creation." The Orlando Sentinel. April 10, 1988.
22. Prizer, Edward L. "The Disney Era in Florida." Orlando-Land. October 1981.
23. Prizer, Edward L. "The Disney Era in Florida." Orlando-Land. October 1981.
24. Wessel, Harry. "The Admiral of 'Can Do.'" The Orlando Sentinel. February 08, 1993.

Chuck Mirarchi

History of the Hoop Dee Doo Musical Revue

Kurtti, Jeff. Since The World Began – Walt Disney World The First 25 Years. Hyperion, 1996.

The Official Disney Fan Club. http://www.D23.com.

Ron Miziker. Personal interview. http://www.miziker.com.

Walt Disney World – The First Decade. Walt Disney Co., 1982.

Walt Disney World. http://www.waltdisneyworld.com.

Wikipedia. http://www.wikipedia.com

Chuck Mirarchi

The History of the Main Street Electrical Parade

Back Stage at Disney: The Main Street Electrical Parade. Disney Channel, 1986.

Dorsey Productions. www.dorseyproductions.com.

Ron Miziker. Personal interview. http://www.miziker.com.

Walt Disney World. http://www.waltdisneyworld.com.

Chuck Mirarchi

The History of the Contemporary Resort & the Polynesian Resort Hotels

Building A Company. Thomas, Bob. Hyperion, 1998.

Disney Files Magazine. Volume 17, No. 3. Fall 2008.

Koenig, David. Realityland: True-Life Adventures of Walt Disney World. Bonaventure Press, 2007.

Pang, May. Instamatic Karma: Photographs of John Lennon. St Martin's Press, 2008.

Ridgway, Charles. "Spinning Disney's World." The Intrepid Traveler. 200

Tikiman Pages. http://www.tikimanpages.com.

Walt Disney World. Preview Edition. Walt Disney World, 1970.

Walt Dated World. http://waltdatedworld.bravepages.com

WDW History. http://www.wdwhistory.com.

Widen Your World. http://www.omniluxe.net/wyw/wyw.htm.

Wikipedia. http://www.wikipedia.com.